Competition Policy

Competition Policy

History, Theory and Practice

Manfred Neumann

Professor of Economics
University of Erlangen-Nürnberg
Germany

Edward Elgar
Cheltenham, UK • Northampton, MA, USA

© Manfred Neumann 2001

Published by
Edward Elgar Publishing Limited
Glensanda House
Montpellier Parade
Cheltenham
Glos GL50 1UA
UK

Edward Elgar Publishing, Inc.
136 West Street
Suite 202
Northampton
Massachusetts 01060
USA

Paperback edition 2002
Reprinted 2003

A catalogue record for this book
is available from the British Library

Library of Congress Cataloguing in Publication Data
Neumann, Manfred
        Competition policy: history, theory and practice / Manfred Neumann.
            p. cm.
        Includes bibliographical references and index.
        1. Competition. 2. Competition, International. 3. Competition—
    Government policy. 4. Industrial policy. 5. Competition—History.
    6. Business cycles. I. Title.

HD41.N39 2001
338.6′048—dc21

                                                            00-062289

ISBN 1 84064 300 5 (cased)
        1 84376 032 0 (paperback)

Printed and bound in Great Britain by Bookcraft, Midsomer Norton

Contents

List of Figures		vi
List of Tables		vii
Preface		viii

1. Aims and Scope of Competition Policy — 1

1.1	Competition in a Market Economy	3
1.2	Horizontal Concentration	17
1.3	Undermining Competition Through Laissez Faire	23
1.4	Approaches to Competition Policy in the US, Germany and the European Union	30
1.5	Conclusion	45

2. Industrial Economics as the Foundation of Competition Policy — 47

2.1	Competition in Oligopoly	47
2.2	Restraints of Competition in Oligopoly	67
2.3	The Structure–Conduct–Performance Paradigm	74
2.4	Monopoly Welfare Loss	85
2.5	Conclusion	98

3. Containing Restraints of Competition — 99

3.1	Collusion	99
3.2	Merger Control	110
3.3	Abuse of Monopolistic Market Power	134
3.4	Regulation, Deregulation and Privatizing	158
3.5	Conclusion	164

4. The Social Framework and Competition Policy — 166

4.1	Freedom of Competition and Property Rights	166
4.2	Competition Policy and International Trade Policy	175
4.3	Financial Markets and Competition on Goods Markets	179
4.4	Public Policy and Competition Policy	183
4.5	Conclusion	189

References	192
Index	211

Figures

1.1   Marginal and average costs in the case of monopoly   8
1.2   Buying power under monopsony   12
1.3   Marginal costs vs average costs   13
2.1   The equilibrium of an individual firm   49
2.2   Reaction curves in Cournot equilibrium   50
2.3   Reaction curves for the case $\alpha_1 = \alpha_2$, $c_1 = c_2$ 60
2.4   Actual vs hypothetical variances of market shares   66
2.5   A general equilibrium approach to monopoly welfare loss   86
2.6   A partial analysis of monopoly welfare loss   87
2.7   The welfare loss in an oligopoly   89
2.8   Static efficiency trade-off   91
2.9   Optimal technical change   96
3.1   Monopolistic price discrimination   137
3.2   A model of successive monopolies   140
3.3   Monopoly and monopsony combined   154
3.4   Fixed costs and a thin market   160

Tables

1.1	Market shares (in per cent) for alternative numbers of firms	20
1.2	Market shares (in per cent) in German food retailing 1993	21
1.3	Market shares (in per cent) of the 20 largest producers of electronic stores and microprocessors 1990	22
1.4	Market shares (in per cent) on the market for motor cars in Germany and the EC 1991	23
2.1	Profitability following a pioneering innovation	54
2.2	Pay-off matrix in a duopoly	69
2.3	Prices and profits at a Bertrand–Nash equilibrium and collusion among two firms ($m = 2$) out of n firms	72
2.4	Annualized welfare loss as depending on interest rate, growth rates and the static welfare loss	94
3.1	Kinds of mergers in the US 1950–77	110
3.2	Kinds of mergers in Germany 1974–90	111
3.3	Kinds of mergers in the UK 1965–89	111
3.4	Prices for multiproduct monopoly and oligopoly, and duopoly in market 1 ($\alpha_1 = 10$, $\alpha_2 = 4$, $c_1 = c_2 = 2$)	149

Preface

Historically, competition policy can be traced back to medieval times. In fact, as put by the historian R.H. Tawney in his treatise *Religion and the Rise of Capitalism* (1926, p. 40), 'a great part of medieval industry is a system of organized monopolies, endowed with a public status, which must be watched with jealous eyes to see that they do not abuse their powers'. The modern history of competition policy took shape only during the later decades of the 19th century, when a free trade era was replaced by a stance of protectionist trade policy under the umbrella of which cartels and trusts began to proliferate. Whereas in the US the political response was antitrust in Europe cartels could develop unimpeded. It was only after World War II that competition policy was introduced in Europe, particularly in Germany, in Britain and at the EC level. More recently for two reasons, internationally, a remarkable convergence of principles and practices of competition policy has emerged. First, globalization of economic relationships gives rise to interdependencies which require a unified approach to face restraints of trade across national boundaries caused by collusion and mergers. Second, in economics a body of theories pertaining to industrial organization has been developed from which standards of evaluation were derived which have come to dominate the standards rooted in the legal tradition of individual countries. Still, because of diverging interests competition policy is subject to political controversies.

Whereas cartels have overwhelmingly been assessed critically, the attitude towards mergers are more ambiguous. In particular recent mega mergers, like mergers one hundred years ago in the United States, have given rise to both concern and admiration, as nicely exemplified toward the end of the nineteenth century in a parody of Finley Peter Dunne (cited in Nevins and Commager 1981, p. 276) 'Th' thrusts are heejous monsthers built up by th' inlightened intherprise ov th' men that have done so much to advance progress in our beloved counthry. On wan hand I wud stamp them undher fut; on the other hand, not so fast'. Frequently smaller competitors are scared by a powerful rival in their market which they do not dare to challenge. A good recent example is the case of Microsoft where only by the opening of antitrust procedures was the ban broken ('The Microsoft Factor', *Business Week* December 7, 1998, p. 64).

Since mergers affect the interests of different people in different ways, competition policy has been subject to political controversies. On one hand mergers and the formation of giant firms are welcomed as allegedly enhancing international competitiveness, and on the other hand the political clout they may wield gives rise to serious concern. The enlargement of markets following globalization seems to require firms to grow in size in order to withstand the challenge of more vigorous competition. Frequently, however, competition is visualized as a zero sum game holding the promise of large gains for a few and losses for many. The mixture of opposing views engenders the demand for industrial policy. However, as admitted by the former EC Commissioner Martin Bangemann, who had been in charge of EC industrial policy, such a hope will largely be in vain. Instead he suggested for internationally active firms to join a common code of behavior to moderate excessive competition, an astounding plead for establishing cartels.

In view of these controversial attitudes and uncertainties regarding the appropriate role of competition policy economic and legal expertise is called for. Whilst at the end of the 19th century legal arguments had taken the lead, more recently the debate has become more heavily influenced by economic reasoning. For competition policy to become effective it must be embodied in the law and has to be implemented by the government and courts. Thus economic and legal expertise must enter a symbiotic relationship. Therefore the present book is addressed at students of both economics and law, at practicing economists and lawyers. It aims first at elucidating the economic arguments pertinent to justifying the necessity of competition policy and second, by providing an overview of legal regulations in the US and Europe, to help acquire an understanding of the rationale and practice of competition policy.

In the first chapter the historical development of competition policy, as displayed in economic and political reasoning and in the development of government regulations, will be outlined. The challenges facing competition policy will be characterized by giving an account of the history of cartelization and industrial concentration in the US and Europe and the response of public policy. Furthermore, by expounding elementary models of economic theory, that is, perfect competition, monopoly and monopsony, the framework provided by economic theory will be set out. It will be elaborated in the second chapter which offers an overview of the present state of industrial economics, the centerpiece of which is the theory of oligopoly, that is, competition among the few. As theoretically-derived relationships are supported by empirical evidence, economic theory turns out to be a reliable foundation for evaluating restraints of competition politically. Competition policy derives its political relevance not least by showing that restraints of competition yield welfare losses which to a large extent can be avoided by adopting an effective competition policy. The third chapter is devoted to expounding the interplay between economic reasoning and the law concerning cartels, mergers, and vertical restraints of trade. Competition policy pertaining to these problems will be analyzed primarily for the US, Germany and the European Union by invoking the relevant law as displayed in legislation and applied by the government and courts. The comparative analysis reveals to what extent, following the impact of economic reasoning, a convergence of the standards of evaluation has developed between the US and Europe. The fourth chapter takes up various elements of the social framework and other policies to discuss how they relate to competition policy. It pertains to the role of property rights, to international trade policy, and to the impact of the prevailing financial system. The chapter closes with a discussion of the relationship between competition policy and the objectives of government policy at large.

I am grateful to many colleagues and friends for encouragement and helpful advice. I should name in particular Horst Albach, Ingo Böbel, Knut Borchardt, Uli Fell, Paul Geroski, Alexandra Gross, Alfred Haid, Harald Otto Lübbert, Ernst-Joachim Mestmäcker, Markus T. Münter, Doris Neuberger, Karl W. Roskamp, and Jürgen Weigand. Caroline Sørensen's copy editing is gratefully acknowledged. Ursula Briceño La Rosa did an excellent job in preparing a print-ready copy of the book. Any remaining shortcomings are my fault.

Manfred Neumann
Nuremberg

1. Aims and Scope of Competition Policy

Competition policy is a cornerstone of economic policy in a market economy, founded on well-defined property rights and freedom of contract, supported by policies aiming at stable money, a high level of employment and social security. The objectives and means of competition policy have been subject to various controversies. On one side there are ardent followers of the gospel of economic freedom as exemplified by the slogan 'Laissez faire, laissez passer le monde va de lui même.' They consider economic freedom and the ensuing competition as ends in themselves. On the other side there are those considering competition policy as a constituent part of an interventionistic industrial policy aiming at establishing market structures and enticing enterprises to behave in a way conducive to the enhancement of economic welfare. Within this range of diverging opinions four objectives to be pursued by competition policy may be identified

- Establishing a competitive order as an end in itself to safeguard economic freedom
- Maintaining a competitive order to foster economic efficiency and technological and economic progress
- Providing for a level playing field of fair competition, which implies prohibition of deceptive and fraudulent practices, threat, extortion and blackmail as well as unfair advantages through government subsidies
- Maintaining a decentralized structure of supply because small and medium-sized enterprises are considered as the backbone of a democratic society.

Some of these objectives are rivalrous whilst others are mutually supportive. The latter is particularly true with respect to the two objectives listed first. The development during the last third of the 19th century gave rise to the conclusion that a laissez-faire stance of economic policy would lead up to undermining a competitive order by the formation of trusts and cartels and thus to the eventual elimination of economic freedom. Therefore maintaining a competitive order by prohibiting restraints of competition was deemed as an objective to be pursued irrespective of the impact on economic efficiency. According to this view, even though the enhancement of economic welfare through competition is welcome it does not in itself justify competition policy (Hoppmann 1966, Pitofsky 1979). At first sight, this view bears a close relationship to the preference for a decentralized structure of the economy, which has been propagated as the Jeffersonian ideal of a democratic society. However, followers of a laissez-faire stance of economic policy would frown upon such a policy aiming at some definite economic structure and criticize it as interventionistic regulation. Consequently, deregulation policies adopted in the US by the administration of President Ronald Reagan led up to a retrenchment of antitrust policy.

Reproaching competition policy as government regulation inhibiting economic freedom is not completely unjustified as far as it is conceived of as part of an interventionistic industrial policy. In fact, the borderline between a freedom-enhancing competition policy and interventionistic industrial policy is somewhat vague. Monopolistic market power is frequently considered as being on the same footing as market failure due to economies of scale, externalities and incomplete information. Attainment of a welfare optimum thus appears to require government interventions. However, in quite a few cases particular interests are coming into play. Interventions which would be justified as correcting for market failures come to be dominated by distributional issues and claims raised in the name of social justice. In the end, without correcting for market failures, government failures arise. For this reason competition policy should content itself with containing restraints of competition and thus establish a competitive order which embodies the rules of the game. Hence competition law assumes the role of a constitution. As put by the German economist Walter Eucken (1959, p. 156, my translation),

> Just as the constitutional state, the competitive order should establish a framework in which individual freedom of action is limited by preserving the sphere of freedom of others such that the individual spheres of freedom will attain an equilibrium.

The major advantage of competition policy can be seen in the role it plays in relieving the government from being burdened with a task it is unable to perform. An anonymous co-ordination of economic activities is substituted for a regulation performed by bureaucracy. As emphasized by Kaysen and Turner (1959, p. 14),

> Competition in this context is desirable because it substitutes an impersonal market control for the personal control of powerful business executives, or for the personal control of government bureaucrats.

Governance by command is replaced by governance by law. Rules are substituted for privileges. This brings economic theory into play. Instituting rules requires predictions of outcomes. Economic theory, however, is best suited for predicting long-run consequences of institutions and modes of behavior. It is less well suited for evaluating short-run relationships which may be analyzed by invoking game theory. Frequently multiple equilibria exist and thus unequivocal predictions are not possible. In the long run, however, some definite outcome may wind up to survive. For competition policy, seeking to establish rules holding in the long run, it is most important to ensure that welfare-enhancing developments are not blocked by restraints of competition. Thus private initiatives will be unleashed to enhance economic welfare.

For competition policy to assume a distinct profile and to emancipate it from political controversies it is necessary to be guided by a unique objective. Posner (1976) and Bork (1965, 1978) therefore suggest that competition policy should adopt welfare maximization as the sole objective. Economic theory allows unequivocal principles for competition policy to be derived from this objective. All the other aims of competition policy mentioned above are to be pushed into the background. Unless they are completely discarded, competition policy may proceed in two successive steps. First, the authorities entrusted with implementing competition policy should by guided by the aim of welfare maximization. In a second step auxiliary and possibly even competing objectives may be taken up. If a trade-off arises, a political decision is required. There is no conflict between maintaining economic freedom and maximization of welfare because a competitive order ensures the attainment of both.

1.1 COMPETITION IN A MARKET ECONOMY

Competition and economic freedom are like two sides of a coin. Philosophically John Locke (1690) propounded the idea that everybody has the unalienable right to pursue happiness and to define his or her interests. This idea gathered political momentum by its propagation in the famous Bill of Rights of Virginia, in the constitution of the United States of America and in the French Revolution of 1789. It finally became the core of all constitutions of the Western world. Individual freedom is deemed to be limited only insofar as the rights of other people must not be infringed. To be sure, as emphasized by Joseph Schumpeter (1942), competition entails 'creative destruction' by displacing existing products and methods of production by new ones. Hence, from day to day there are both winners and losers. Still, in the long run, all can become winners unless the right to participate in market activities is curtailed. Freedom to join the competitive process must therefore by safeguarded by law. In his popular essay *On Liberty* John Stuart Mill (1859, pp.

16f) has propounded this principle in admirable clarity,[1]

> The only freedom which deserves the name is that of pursuing our own good in our own way, so long as we do not attempt to deprive others of theirs or impede their efforts to obtain it.

Given economic freedom the scope of economic activity, the level of production and the distribution of income follow from autonomous decisions of individuals. As convincingly expounded by Hayek (1973, p. 41), individual freedom gives rise to a spontaneous order which has not been deliberately designed by anyone.

> Since a spontaneous order results from the individual elements adapting themselves to circumstances which directly affect only some of them, and which in their totality need not be known to anyone, it may extend to circumstances so complex that no mind can comprehend them all.

The spontaneity of individual behavior gives rise to an open-ended process, the outcome of which cannot exactly be predicted. There is no way to determine in detail what the objective of the economy is. Therefore a common weal is impossible to narrow down. It nevertheless remains true that economic freedom is best suited for safeguarding the individual welfare to be achieved. Even though a welfare maximum cannot be identified in advance, competition can be understood as a process approaching a maximum. The neoclassical theory of maximizing behavior of individuals which under competitive conditions yields a welfare maximum can be used as a paradigm of an evolutionary process. In fact the evolutionary process, characterized by survival of the fittest, is a process of groping for a superior outcome and can thus be understood as the equivalent to solving a maximization problem. Depicting it by setting up and utilizing a mathematical model amounts to simplifying matters, but at the same time helps to understand what is going on. Spontaneity, as alluded to by Hayek, implies that the outcome cannot be predicted because 'we cannot anticipate today what we shall know only tomorrow' (Popper 1957, p. x). Although the specific outcome is thus unknown, it is helpful to utilize a model as mentioned above to identify circumstances under which a maximum of economic welfare is attained. Theory thus gives guidance to devise the framework and the rules of the game to be applied. The choice of the rules must not be left to emerge spontaneously from the interplay of individual interests. That would amount to subscribing to the

---

[1] In *Utilitarianism* (1861, p. 22) Mill gave it a positive turn by citing the golden rule of Jesus of Nazareth (Matthew 7, 12) 'To do as you would be done' as being the ideal perfection of utilitarian morality.

principle of laissez-faire. Safeguarding economic freedom, as propounded by John Stuart Mill, must not be confused with laissez-faire. Laissez-faire provides scope for a dominant firm or a cartel to interfere with the liberty of other people and may eventually eliminate economic freedom altogether. Therefore competition policy must be geared to prohibit the abuse of economic power.

Competition as Institution Needs Protection

Although in a free economy the individual pursuit of profit is the engine of economic development, freedom alone does not suffice. For the pursuit of profit to be compatible with the advancement of economic welfare a competitive order must be established. Through competition variegated individual capabilities and powers are harnessed and put into motion to serving the common weal. Adam Smith illustrated the relationship between the pursuit of self interest and economic welfare forcefully by invoking the parable of the invisible hand. Provided competition exists, an entrepreneur following self-interest is 'led by an invisible hand to promote an end which was not part of his intention' (A. Smith [1776] 1950, vol. 1, pp. 477f). This is indeed a remarkable insight. For economic welfare to be enhanced, individuals need not pursue this objective. On the contrary, it would be presumptuous for individuals to claim that their command of knowledge and capabilities would enable them to act in the interest of the society. Moreover, frequently people in possession of power invoke the public interest only for being able to serve their own interest more successfully. To provide scope for the invisible hand to accomplish its task, competition policy must aim at securing undistorted competition. Since it involves creative destruction competition policy must not be concerned with protecting the individual competitor but with protecting competition as an institution.

The necessity of competition policy derives from the experience that everybody quite naturally strives for obtaining a position uncontested by competition (North 1981). Countless admonitions of churchmen from the Middle Ages and the Early Modern Times (Tawney 1926, passim) against greed and avarice, as revealed by exercising monopoly power, are convincing proof of the prevalence of the reprehended behavior. The experience with the economic practice of his time led Adam Smith ([1776] 1950, vol. 1, p. 144) to observe,

> People of the same trade seldom meet together, even for merriment and diversion, but the conversation ends in a conspiracy against the public, or in some contrivance to raise prices.

In fact Ashton (1964, pp. 89–91), in his history of the Industrial Revolution in England, mentioned quite a few cartels in various industries and thus supports the evaluation to be found in Adam Smith. What was true in England of that time applied as well to other countries.

Cartels existed also in the United States (Kintner 1980a), and the last third of the 19th century saw the emergence of trusts. The trust used to be a legal form where the voting rights of shareholders of the participating firms were transferred to a trustee such that unified decision-making was ensured. Hence, trusts were tightly knit cartels. The start was made by John D. Rockefeller who founded the Standard Oil Company in 1882. By eliminating most of his competitors he created the largest monopoly of the country. His example was followed by the creation of other trusts pertaining to lead, whiskey, sugar, matches, tobacco and rubber. By 1904 there were 319 industrial trusts which 5300 formerly independent companies had absorbed (Nevins and Commager 1981, pp. 269ff).

In Germany, at that time, cartels were created first in coal mining and the iron industry, and later on in various other industries, as will be reported below in more detail. This historical experience as well as collusion repeatedly uncovered up to the present time proves that Walter Eucken (1959, p. 37) was right in suggesting a 'propensity to monopolize' exists which tends to undermine a competitive order. A competitive order must therefore be protected by an appropriate competition policy.

To elucidate the effects attributable to competition, and to confront them with the consequences following from restraints of competition, it is helpful to consider two opposing cases, namely perfect competition and monopoly. The analysis of these extreme cases, which themselves are hardly ever to be found in reality, allows for the development of standards of evaluation which also apply in the more realistic setting of an oligopoly to be treated in the next chapter.

Perfect Competition

Put most simply, competition and monopoly are distinguished by the presence or absence, respectively, of power to fix prices. Whereas a monopolist has the power to fix the price such that his own interest is served best, competition curtails this power to set prices, and in the extreme case of perfect competition there is no power at all. According to Frank Knight (1921) perfect competition prevails if buyers are perfectly informed about the quality of the product and the prices charged by competing suppliers, and if no barriers to entry exist such that actually or potentially the number of competitors is large, in the extreme infinitely large. Firms are assumed to be driven by self-interest. Since prices are given, firms choose the level of output such that profits are maximized. This requires marginal costs, that is, additional costs for an extra unit of output, to equal the price.[2]

Given perfect competition, in the long run, the price cannot exceed average costs of production. Otherwise profits would entice new firms to enter the market. Supply would increase and the market price would decline until it covers average costs and profits disappear. If demand for a commodity or service increases, at a given supply, the price goes up and profits arise. Following the entry of new competitors, during a period of adjustment existing firms can still earn profits, called quasi rents, but eventually they are eroded by the entry of new competitors.

The model of perfect competition has frequently been criticized for its static assumptions regarding demand and costs. As suggested by Schumpeter (1912) competition unfolds itself by innovations, that is, by the introduction of cost-reducing processes, new products and new ways to organize economic activity. At a close look, however, this criticism turns out to be unfounded. Starting from the model, as expounded above, to account for the facts emphasized by Schumpeter, innovations are easily incorporated. Between the notion of competition as rivalry unfolding in the dynamics of innovations and the ensuing change in prices on one hand, and the model of perfect competition, as suggested by Knight, on the other, a fundamental difference does not exist as frequently asserted (DiLorenzo and High 1988). Since competition entails profits to be eroded by the entry of competitors, each firm has the chance and an incentive to reduce costs or to elicit new demand by adopting process or product innovations and thus to improve profitability. Each enterprise is assumed to choose the level of output such that at a given price, which cannot be raised by an individual firm, profits are maximized. Following a cost-reducing innovation profits increase as long as marginal costs fall short of the given price. In this way total production increases which yields a decline in the market price. Firms that have failed to reduce their costs are coming under pressure and must eventually leave the market once the price falls short of their average costs. Schumpeter (1942) has called this 'creative destruction'. Old ways of doing things are displaced by new ones.

Still, not all firms with average costs exceeding the market price, which has fallen following innovations, are driven from the market immediately. At each time producers with different costs usually exist side by side because physical capital as well as human capital incorporated in organizational structures is long-lived and sunk. It cannot therefore be removed in the short

---

[2] Maximizing profits, $\Pi = pq - C(q)$, where p is price, q is output, and $C(q)$ are costs depending on the level of output, requires $d\Pi/dq = p - C'(q) = 0$, $d^2\Pi/dq^2 = -C''(q) < 0$, $C'(q)$ being marginal costs.

term from their present location to a new one. Following cost-reducing innovations existing plants and equipment are shut down only once the average
total costs of a new process fall short of the average variable costs of the
previously installed capacity. Since technical progress usually entails rising
wages it also gives rise to increasing average variable costs. Thus old and less
efficient plants and equipment become economically obsolete. In industries
with a high rate of technical progress, and consequently rapidly decreasing
relative prices and average costs, the rate of obsolescence is also high and the
average age of capital goods is comparatively low.

It should be emphasized that shutting down obsolete equipment and replacing it with new capital goods has very little to do with a progressive attitude of the management of the respective firms. It is primarily imposed by the
forces of competition. If a market is populated by a large number of competitors the likelihood for some of them to adopt innovations is high. This
yields a threat to be driven out of the market for those firms which do not
keep pace with the innovative process. Such a force to adopt technical change
does not exist in the case of monopoly. Competition thus provides for two
driving forces which may be called 'stick and carrot', that is, the incentive
given by rewards for successful innovations and the threat of being driven
from the market. Whilst 'carrot' works in the case of monopoly, too, 'stick' is
missing. Therefore the likelihood of innovations is raised by competition.

Monopoly

In the case of monopoly the price may permanently exceed both marginal and
average costs, as shown in Figure 1.1. For illustrative purposes the inverse

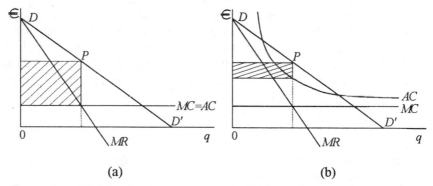

(a)   (b)

Figure 1.1   Marginal and average costs in the case of monopoly

demand curve, DD', is assumed to be linear. It slopes downward such that
demand increases as the price is reduced. In Figure 1.1(a) marginal costs,

MC, are assumed to be constant and identical with average costs, *AC*. In Figure 1.1(b) total costs are composed of both variable costs and fixed costs. This implies that average costs exceed marginal costs.[3]

Although a monopolist has the power to fix the price he must take into account that demand declines if the price is raised. The response of demand elicited by a rising price is measured by the price elasticity of demand, $E := -(p/q)(dq/dp)$, which denotes the percentage change in demand following a 1 per cent increase in price. Profits are maximized if marginal costs equal marginal revenue,[4] which is the extra revenue attributable to an additional unit of output sold. Marginal revenue, as given by the formula $MR = p(1 - 1/E)$, falls short of the respective price.

As shown in Figure 1.1 the price charged by a monopoly is always higher than marginal costs. Therefore, as suggested by Abba P. Lerner (1933–4), the power of a monopoly can be quantified by the price–cost margin (*PCM*) which is the difference between price and marginal costs in relation to the price. For a monopoly maximizing profits the price–cost margin equals the reciprocal of the price elasticity of demand, hence

$$\frac{(p - MC)}{p} = \frac{1}{E} \, .$$

Since the price elasticity of demand denotes the response of demand elicited by an increase in price it reveals to what extent buyers are dependent on the monopoly. Dependence is low if for a buyer a large number of alternative sources of supply exist to satisfy demand. The alternatives may be commodities which are substitutes for the given supply of the monopoly.[5]

As shown in Figure 1.1 under monopoly the output is lower than under competition. Two different cases can be distinguished. In Figure 1.1(a) marginal costs are assumed to equal average costs. In this case, under perfect competition, the equilibrium output is determined by the intersection of the inverse demand curve with the curve depicting marginal costs. In Figure 1.1(b), where fixed costs are assumed to exist, marginal costs fall short of

---

[3] In Figure 1.1(a) the cost function is $C(q) = cq$, where q denotes output and $dC/dq = C/q = c$ are marginal costs and average costs, respectively. In Figure 1.1(b) the cost function is $C(q) = F + cq$ with F denoting fixed costs. Hence marginal costs, c, are lower than average costs, $C/q = c + F/q$.

[4] Maximizing profits, $\Pi = R(q) - C(q)$, where $R(q) = p(q)q$ is revenue, by choosing the level of output, q, requires marginal revenue to equal marginal costs, that is, $R'(q) = C'(q)$, or in slightly different notation $MR = MC$.

[5] In the next chapter the price elasticity of demand as seen by the seller will be shown to increase with an increasing number of competitors.

average costs. The existence of a competitive equilibrium depends on whether fixed costs are sunk. Costs are sunk if they are incurred following an irreversible investment and cannot therefore be recouped if production is shut down. If fixed costs are sunk a competitive equilibrium does not exist. As can be seen easily by inspecting Figure 1.1(b), pricing at marginal costs would always yield a loss. Hence a natural monopoly arises. By contrast, if fixed costs are not sunk, freedom of entry leads up to an equilibrium at the intersection of the average cost curve with the inverse demand curve where average costs are lowest. Even though only a single firm exists it does not possess monopoly power. If the 'monopolist' raises the price he will immediately be undersold by an entrant who, since costs are not sunk, can leave the market without costs once the monopolist reduces the price to the previous level. As the monopolist anticipates being challenged by an entrant he will charge a price which does not exceed average costs from the very beginning. If, in the absence of sunk costs, entry and exit is possible without extra cost the market has been called 'contestable' (Baumol, Panzar and Willig 1982).

Whilst under perfect competition and in the case of contestability profits are zero, monopoly power yields a profit, as depicted in Figures 1.1(a) and 1.1(b) by the respective shaded areas. The existence of monopoly power implies that the income accruing to labor and capital, that is, wages and interest, is lower than under competition. This applies not only to those industries where monopoly exists but throughout the entire economy. Consequently, those people holding the property rights to the monopoly receive an extra income. Recipients of this monopoly rent are mostly capitalists. In quite a few cases, however, monopoly rents can also be acquired for workers by the activities of trade unions.

Lerner's formula for measuring monopoly power suggests that the power a monopolist can wield depends on the relevant price elasticity of demand. The concept of monopolistic market power must therefore be distinguished from the concept of power as used in sociology which denotes a relationship between individuals. For sociology Max Weber (1956, p. 8) defined power as follows,

> Power denotes each possibility within a social relationship to impose their own will on others even against their opposition regardless of why this possibility exists. (My translation.)

Power in this meaning certainly plays some role in economic relationships as well. It must not, however, be confounded with the concept of monopolistic market power. How much power can be wielded depends on how many alternatives are available for buyers, how many competitors are around and how many products are offered which cater to a given demand. Since monopolistic market power is thus a matter of degree, the existence of such market power does not exclude price competition from prevailing. Conversely, the existence of price competition does not disprove that monopolistic market power exists.

Focusing on monopoly and competition has sometimes been criticized on the ground that in particular the concept of perfect competition would fail to characterize competition as experienced in the markets of the real world. Competition, so the criticism goes, is rivalry, it is fighting for control of a market and not adjusting output at given prices. Robert Liefmann, well known for his pioneering book on cartels and trusts (1927) had written in an article published in 1915 in the *Quarterly Journal of Economics*, 'The climax of competition is monopoly, and all competition is nothing but striving for monopoly'.

This is a thesis repeatedly to be encountered in the management literature of our own days. Management is prodded into striving for excellence because allegedly it is only rank number one which really counts. However, in view of the rediscovered objective of maximizing shareholder value, that is, the present value of expected profits, striving for the highest market share cannot be considered but as an intermediate goal. Maximizing shareholder value encompasses profit maximization and may be achieved both by innovating activities and by collusion. Not the least for this reason Allyn Young (1915) replied to Licfmann that there is 'a substantial difference between competing and "attempting to monopolize"'.

Which one of the two options is chosen depends on the institutional and legal framework. Enterprises and their spokesmen may attempt to change the framework by lobbying activities such that monopolistic market power arise and can be exercised. Competition policy aims at inhibiting those tendencies.

Monopsony

Market power can also arise on the side of demand. The extreme case of buying power is called monopsony where a single buyer faces a large number of sellers. The buyer himself may be a monopolist as a seller or he may be subject to competition. To focus on the consequences of buying power we shall assume a buyer selling his output under perfect competition at a price which he is unable to affect. Subtract from this price the marginal selling cost of the buyer to obtain the net selling price, p, as shown in Figure 1.2.

As a matter of simplification the quantity of the purchased commodity is assumed to be proportionally related to the output of the monopsony. That allows for both input and output of the monopsony to be depicted by q on the horizontal axis. Let the supply of the input be shown by the upward sloping curve SS'. The monopsony fixes the purchase price w which elicits a supply

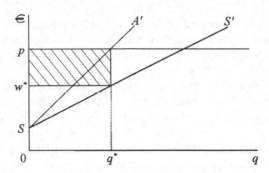

Figure 1.2   Buying power under monopsony

given by the supply curve. A higher price w gives rise to a larger supply.

A profit maximum for the monopsony is attained where the net selling price equals the marginal expenditure which always exceeds the purchase price. Given the inverse supply curve $w = w(q)$ with $w'(q) > 0$, total expenditures are $A(q) = w(q)q$ and marginal expenditures amount to

$$A'(q) = w + qw'(q) = w(1 + 1/\eta)$$

where $\eta := (w/q)(dq/dw)$ is the elasticity of supply with respect to the purchase price w. It denotes by how much supply increases following a 1 per cent rise in the price w. A profit maximum of the monopsony is attained where in Figure 1.2 the marginal expenditure curve, SA', cuts the horizontal line denoting the net selling price. Hence, at a profit maximum

$$w(1 + 1/\eta) = p,$$

which yields a profit depicted by the shaded area in Figure 1.2.

Monopsonistic buying power may, in analogy to the measure of monopoly power suggested by Lerner, be quantified by the difference between the net selling price and the purchase price as related to the net selling price. Profit maximization entails

$$(p - w)/p = 1/\eta.$$

Buying power is thus greater the smaller the elasticity of supply. Once more this elasticity can be interpreted as a measure of the availability of alternatives open to suppliers. The more alternatives are available the higher is the elasticity of supply and the lower is the ensuing buying power of the monopsony.

Short Run vs Long Run

In the short run frequently marginal costs and average costs are different because on one hand the technology involves indivisibilities and on the other hand bottleneck facilities give rise to increasing average costs following an increase in output. If neither case applied marginal costs and average costs would be equal and the supply curve would be a horizontal line, as shown in Figure 1.1(a). In the absence of indivisibilities even the smallest productive unit would be able to compete with a large factory on an equal footing because average costs would be equal. Of course, this fictitious world does not exist in reality because buildings, machinery and the division of labor within organizations are indivisible, at least to some extent. Therefore, average costs decline following an increase in output until beyond some level of output bottleneck facilities become operative and cause average costs to increase. Hence, as illustrated in Figure 1.3, marginal costs fall short of average costs until a minimum efficient size is reached. Beyond this point average costs rise and exceed marginal costs.

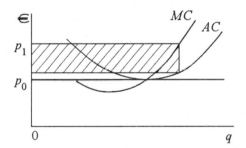

Figure 1.3   Marginal costs vs average costs

If the market price equals minimal average costs, profits are zero. The invested capital is rewarded by a rate of return which could have been earned on the capital market, and a self-employed entrepreneur receives a remuneration for his labor which equals the wage rate he could have earned elsewhere. If the market price exceeds the minimal average costs the shaded area in Figure 1.3 denotes a pure profit. Free entry would induce the emergence of new competitors. Hence the total output of the market would increase and the price would be forced down. If this were to happen instantaneously, the price would be bound to equal minimal average costs all the time. In reality various impediments may cause this process to occur only sluggishly.

Moreover the expansion of output may be inhibited by the limited availability of resources which cause the long run supply curve to slope upwards. For an equilibrium to be attained, the market price must cover the average

costs of the least efficient firm which is required to satisfy forthcoming demand. The more efficient firm then earns a permanent profit which is called a
rent. By contrast profits arising only temporarily during an adjustment
towards a competitive equilibrium are called quasi rents.

Competition as a Process of Discovery

Competition yields discoveries. Which technique is the most efficient one
and which products appeal most to consumers cannot be anticipated with
certainty. Initially unknown and untried techniques and novel products are
put to the test of the market. The price a successful product commands may
exceed average costs. Success is thus rewarded by profitability which in turn
provides incentives for further innovations. A deficient state of knowledge is
thus overcome by competition as a process of discovery.

Profits of a successful enterprise may firstly be due to costs being lower
than those of competitors or to the superiority of products. Profits may sec-
ondly arise because of a temporary monopoly enjoyed by the pioneering
enterprise. Under competition, however, nobody can rest on his laurels since
the entry of new competitors is apt to undermine a once achieved market
position. In fact, the likelihood of competing innovations to emerge increases
with the number of competitors. The more enterprises are seeking independently to innovate, the larger is the probability that at least one of them will
be successful.[6]

Profits in the Long Run

Following the emergence of a new market the successful pioneer first enjoys
excess profits. His leading position, however, is contested by new competitors unless he is able to maintain his lead by follow-up innovations. He may
adopt new techniques which yield lower costs, he may improve his product or
he may himself shift to entirely new products. So new profit opportunities are
created which are subject to erosion in the competitive process.

Thus two opposing tendencies are at work, innovation and erosion of profits. It is therefore possible that in historical time profits never disappear. In
fact in most industries a remarkable persistence of profits has been observed
(Mueller 1986, Geroski and Schwalbach 1991, Audretsch 1995). A priori
such a persistence of profits need not be taken as disproving the characteris-

---

[6] If N independent experiments are conducted with probability $\pi < 1$, the probability for at least
one of them to be successful is $P = 1 - (1 - \pi)^N$. It is the higher the larger the number of experiments.

tics of the competitive process as depicted above. On the other hand, it cannot be ruled out that the evolutionary process is subject to some inertia. The entry of new competitors proceeds only sequentially since it takes time to acquire information about profitability and to build up new productive capacities. For this reason incumbents may enjoy temporary monopoly power despite potential, and eventually even actual, entry of competitors (Gaskins 1971). Temporary monopolies need not be of concern for competition policy insofar as they are contested by potential and actual entry.

Regarding the role performed by entry and exit, two different phases of the development of a market have to be distinguished (Münter 1999). At the beginning of the life cycle of a product a large amount of experimentation occurs. Market structure is subject to dramatic changes. New firms emerge, increase their market share and displace existing suppliers. For depicting what is going on it is helpful to invoke the metaphor of a forest where new trees grow up. Old trees decay and are eventually supplanted by new ones. This picture, however, no longer applies if one looks at a mature industry. Following experimentation a dominant design with regard to products and processes has asserted itself. Surviving firms have achieved a decisive lead in experience against newcomers. Best suited for describing the situation is the metaphor of a revolving door. Inside the building, that is, in the existing market, one finds the incumbents. Newcomers enter by the revolving door but most of them are turned around and thrown out without being able to establish themselves in the building. Although in mature industries quite a few entries occur, most of them turn out to fail, and thus the market shares of incumbents are hardly affected (Mueller 1991, p. 12)

> Despite the seemingly large amounts of entry and exit that occur in most industries, neither has much of a measurable effect on their basic structural characteristics. ... The leading firms in most industries stand calmly in the center, as if in the eye of a tornado, while a myriad smaller challengers whirl in and out along the periphery.

The stability of market shares of incumbents to be found in mature industries may result as the outcome of the competitive processes where the opposing forces of innovation and the erosion of profits are just balancing. It cannot be ruled out, however, that the permanent incumbency of leading firms follows from the exercise of market power. Leading firms may abuse their dominance to inhibit the entry of new competitors. This poses a challenge for competition policy.

Monopoly Profits and Quasirents as Concerns for Competition Policy

Traditionally restraints of competition have been evaluated primarily, albeit not exclusively, with regard to efficiency. For representatives of the so-called Chicago School efficiency is even claimed to be the only legitimate standard of evaluation. According to their view it is only the misallocation of resources and the entailed welfare loss which should be of concern. Competition policy should not be concerned with the transfer of income towards those holding a monopoly because allegedly distributive effects can only be evaluated by reference to 'ultimate values' which cannot be justified within the framework of economic theory (Bork 1965, pp. 837ff). Even though this opinion has some merit, a close look at the problem will reveal that economic reasoning does have some bearing on distributive issues.

It helps to remember the distinction between commutative and distributive justice suggested by Aristotle. Commutative justice refers to rewarding achievement such that the accrual of income can be attributed to performance. In economics this principle is applied by explaining income distribution by reference to the marginal productivity of factors of production. Given perfect competition throughout the economy, factors of production like labor and capital are rewarded by the value of their respective marginal productivity. If monopoly power comes into play factor rewards and the income shares of labor and capital are lower. In addition to that, the actual distribution of income is affected by various causes which cannot be identified in detail and which therefore are attributed to random effects. As far as income distribution turns out to become unequal in consequence of those effects, that is, good luck or bad luck, respectively, the outcome may be considered as unjust and in need to be corrected. A value judgement of this kind belongs to the realm of distributive justice. It is beyond the reach of economics. However, not all inequities of distribution are attributable to random effects. Some of them are deliberately created and thus amenable to being evaluated by standards of commutative justice. In this regard monopoly profits and quasi rents come to mind.

From the viewpoint of commutative ethics a monopoly profit is legitimate if it performs a useful task for society. This may apply insofar as the chance to earn a monopoly profit creates an incentive to innovation and if the profit is subject to ensuing erosion by imitation. A temporary monopoly is tolerable because the profit is a reward for a valuable achievement. By contrast, in other cases a monopoly profit may be unjustifiable by reference to commutative ethics. A monopoly will hardly ever come into existence at random. Most monopolies are deliberately created or strived for if the legal framework allows monopolies to emerge, or if a monopoly is even granted by government decree. It also depends on the legal framework, in particular on the existence and stance of competition policy, how fast temporary monopolies, originally based on superior performance, are eroded by the forces of competition. The same applies to quasi rents which are subject to being swept away if the market is open for new competitors. In light of these considerations monopoly profits cannot be considered as pure transfers of income between different individuals beyond the scope of economics. In quite a few cases a differentiated analysis leads to a clear-cut condemnation of monopoly profits.

1.2 HORIZONTAL CONCENTRATION

A necessary condition for monopoly power to exist is a small number of suppliers. Monopoly power is thus predicated on a high level of horizontal concentration. Horizontal concentration which entails high market shares of the leading firms may be caused by restraints of competition which convey the power to fix prices. Horizontal concentration is not sufficient, however, to create monopoly power. It may lose its force by virtue of potential entry.

Potential vs Actual Competition

As explained above, in the case of a perfectly contestable market (Baumol, Panzar and Willig 1982), where costs are not sunk, a single supplier suffices to ensure that the price of a commodity can not exceed average costs. Actually, however, in most cases fixed costs are sunk. An incumbent monopoly is then able to charge a monopoly price and earn a monopoly rent without enticing the entry of competitors. If a competitor did enter, the price would eventually be driven down to the level of average costs. Upon exiting the market sunk investments are definitely lost. A potential entrant therefore knows that the envisaged profit opportunity is but a Fata Morgana which disappears once entry occurs. Although the incumbent monopoly earns excess profits, entry is blocked. Potential entry has no effect whatever.[7]

Measuring Horizontal Concentration

In practice horizontal concentration is frequently depicted by the combined market share $CR3$ ($CR4$, $CR6$, $CR8$, and so on) of the leading 3 (4, 6, 8, and

---

[7] Stiglitz (1994, p. 124), to support this argument, pointed out the case of the US airline industry which the advocates of the contestability doctrine used to mention and which, not least because of the influence of this doctrine, has been deregulated. Although initially numerous new firms entered the market, in the meantime, following a shake-out just three major airlines remained in the US.

so on) firms of an industry. Data for this measure are easy to collect. A more subtle measure is the Herfindahl index

$$H = \sum_{i=1}^{n} s_i^2$$

where s_i is the share of firm i in sales of the respective industry which is composed of n firms.

The Herfindahl index can be decomposed into one part representing the number of firms and another one reflecting the variance of market shares. The variance of market shares is $V = [\sum_{i=1}^{n}(s_i - \bar{s})^2]/n$, where $\bar{s} = 1/n$ is the average market share of the n firms under consideration. After multiplication and rearranging one obtains

$$H = 1/n + nV.$$

The Herfindahl index is $H = 1$ in the case of monopoly. It is $1/n$ if all firms are alike and in this case approaches zero if n goes to infinity. The Herfindahl index rises ceteris paribus with the variance of market shares and thus takes account of the size distribution of firms.

Gibrat's Law

Horizontal concentration does not necessarily entail monopolistic market power, as explained above. Nor can horizontal concentration be always conclusively attributed to monopolizing strategies. Horizontal concentration may be caused by random effects. For the sake of argument assume technology to display perfect divisibility and additivity such that neither economics to scale apply nor rising average costs due to bottleneck facilities. Then, in the absence of artificial barriers to entry, perfect competition exists irrespective of the actual number of firms. Nevertheless over time random effects will cause horizontal concentration to arise. Since constant returns to scale leave the size of individual firms technologically indeterminate, the size distribution of firms depends on how much demand accrues to the individual supplier. All firms enjoy identical chances to capture demand. If demand grows, the actual rate of change of individual firm size depends on random effects. The statistical expectation of firm size is thus independent of the initial size. If, in some period, firm A by chance grows faster than firm B, at the beginning of the next period it starts from a higher level from which an identical proportionate rate of growth yields a larger increment of size. Furthermore, since the probability to achieve a more than average rate of growth in successive periods declines with the number of periods for which this may hold, an unequal size distribution can be expected to emerge. Even though the chances to grow are equal among the firms under consideration, horizontal concentration increases. In fact the size distribution approaches a logarithmic normal distribution. That is Gibrat's Law (see Sutton 1997) according to which the emerging size distribution is skew with only a few big firms and a large number of smaller ones.[8]

Gibrat's Law has been used for explaining the actual size distribution of firms and thus horizontal concentration in various industries. In some cases fairly accurate predictions could be achieved; in other cases the outcome was not so good. Still, Gibrat's Law holds an important lesson. Horizontal concentration may emerge by chance and it would be premature to infer from observing high concentration alone that restraints of competition exist. On the other hand, a failure of Gibrat's Law to deliver a sufficiently good prediction of the size distribution strongly suggests that the size distribution does not emerge from random effects alone, but may also be affected by restraints of competition. Given the ambiguity of empirical results it would be desirable to have a model which allows more precise predictions.

Mosteller's Law

A promising alternative to Gibrat's Law is Mosteller's Law (1965). It does not pertain to the size of firms but to their market shares. By comparing an actual distribution of market shares with the distribution which can be expected to arise purely at random, Mosteller's Law can be utilized to uncover circumstantial evidence for the presence of restraints of competition. If the chances of success are equally distributed and if, in particular, they are not distorted by restraints of competition which favor dominant firms, the distribution of market shares can be expected to follow Mosteller's Law. Average costs depend on innovative activities, and sales depend in addition on how well the products of a firm appeal to consumers' wishes. Both are subject to countless random effects. If they are taken into account an unequal distribution of market shares is likely to arise following the formula

---

[8] Let x denote the size of a firm in period t. If the rate of growth ε_t is a random variable one obtains $x_t = (1+\varepsilon_t)x_{t-1} = x_0(1+\varepsilon_1)(1+\varepsilon_2)...(1+\varepsilon_t)$. Given a small distance between t and $t-1$, as $\ln(1+\varepsilon_t) \cong \varepsilon_t$ holds approximately, $\ln x_t = \ln x_0 + \varepsilon_1 + \varepsilon_2 + ... + \varepsilon_t$. Provided the rates of growth are stochastic and independently distributed a lognormal distribution results (see Sutton 1997, pp. 40f).

$$s_j = \frac{1}{n}\sum_{i=j}^{n}\left(\frac{1}{i}\right)$$

(Mosteller 1965, Gilman 1992).[9]

Applying this formula yields a distribution of market shares as illustrated in Table 1.1.

Table 1.1   Market shares (in per cent) for alternative numbers of firms

Number of suppliers	Rank order of suppliers						Herfindahl Index	Variance of market shares
	1	2	3	4	5	6		
1	100						1.0	
2	75	25					0.6250	0.0625
3	61	28	11				0.4626	0.0431
4	52	27	15	6			0.3694	0.0299
5	46	26	15	9	4		0.3114	0.0223
6	41	24	16	10	6	3	0.2658	0.0165

At random a distribution of market shares can be expected to emerge such that the Herfindahl index of horizontal concentration declines following an increase in the number of suppliers. Moreover, as shown in Table 1.1, the variance of market shares is a declining function of the number of competitors. Thus if the number of suppliers increases they can be expected to become more equal in size.

Mosteller's Law predicts a rank order of market shares to emerge without giving information about the identity of the firms occupying a particular rank. It is quite possible for a firm which in some period holds a leading position to fall back to a lower rank in some later period. Since the ensuing rank order yields a prediction for the distribution of market shares which would eventu-

---

[9]   The formula is derived from the following model (Gilman 1992). 'Let a stick of wood represent a market. Break the stick at some random place along its length. This represents dividing the market into two shares. Repeat this many times to represent the large number of factors that determine market shares (location, advertising, pricing, quality, service, product design, and so on). After many sticks have been randomly broken, measure the lengths of the smaller and the larger pieces resulting from each break; then determine the averages. ... The average for the whole length will be 1/4 and 3/4 pieces. ... Similar reasoning can be applied for any number of companies participating in a particular market. For example, suppose there are three companies. This corresponds to two random breaks. The average shares are then 11/18, 5/18 and 2/18.' If the market is shared by n firms the individual market share to be expected is given by the above formula.

ally come about given undistorted competition, deviations from the expected distribution give rise to the suspicion that restraints of competition may be present. The relationship between the theoretically expected distribution of market shares and the actual one will be illustrated by some examples.

In German food retailing in 1993, as shown in Table 1.2, the actual distribution of market shares came pretty close to the distribution to be expected by Mosteller's Law. The second example pertains to worldwide market

Table 1.2   Market shares (in per cent) in German food retailing 1993

Firm		Actual market share	Mosteller's Law
Metro		17.39	15.27
Rewe		11.67	11.27
Edeka		11.33	9.27
Aldi		8.38	7.94
Tengelmann		7.45	6.94
Karstadt		6.09	6.14
Spar		4.38	5.47
Lidl & Schwarz		4.22	4.90
Hertie		2.20	4.40
Allkauf		1.89	3.96
	Sum	75.00	75.56
Correlation		0.986	
Herfindahl Index		0.0775	0.0684

Source: dpa.

shares of electronic stores and microprocessors in 1990. Whereas electronic stores display a good conformity between the actual and the theoretically expected distribution, in the case of microprocessors Intel stands out as having an excessive market share. This may be attributable either to Intel having been successful in remaining a pioneer, or to its using restrictive practices to shield a once attained lead from the inroads of contenders.

For a third example look at the market shares for motor cars in Germany and the EC 1991. In Germany the actual distribution is very similar to the one expected according to Mosteller's Law. This is not so in the EC, where six firms were holding almost identical shares. This finding lends support to the suspicion that the European market for motor cars may be subject to collusive restraints of trade.

Table 1.3   Market shares (in per cent) of the 20 largest producers of electronic stores and microprocessors 1990

Electronic stores			Microprocessors	
Firm	Actual share	Mosteller's Law	Firm	Actual share
Toshiba	12.3	12.11	Intel	27.0
NEC	10.7	9.17	NEC	10.7
Hitachi	9.9	7.70	Motorola	9.9
Fujitsu	8.2	6.72	Hitachi	6.4
Mitsubishi	7.3	5.99	Mitsubishi	4.6
Samsung	7.1	5.40	Toshiba	4.5
Texas Instruments	5.4	4.91	Texas Instruments	3.2
Sharp	4.0	4.49	Matsushita	2.4
Motorola	3.0	4.12	Fujitsu	2.4
Oki	2.9	3.79	National Semiconductor	2.4
Intel	2.5	3.50	Chip & Technologies	2.3
Siemens	2.5	3.23	Advanced Micro Devices	2.0
Matsushita	2.3	2.99	Philips	1.9
SGS-Thompson	2.2	2.76	SGS-Thompson	1.7
Micro Technology	2.1	2.55	Western Digital	1.5
Advanced Micro Devices	2.1	2.35	Oki	1.5
Sony	1.9	2.17	AT & T	1.4
NMB Semiconductor	1.5	1.99	Sharp	1.3
Cypress Semiconductor	1.2	1.83	Cirrus Logic	1.3
National Semiconductor	1.1	1.67	Harris	1.1
Sum	90.2	89.44		89.4
Correlation		0.974	0.914	
Herfindahl Index	0.0559	0.0542		0.1078

Source of Data: Monopolkommission (1992, p. 394).

Table 1.4 Market shares (in per cent) on the market for motor cars in Germany and the EC 1991

Germany			EC	
Firm	Actual share	Mosteller's Law	Firm	Actual share
VW	21.1	15.3	Peugeot/Citroen	12.9
Opel	16.3	11.3	Opel	12.4
Ford	10.0	9.3	Ford	11.6
Mercedes-Benz	8.3	7.9	Renault	11.0
BMW	6.7	6.9	Fiat/Alfa/Lancia	10.8
Audi	5.2	6.1	VW	10.3
Renault	5.2	5.5	Mercedes-Benz	3.6
Peugeot/Citroen	4.6	4.9	Nissan	3.3
Fiat/Alfa/Lancia	3.8	4.4	BMW	3.3
Nissan	2.7	3.9	Rover	3.2
Toyota	2.5	3.5	Audi	2.6
Mazda	2.3	3.2	Toyota	2.6
Seat	2.0	2.9	Seat	2.5
Honda	1.6	2.5	Volvo	1.7
Mitsubishi	1.5	2.3	Mazda	1.5
Volvo	0.8	2.0	Honda	1.4
Rover	0.5	1.7	Mitsubishi	1.0
Skoda	0.5	1.5	Skoda	0.5
Saab	0.2	1.3	Saab	0.4
Sum	95.8	96.4		96.6
Correlation		0.988	0.914	
Herfindahl Index	0.1043	0.0736		0.0872
C3	47.4	35.8		36.9
C6	67.6	56.8		69.0

Source: Frankfurter Allgemeine Zeitung (Kraftfahrtbundesamt and Aea).

1.3 UNDERMINING COMPETITION THROUGH LAISSEZ FAIRE

What is the appropriate role for competition policy to play? Since competition is a constitutive element of a market economy and undoubtedly contributes to enhance economic welfare the question arises how competition policy should be conducted to maintain a competitive order. An extreme opinion holds that guaranteeing freedom of contract would be sufficient since it implies freedom of entry. According to this view a cartel which charges monopoly prices would elicit the entry of new competitors which would undermine monopoly power and render the cartel as useless for its members. Rational producers would not join a cartel in the first place (Selten 1973). This reasoning finds some support by the experience of the cartel of oil exporting countries (OPEC) which succeeded twice during the 1970s in raising the price dramatically, but also elicited the emergence of new producers which did not join the cartel and eventually undermined the power of OPEC. The high prices enforced by the cartel led to opening up new oil fields which exerted pressure on oil prices. This process took about 20 years to evolve, however.

Controversial Evaluation of Cartels

Towards the end of the 19th century most economists looked at cartels approvingly as being the appropriate organization of industries. Cartels were assumed to play the role which in the Middle Ages and the Early Modern Time had been played by guilds. In fact, during the second half of the 19th century a substantial change in technology had occurred. The Industrial Revolution, which originated in England one hundred years earlier, led to the foundation of a few large enterprises. However, in general it was still small and medium-sized firms which were representative for the economy of the earlier decades of the 19th century. Only from the middle of the century did really big firms make their appearance, first railway companies, followed by enterprises in manufacturing industries. A characteristic feature was the increase of fixed costs (Piore and Sabel 1984). Bigness lent economic superiority vis-à-vis traditional small firms. Fixed costs, however, made them more vulnerable in business cycle recessions.

From this perspective the monopolistic element inherent in cartels, which by the way also applied to medieval guilds, used to be overlooked. It was the necessity to provide protection for weak members of the guilds from the destructive consequences of competition which primarily drew the attention of contemporary observers. Since competition entails 'creative destruction', as suggested by Schumpeter (1942), the innovations coming forth during the latter decades of the 19th century threatened the traditional structure of industry. Cartels were considered as a means to slow down this process and thus to entail beneficial effects. Since structural change announces itself frequently in business cycle recessions, for many people cartels appeared to be 'children of distress'. The Austrian economist Kleinwächter (1883) who coined this characterization of cartels considered them to be indispensable for achieving an orderly adjustment of production to volatile demand. Some people considered cartels even in a romantic light as safeguarding social stability and avoiding the chaotic conditions of competition. At the meeting of the *Verein für Socialpolitik,* that is, the German Economic Association, in Mannheim 1905, Gustav Schmoller, the head of the Younger Historical School of German economists, although not uncritical of cartels, pleaded for abuse control but vehemently opposed prohibiting them. According to him, such suggestions can only come from infantile hotspurs, that is, economists unaware of the evils of the old free competition. Another prominent economist of the Historical School, Karl Bücher (1895, p. 138), said,

> I consider the change initiated by cartels to be welfare enhancing and necessary because it entails a return from anarchy to order of production, social and economic disciplining of society for higher tasks of culture to be expected in the future. (My translation.)

Politically leftist circles welcomed cartels for quite another reason. The leader of the Social Democratic opposition in Germany, August Bebel, considered cartels as a welcome step into the direction of Socialism (Möschel 1972, p. 15).

Among US economists, trusts met with approval for similar reasons. John Bates Clark wrote in 1887 (see Neale 1966, p. 25),

> Combinations have their roots in the nature of social industry and are normal in their origin, their development and their practical working. They are neither to be deprecated by scientists nor suppressed by legislation.

He gave expression to an opinion overwhelmingly held by professional economists of his time (DiLorenzo and High 1988).

This opinion also lay at the bottom of the decision in 1897 of the German Imperial Court of Justice (Reichsgericht) by which cartels became de facto legalized in Germany. The case at stake was a cartel 'Sächsischer Holzstoff-Fabrikanten-Verband' (Association of Saxonian Woodpulp Producers) for woodpulp, the statutes of which provided for the avoidance of what was deemed destructive competition. A member of the cartel had been fined by the cartel for cheating and had sued the cartel for violating the legal principle of freedom of economic activity (Gewerbefreiheit). The Imperial Court, as a court of last resort, turned down the complaint on the ground that, against the good intention of the law to provide for economic freedom, the danger of ruinous competition would justify the formation of cartels to safeguard existence. The Court also argued that preventing ruinous competition is in the public interest.[10]

---

[10] Böhm (1948) criticized the ruling of the Court as being a clear violation of the law. However, as argued by Möschel (1972, p. 21), the existing law (Gewerbeordnung) aimed primarily at dismantling government restrictions of economic activities. The conclusion, drawn by Böhm,

The emergence of cartels in industries characterized by high fixed costs and volatile demand may be understood by recalling that in a business cycle recession the price may fall short of average costs, and thus a competitive equilibrium no longer exists, as suggested by Bittlingmayer (1982) and McWilliams and Keith (1994) for explaining the emergence of trusts in the US. In such a case cartels may in fact be 'children of distress' as claimed by advocates of cartels in Germany. Thus, the Imperial Court of Justice in Germany, in its defense of cartels, was led by the assumption that cartels are suitable to avoiding price cutting and excess production and would thus also serve the public interest (Möschel 1972, p. 8).

Characterizing cartels as being 'children of distress', though, cannot be generally true. Whereas in Germany during the later decades of the 19th century cartels were founded primarily in mining, iron and steel, the chemical industry and the cement industry where indeed fixed costs are high, later on, particularly during the 1920s, cartels were established in many labor-intensive manufacturing industries where the aforementioned justification does not apply.[11]

Following the ruling of the Court, in Germany cartels proliferated tremendously. In 1890 137 cartels were counted, 364 in 1910, and 1539 in 1925 (Feldenkirchen 1985, p. 154). According to another source the number of cartels amounted to 2000–2500 in 1925 (Fischer 1954, p. 443). In this way Germany became a country of cartels. Eventually membership in a cartel was declared mandatory by the Nazi government, and toward the end of the 1930s all cartels were changed into agencies of the centrally planned war economy. It turned out as an irony of history that the forecast of August Bebel mentioned above (p. 25) came true in quite another way than expected by him.

The emergence of cartels in Germany and trusts in the US was supported by protectionism which during the latter decades of the 19th century gained ground in all industrialized countries. Up to the 1870s international trade policy was governed by the free trade gospel which had scored its major victory by the repeal of the Corn Laws in Britain in 1846 and spread to the European continent and gained ground also in the US. During this time cartels had hardly any chances to develop and therefore could not play a dominant role. By contrast, the barriers to free trade built up during the era of imperialism gave rise to a protective wall behind which cartels could survive and proliferate. This observation again proves cartels to be monopolistic organizations.

that the law implied a prohibition of private restraints of competition would amount to 'making law' instead of applying it.

[11] About two-thirds of the 1500 cartels estimated by Liefmann (1927, p. 39) for 1923 were to be found in consumer goods industries.

This conclusion agrees with the evaluation of contemporaries. One of the leading German economists of the 1920s, Werner Sombart (1921, p. 316), observed,

> Cartels are not children of distress, as frequently assumed. It is not the time of deep depression (as one might think) when enterprises of a certain industry are ready to strike an agreement on prices or other conditions of trade (in those times everybody tries to fight out the problems on his own) but rather the time of an upswing, when sales at prices exceeding costs are assured. (My translation.)[12]

More recently this interpretation has been questioned by Rotemberg and Saloner (1986). Using game theory they claimed that price cutting causing cartels to break up occurs primarily during a business cycle upswing. Their conclusion, though, is predicated on the assumption of demand shocks being independently and identically distributed random events. Actually, however, during business cycles, prices and quantities are serially correlated such that the underlying assumption of the Rotemberg/Saloner model is violated. Dropping their basic assumption, Haltiwanger and Harrington (1991) found cartels to be particularly vulnerable to decay during recessions. In further empirical studies this tendency, which had been pointed out by Sombart, was confirmed for US industries by Dick (1996) and Bagwell and Staiger (1997). It is also supported by the finding of Neumann, Böbel and Haid (1983) according to which in a cross-section of West German industries a favorable influence of horizontal concentration on the price–cost margin could only be observed during business cycle upswings but not in recessions. Sombart's thesis thus appears to be well founded both theoretically and empirically.

Competition Policy is Necessary

In fact a laissez-faire policy towards cartels appears to be conducive to their proliferation. It may still be objected that the development of cartels in Germany as well as the emergence of trusts in the US has been supported by protectionism in international trade policy. Had the former free trade policy been maintained, cartels would have crumbled and possibly would not have been founded in the first place. This may be true. Nevertheless, the adoption

---

[12] Similarly, Liefmann (1927, p. 3) observed, 'Under free competition the individual entrepreneur, even in favorable times, hesitates to raise prices for fear of losing sales because competitors do not follow suit. By contrast, cartels allow for firms to raise prices immediately once demand rises. Thus not only times of distress but also favorable times are conducive to establish cartels, as experienced during the years of business cycle upswing 1888–90, during the boom from 1895 to 1900, as well during the favorable years 1904–7, and 1910–13.' (My translation.)

of protectionism under the aegis of imperialism and the permissive stance adopted in Germany by the Imperial Court presumably set into motion an irreversible process. Cartels gave rise to interest groups which were conducive to the maintenance of protectionism. In Germany it was only after the total collapse of the political system (see also Olson 1965) that, first under the US military government and later on in the Federal Republic of Germany, a strict competition policy was introduced and, together with all of the Western World, a liberalized international trade policy has been established within GATT and WTO.

This experience provides overwhelming evidence for competition policy to be indispensable for maintaining competition. It also elucidates the interdependence between competition policy and international trade policy. It would, however, be foolish to be indulgent towards restraints of competition on the ground that the vigor of competition increases following globalization. Although international trade policy presently conducted in the spirit of free trade serves as a supportive companion piece for competition policy, it is not, however, immune from being weakened by protectionist interests. Thus adopting a laissez-faire stance of competition policy bodes the danger for a free market economy to be corrupted and its social legitimacy to be undermined.

Competition Policy and Industrial Policy

Therefore competition policy is to be shaped such as to ward off both restraints of competition and restraints of international trade. By contrast, competition policy is frequently conceived of in the spirit of regulating economic activities. In view of prevailing fixed costs perfect competition as defined by Knight (1921) can hardly ever be expected to exist. Therefore the government is supposed to be responsible for attaining economic welfare by aiming at an industrial structure which is believed as being welfare enhancing. Thus John Maurice Clark (1940, 1961) propagated 'workable competition' as a goal to be recommended which, although falling short of the ideal of perfect competition, could still be expected to be conducive to an outcome which would approach a welfare optimum as closely as possible in the real world. In the same vein, Kantzenbach (1967) recommended a situation dubbed 'wide oligopoly' to be aimed at by competition policy. A wide oligopoly was assumed to entail some heterogeneity of products, moderate transparency and the number of competitors larger than in the case of a so-called 'narrow oligopoly'. A wide oligopoly was assumed to provide sufficient incentives for innovating. John Maurice Clark emphasized, similarly to Eucken (1959), the dynamics of competition as revealed in an unending succession of moves and responses. The advocates of workable competition thus propagated an image of a welfare-enhancing economic structure to be achieved by an appropriate policy.

This stance of policy is opposed to the view that competition should fend off restraints of competition. At first glance the contrast is not obvious. For competition policy it is necessary to decide in individual cases whether a contract between firms, irrespective of whether it is a cartel, a merger or some vertical agreement, is to be tolerated or dismissed. This might appear as leading up to the problem of deciding whether a glass of water is half full or half empty. This is not true, however, as will become clear upon a close look at the problem. To clarify the issue two opposing approaches should be distinguished, namely the constructivistic and the evolutionary approach, respectively (Neumann 1990).

According to the constructivistic approach competition policy is a branch of industrial policy aiming at an industrial structure most conducive to economic welfare (Maillet 1984). According to this view, which can also be found to be held by prominent German jurists (see Badura 1966), competition is an arrangement established by the government. The evolutionary view, by contrast, is based on the insight that competition is a dynamic process of discovery driven by individual self-interest. The difference between the two opposing approaches is simply that according to constructivism everything is prohibited unless it is explicitly permitted, whereas evolutionists would consider everything to be allowed unless it is explicitly forbidden. The followers of the evolutionary view, instead of striving at the attainment of an optimal allocation of resources and an optimal rate of technical change through government regulation, hold that neither the objectives of the economy nor the means for their attainment are known a priori. It is only through the competitive process that new ways of doing things are discovered, new markets are opened and new products are developed. There is no government which might be able to outguess entrepreneurs regarding the potential of the future, and there is no government which, like a benevolent dictator, might be able to pursue economic welfare by adopting non-partisan policies.

Even though market structure and performance are related, the market structure, too, is the outcome of competition. From the view of the evolutionary approach constructivists are guilty of committing a logical error. Given that the future is unknown its potential cannot be explored other than by trial and error. It can only be discovered stepwise by adopting innovations and subjecting them to the test of the market. It is thus an illusion to expect the government to anticipate today what can only be known tomorrow (Popper 1957, p. xii). An active industrial policy is thus guilty of being presumptuous and will frequently cause more harm than good. Once firms act in good faith on an official forecast the government can hardly refuse to compensate firms for losses if the forecast turns out to be erroneous. Following unavoidable errors industrial policy is thus conducive to a proliferation of subsidies and accompanying distortions of competition.[13]

Frequently industrial policy is held to improve the international competitiveness of a country. This end used to be achieved by singling out some enterprises as 'National Champions' which are supported by government aid. The outcome, however, is dubious because such a policy gives rise to distortions and restraints of competition. Selectively subsidizing particular industries or firms amounts to returning to the policy of privileges as employed during Mercantilism. This policy has been castigated harshly by Adam Smith, not least on the ground that it gave rise to monopolies. Moreover, as shown by Porter (1990) in a comparative study, international competitiveness appears to be most effectively promoted by maintaining competition at home through a strict competition policy.

1.4   APPROACHES TO COMPETITION POLICY IN THE US, GERMANY AND THE EUROPEAN UNION

The following section is devoted to outlining the principles of competition policy in the US, Germany, the UK, France and the EC. It will be shown to display a remarkable convergence. In the US the beginning of antitrust was set by the Sherman Act of 1890. In the Federal Republic of Germany a national competition policy was initiated by the Act against Restraints of Competition (GWB Gesetz gegen Wettbewerbsbeschränkungen) of 1957. At the European level the treaties concerning the European Community of Steel and Coal (ECSC) of 1951 and the European Economic Community (EEC) of 1957 contained provisions against restraints of trade and competition. The competition policy of the European Community has been shaped by the same principles as the German competition policy which in turn was influenced by US antitrust. In the meantime the law of the European Community has assumed increasing weight and has exerted a determining influence on the national laws of the member states of the European Community which gives rise to a harmonization of competition law within the EC. The EC law has in particular exerted pressures on the member states to abandon exemptions and specific regulatory regimes applying to certain industries, such as telecommunications, traffic, banking, insurance, postal services and public utilities, and to subject them to the general rules of competition policy.

---

[13] An outstanding example is the European steel industry. See Chapter 4, Section 4.4.

US Antitrust

Competition policy in the United States of America is based on the Sherman Act of 1890, the Clayton Act and the Federal Trade Commission Act, both of 1914. Although this legislation stood in the tradition of the common law prohibition of monopolies it gave rise to an important change. The English common law courts used to uphold restraints of competition unless they were motivated by sheer malice towards third parties. In the US only a few courts went that far, however. The prevailing trend was hostile to restrictive practices even when they were alleged to put an end to 'ruinous' competition (Neale 1966, p. 26). The monopolistic character was clearly perceived. In the case of Central Ohio Salt Co. v. Guthrie (1880) concerning a common sales organization combined with a pooling agreement (Kintner 1980a, p. 89) the court found that

> The clear tendency of such an agreement is to establish a monopoly, and to destroy competition in trade, and for that reason, on grounds of public policy, courts will not aid in its enforcement.

The denial of protection by the law for cartels, as practiced by most US courts, destabilized cartels[14] without, however, being able to prevent them altogether. If cartels are denied the protection of the law, their members usually attempt to create their own law and to enforce it by information exchange, monitoring the allegiance and punishing defectors. Even though the duration of cartels used to be low in the US there were notable exemptions where cartels were stabilized by particular conditions.

Probably the most successful cartel of US history was the 'railroad express cartel' of the parcel service. It asserted itself for more than 50 years, that is, from 1851 to 1913, by setting up a network which provided for economies of scale and scope for its members and left no chances for outsiders (Grossman 1996). A second instructive example was the US bromine cartel which existed from 1885 to the beginning of World War I. It was stabilized not least by an agreement with the corresponding German cartel called 'Deutsche Bromkonvention' about mutually respecting the national sales territories. As reported by Levenstein (1997, p. 135), during about 30 years of its existence there were numerous cases where defectors were punished, but only two episodes where cartel coherence temporarily broke down. One of them was triggered off by a quarrel with the 'Deutsche Bromkonvention'.

These examples are exceptions to the rule that denial of protection of law is conducive to destabilizing cartels. If courts decline to enforce restrictive

[14] For a theoretical explanation see Chapter 2, Section 2.2.

agreements private firms will look for alternatives other than cartels to achieve their goal. In the US that was first tried by forming trusts and subsequently holding companies and eventually by outright merger. In view of this experience the sometimes held opinion that it would suffice for competition policy to deny protection of law to ward off the emergence of restraints of competition is clearly erroneous. If firms intend to restrict competition they will invariably look for solutions which can be enforced by law.

The legislation opened by the Sherman Act aimed at stopping this trend. It was the response to the emergence of trusts and the ensuing consolidations in giant corporations which in parliamentary debates were censured as threats to civil liberties. Hence Senator Sherman, upon bringing in the bill which later was passed as the Sherman Act, said (Audretsch 1999, p. 229), 'If we will not endure a King as a political power we should not submit to an autocrat of trade with power to prevent competition and to fix the price of any commodity.' This statement clearly aimed at stirring up emotions serving to support a fundamental decision in economic policy. The Sherman Act came into existence after a decade full of social unrest, strikes and anarchist agitation. The bill initiated by Senator Sherman turned against these tendencies. He claimed 'You must heed their [the voters'] appeal or be ready for the socialist, communist, and the nihilist' (Pitofsky 1979, p. 1057). Competition policy was thus clearly visualized as a constitutive element of a market economy. It may remain an open question whether behind these arguments, which appealed to the public, there was some deep rooted economic reasoning.[15]

Whatever the motivation for initiating antitrust may have been, it is certainly true that in the meantime courts in their ruling were ever more guided by the aim of enhancing economic welfare by maintaining competition. This development is to some extent attributable to an increasing influence of economic theory. On the other hand, for implementing competition policy clearly defined goals are indispensable. As remarked by Bork (1965, pp. 837f), 'The choice of the wealth-maximization policy (has) the additional benefit of

---

[15] Posner (1976) and Bork (1965, 1978), two prominent representatives of the Chicago School of antitrust, argued that the legislation was ultimately driven by the objective to enhance economic efficiency and welfare. This interpretation appears somewhat questionable in view of the above mentioned assessment of trusts by professional economists of the time, as revealed for instance by the citation of John Bates Clark. Members of Congress, most of them being lawyers, can hardly be expected to have held fundamentally differing opinions. The same evaluation as the one expressed here, can be found in Hazlett (1992), Duménil, Glick and Lévy (1997), and Stiglitz (1994, p. 127). This view is furthermore supported by recalling that the criticism of monopolies has a long tradition, going back to the Middle Ages where monopolistic practices used to be condemned as sinful greed and avarice (Tawney 1926, pp. 40ff). Using modern terminology they were condemned for distributive reasons and not on efficiency grounds.

making the law more easily predicted, enforced, and applied.'[16] By contrast, 'The choice of ultimate values ... is usually regarded as a function of the legislature and not of the courts'.[17] It must not be overlooked, though, that the political movement leading up to antitrust was driven by the desire to prevent the emergence of monopolistic exploitation of consumers and small business by powerful private firms. Despite the warnings expressed by Bork US courts did pay tribute to these aspects.[18]

The Sherman Act prohibits restraints of competition in most general terms.

Section 1. Every contract, combination in the form of trust or otherwise, or conspiracy, in restraint of trade or commerce among the several States or with foreign nations, is declared to be illegal. Every person who shall make any contract or engage in any combination or conspiracy hereby declared to be illegal shall be deemed guilty of a felony, and, on conviction thereof, shall be punished by fine not exceeding ten million dollars if a corporation, or, if any other person, three hundred and fifty thousand dollars, or by imprisonment not exceeding three years, or by both said punishments, in the discretion of the court.

Section 2. Every person who shall monopolize, or attempt to monopolize, or combine or conspire with any other person or persons, to monopolize any part of the trade or commerce among the several States, or with foreign nations, shall be deemed guilty of a felony, and, on conviction thereof, shall be punished by fine not exceeding ten million dollars if a corporation, or, if any other person, three hundred and fifty thousand dollars or by imprisonment not exceeding three years, or by both said punishments, in the discretion of the court.[19]

Thereby criminal offences were defined to be punished by imprisonment and fines. Moreover damaged parties are entitled to claim treble damages. The thrust of the Sherman Act is directed against a behavior which entails restraints of competition, irrespective of whether horizontal agreements, that is, cartels, are concerned, or vertical agreements or mergers and acquisitions. The Sherman Act does not prohibit monopolies as such, but behavior conducive to establishing a monopoly. A monopoly based on applying a superior technique or offering novel products is not subject to the Sherman Act.

The Sherman Act was a popular piece of legislation but it was poorly

---

[16] Kintner (1980a, p. 342) documents how this principle has been applied by US courts.

[17] In fact the Robinson–Patman Act of 1936 was clearly motivated by the goal to protect small business.

[18] See the outstanding case of the Chicago Board of Trade (1918) and Appalachian Coals of 1933 (Bork 1965). The decision in the latter case, however, is no longer accepted as a valid precedence (Elzinga 1977, p. 1204). Arguments beyond economic reasoning played some role also in the famous Alcoa case (see below).

[19] Originally the offence was classified as 'misdemeanor' to be punished by imprisonment of one year and/or a fine. Since 1974 the offence is treated more severely as a felony to be punished with imprisonment up to three years and/or a fine.

drafted and very vague. The terms 'restraint of trade', 'combination', or 'monopolize' may appear obvious to the layman but were not so to the courts who were charged with enforcing the act. Therefore the courts have been free to interpret the act. The result has been that antitrust law changes according to the prevailing mood of legal opinion. Because this is in part a function of politics of the day, antitrust law has always been one of the most politicized portions of the legal code.

Antitrust policy was given a new thrust by the Clayton Act which outlawed specific restrictive practices,

- price discrimination,
- exclusive dealing and tying contracts,
- acquiring of competing companies,
- interlocking directorates,

if their 'effect may be to substantially lessen competition or to tend to create a monopoly'. As far as mergers are concerned the Clayton Act prohibited only the formation of holding companies. It was only by the Celler–Kefauver Act of 1950 that a more encompassing definition of mergers was adopted. Similarly to the Sherman Act, the Clayton Act was motivated not only by economic reasons but also aimed at curtailing the emergence of economic power (Pitofsky 1979, pp. 1062f). Whereas the Sherman Act was intended to fend off the harmful effects of monopoly power and, being antitrust policy in a literal sense, was defensive in character, US antitrust by the Clayton Act was given a positive thrust. Neale (1966, p. 29) cites Chief Justice Stone stating that 'public interest is best protected from the evils of monopoly and price control by the maintenance of competition'. Hence competition as an institution is to be protected.

It is important to understand the historical background of the Clayton Act. After the Sherman Act had remained without visible effect for several years in 1898 the Sixth Circuit Court of Appeals in the case of US v. Addyston Pipe and Steel Company established the so-called *per se* doctrine according to which horizontal agreements, such as cartels, are always illegal. This doctrine has later on been confirmed by other courts as well (see Chapter 3 for further details). Hence trusts, which actually were cartels, ran into danger of falling under the verdict of the *per se* doctrine. A welcome legal expedient, opened in particular by the State of New Jersey, was merger. Thus, as stated by Chandler (1977, p. 319), 'the New Jersey holding company took the place of the trust as the form used to merge a number of single unit enterprises'. That paved the way for the first great merger wave which occurred around the turn of the 19th century. The reaction of competition policy came in 1903 when the Supreme Court dissolved the Northern Securities Company by which two competing railways were to be merged into a holding company. This decision was a landmark of US antitrust. In previous years the US government had adopted a laissez-faire attitude. In his popular history of America Alistair Cooke (1973, p. 299) wrote about the time around the turn of the century,

> We have barely mentioned a President since Lincoln. This is not an oversight. For forty years after the Civil War the true national power lay with the oil monopoly, the steel trust, the railroad combines.

The new stance of antitrust was introduced by President Theodore Roosevelt when in 1902 the initiator of the Northern Securities Company, the influential banker J. Pierpont Morgan, heard that the government was about to intervene against the newly created company. When Morgan complained to the President that he had not been consulted and assured 'If we have done something wrong, send your man to my man and they can fix it up', the Attorney General's reply, 'We don't want to fix it up, we want to stop it' (Hughes 1973, p. 426) told the story of economic and political change.

The second landmark decision of the Supreme Court came in 1911 in the case of John D. Rockefeller's Standard Oil Company of New Jersey which held a virtual monopoly for refining petroleum. For this decision, which led to the dissolution of the Standard Oil Company, the rule of reason was developed. It implies that neither bigness nor the possession of monopoly power as such is an offence. The Sherman Act is directed against intent and purpose to monopolize, that is, against a behavior which is beyond the normal methods of industrial development.

The problem with the assumption that size as such is not deemed an offence comes to light by looking at the case of US Steel (Comanor and Scherer 1995), a merger of some 170 firms consummated in 1901, which led to a market share in the US iron and steel market of 66 per cent. In 1920 the Supreme Court rejected the reproach of monopolization on the ground that even though US Steel enjoyed substantial market power it worked also to the benefit of competitors. Actually, competitors under the umbrella of the price policy of the leader could successively raise their market share such that the market share of US Steel had by 1990 decreased to no more than 20 per cent.[20] This case elucidates the problem associated with drawing a proper dividing line between permissible and illegal mergers.

The Clayton Act, on one hand, provides for mergers to be prohibited in its

---

[20] As demonstrated by Gaskins (1971), this outcome can be modeled as resulting from maximizing the value of the leading firm facing inevitably occurring successive entry of competitors. See also Yamawaki (1985).

incipiency and not only ex post. The Sherman Act requires abusive conduct to be proved for a merger to be declared illegal, in which case the merged firm has to be dissolved. The Clayton Act aims at prohibiting the consummation of an illegal merger ab initio. On the other hand it is not necessary to proceed against negligible restraints of competition. For the prohibitions of the Clayton Act to become effective requires a substantial restraint of competition to be expected. The wording 'may be' could imply a substantial restriction to be likely or only possible. A clarification was furnished by the decision of the US District Court for the Northern District of Illinois of 1954 in the case of US v. du Pont according to which section 7 of the Clayton Act applies if 'the reasonable likelihood appears that the acquisition will result in a restraint of commerce' (Neale 1966, p. 214). Anyway, the Clayton Act introduced a merger control predicated on some normative idea about the desirable degree of competition to prevail in the respective market. Thus competition policy following from the Clayton Act may, but need not, be conducted in the spirit of constructivism. It certainly involves an element of industrial policy. It may nevertheless be confined to fending off substantial restraints of competition. Still there is a danger of it being misused as an instrument of government interventionism.[21]

During the Great Depression of the 1930s the Robinson–Patman Act was passed which provided for protective measures against big retailers in favor of proprietary retailing and small business firms in manufacturing industries. Antitrust policy was relaxed and replaced by interventionistic industry policies. These, however, were removed by the Supreme Court as unconstitutional. The return to antitrust led to increasingly invigorating the stance of competition policy by the 1950s and 1960s until in the 1970s and 1980s, intellectually supported by the notion of contestable markets (Baumol, Panzar and Willig 1982), a more lenient approach to merger control came to be adopted. As the predictions maintained by the adherents of the contestability approach did not pay off as expected, more recently some intensification of antitrust can be observed.

When during the 1940s and 1950s horizontal mergers were judged by increasingly severe standards, such that even at very low market shares achieved mergers and acquisitions were disallowed, the number of horizontal mergers decreased. Increasingly conglomerate mergers came to the fore where big firms diversified by acquiring smaller firms operating in diverse industries outside the previous field of activity of the acquiring company. Since more recently horizontal merger were judged less critically by the US

---

[21] For this reason during the presidency of Ronald Reagan antitrust policy following from the Clayton Act used to be denounced as government regulation. In the light of deregulation policies it looked faulty and thus gave rise to a permissive stance of merger control.

authorities their number once more increased, and diversified conglomerates have been selling off parts of their empire to strengthen their core business.

Germany

After the decision of the Imperial Court in 1897 which de facto legalized cartels they did not proliferate without meeting with opposition in public opinion. In 1923, at the height of the hyperinflation, which by the way led to a devaluation of the German currency to four trillion Marks for the US Dollar, a law against abuse of economic power (Verordnung gegen den Miß-brauch wirtschaftlicher Machtstellungen) was passed. It contained two provisions. The first one was directed against excessive pricing. This provision had very little effect, first, because the conditions to be satisfied for its application were rather demanding, and second, because the inflation which the law was intended to fight was not primarily caused by restraints of competition but rather by an ill-devised monetary policy. Even though the rise in demand following the excessive monetary expansion entailed some scope for the exercise of monopoly power this effect was dwarfed by the inflationary effect of monetary expansion. The second goal of the law was to prevent unjustified restraints of trade for members of cartels. Even in this respect the law is reported to have fallen short of prior expectations (Bremer 1985, pp. 124ff).

After World War II in the Federal Republic of Germany, that is, West Germany, during the first ten years competition policy followed antitrust regulations introduced by the Allied Forces Government immediately after the war. In the meantime a group of German economists and jurists, which later came to be known as the Ordo Liberal School, had developed principles which were to shape competition policy in Germany. The best known representatives of this group were the economist Walter Eucken and the jurist Franz Böhm. The ideas of this group later on, under the label 'Soziale Marktwirtschaft' (Social Market Economy), as coined by Alfred Müller-Armack, were politically propagated and implemented by Ludwig Erhard, the first Minister of Economics of the Federal Republic of Germany. The notion of the Social Market Economy has been conceived of as opposing both socialism and interventionism, as it had proliferated during the time between the two World Wars.

Initiated by the Ordo Liberal School the Law Against Restraints of Competition (Gesetz gegen Wettbewerbsbeschränkungen – Kartellgesetz) was passed in 1957 and thus became the foundation of German competition policy. Except for a few exemptions practicing cartels and some other types of restrictive conduct as well as the abuse of a dominant position were prohibited. The latest amendment of the law in 1998 brought it in line with EC law, which contains a *per se* prohibition of cartels.[22]

In contrast to US law, practicing an illegal cartel – with the exception of participating in a submission cartel – is not a criminal offence. It is deemed an act against the public order to be punished by a penalty. Practicing a cartel, however, may be prosecuted as a fraud. Firms holding a dominant position are subject to an abuse control. A dominant position is assumed to exist if a firms is not subject to any competition or not subject to substantial competition, or if it is holding a superior market position *vis-à-vis* its competitors. Whereas an abuse of a dominant position previously could be prohibited and contracts could be declared void by the authorities they are now, according to § 19 KartellG, illegal from the beginning. Violations are to be fined and damaged parties may sue for compensation. In addition the cartel authority may lay claim to excessive profits (§§ 33, 34 KartellG).

A merger control had been planned by the Ordo Liberal proponents of the German cartel law, it could not, however, become law because of opposition from industrial interest groups arguing that a prohibition of mergers would be harmful since benefits to be enjoyed by exploiting economies of scale had to be sacrificed. So a typical trade-off argument of industrial policy was used by pressure groups to talk the parliament out of passing a provision for merger control. An amendment providing for merger control was passed only in 1973 after the conservative coalition of the first two decades of the Federal Republic of Germany had been replaced by a coalition of the Social Democrats (SPD) and the Free Democrats (FDP). It opened for the authorities the possibility of preventing the emergence of a dominant position in its incipiency. The law specifies the conditions under which dominance is presumed to exist. If they are satisfied the Federal Cartel Office (Bundeskartellamt) has to stop the merger. The wording of the law, at first sight, gives the impression that, similarly to the US Sherman Act, monopolizing of markets shall be prevented. The legal criteria for presuming dominance and the following practice of the authorities as well as the administration of justice by the courts, however, suggest that only substantial restrictions of competition are to be prohibited. Similarly to the US Clayton Act merger control in Germany involves industrial policy.

When it comes to evaluating German competition policy the question arises which kind of competition is to be protected. In view of the administration of justice by the courts the answer is ambiguous. Referring to the justification for the bill which later became the Law Against Restraints of Competition (GWB) the Federal Court of Justice (Bundesgerichtshof) noted in 1961 that, from a legal point of view, contracts are not to be objected to

---

[22] The new drafted law will subsequently be referred to as KartellG, whereas the original law is referred to as GWB.

insofar as they only intend to prevent unfair competition, since the law only aims to protect fair competition from being restrained but not unfair or illegal competition (Mestmäcker 1984, p. 90). The Law Against Unfair Competition (Gesetz gegen unlauteren Wettbewerb, UWG) to which the Court refers goes back to 1896 and in its revised version of 1909 is still valid. That was the time when cartels were blooming in Germany. The general clause of the Law (§ 1 UWG) refers to the custom of trade as the standard of fairness. It thus entails a touch of collusion to be accepted as fair conduct. This standard of judgement cannot be derived from economic theory. It is an autonomous standard founded on purely legal reasoning. The reference to fairness justifies associations of industry being entitled to set up rules of conduct for their members (§ 24, 2 KartellG) which, from an economic point of view, are collusive arrangements.

European Union

The history of competition policy in the European Community followed similar lines to that of Germany. The beginnings are to be found in the European Community of Steel and Coal (ECSC). In Articles 65 and 66 of the ECSC Treaty of 1951 cartels are prohibited. Mergers are subject to control by the High Authority of the ECSC. By contrast, the EC Treaty of 1957 provides only for a prohibition of contractual restraints of competition, subject to various exemptions, and the abuse of a dominant position. Merger control was being introduced only in 1989. The validity of the ECSC Treaty expires in 2002. Thereafter coal mining and the iron and steel industry will also be subject to the EC Treaty. The major provisions of the treaty are contained in Articles 81 and 82.[23]

Article 81
(1) The following shall be prohibited as incompatible with the common market: all agreements between undertakings, decisions by associations of undertakings and concerted practices which may affect trade between Member States and which have as their object or effect the prevention, restriction or distortion of competition within the common market, and in particular those which:

    (a) directly or indirectly fix purchase or selling prices or any other trading conditions;
    (b) limit or control production, markets, technical development, or investment;
    (c) share markets or sources of supply;
    (d) apply dissimilar conditions to equivalent transactions with other trading

---

[23] The numbering has been changed by the Treaty of Amsterdam 1997. Articles 81 and 82 used to be 85 and 86. Subsequently only the new numbering will be used.

parties, thereby placing them at a competitive disadvantage;
- (e) make the conclusion of contracts subject to acceptance by the other parties of supplementary obligations which, by their nature or according to commercial usage, have no connection with the subject of such contracts.

(2) Any agreements or decisions prohibited pursuant to this Article shall be automatically void.
(3) The provisions of paragraph 1 may, however, be declared inapplicable in the case of:

- – any agreement or category of agreements between undertakings;
- – any decision or category of decisions by associations of undertakings;
- – any concerted practice or category of concerted practices,

which contributes to improving the production or distribution of goods or to promoting technical or economic progress, while allowing consumers a fair share of the resulting benefit, and which does not:

- (a) impose on the undertakings concerned restrictions which are not indispensable to the attainment of these objectives;
- (b) afford such undertakings the possibility of elimination competition in respect to a substantial part of the products in question.

Article 82
Any abuse by one or more undertakings of a dominant position within the common market or in a substantial part of it shall be prohibited as incompatible with the common market insofar as it may affect trade between Member States.
Such abuse may, in particular, consist in:

- (a) directly or indirectly imposing unfair purchase or selling prices or other unfair trading conditions;
- (b) limiting production, markets or technical development to the prejudice of consumers;
- (c) applying dissimilar conditions to equivalent transactions with other trading parties, thereby placing them at a competitive disadvantage;
- (d) making the conclusion of contracts subject to acceptance by the other parties of supplementary obligations which, by their nature or according to commercial usage, have no connection with the subject of such contracts.

The primary objective of the regulations regarding competition in the EC Treaty has been the prevention of private contracts to re-establish the borders between Member States which had been abolished by the European Community. For the rest there is a far reaching parallelism to the German Law Against Restraints of Competition. Similarly to the German law, as it was passed in 1957, the EC Treaty did not provide for explicit merger control. However, the European Court of Justice, in two leading cases, paved the way for establishing merger control at the EC level. In the Continental Can case of

1973, where Continental Can took control of the leading Belgian producer of metal cans, the Court referred to Article 82 (then Article 86) of the EC Treaty as the legal basis for prohibiting a merger on the ground that it constitutes an abuse of a dominant position. Regarding Article 82 the Court said that (Jacquemin 1990, p. 29)

> (the) provision is not only aimed at practices which may cause damage to consumers directly, but also at those which are detrimental to them through their impact on effective competition structure, such as is mentioned in Article 3(f) of the Treaty. Abuse may therefore occur if an undertaking in a dominant position strengthens such a position in such a way that the degree of dominance reached substantially fetters competition, i.e., that only undertakings remain in the market whose behaviour depend on the dominant one.

In addition, in the Philip Morris case of 1987, the Court decided that the acquisition of a minority shareholding in a competitor may come within the ambit of Article 81 (then Article 85) (Jacquemin 1990, p. 30).

These rulings established a legal situation which parallels the one which existed in the US after the passage of the Sherman Act. A merger control, as provided by the Clayton Act of 1914 in the US, and the amendment to the Law Against Restraints of Competition of 1973 in Germany, was introduced in the EC only in 1989 by adopting the 'Merger Control Regulation' based on Articles 87 and 235 of the EC Treaty. According to this law mergers are subject to control by the EC Commission in particular if worldwide sales of the participants to a merger exceed 5 billion Euro, and at least two participating firms have sales in the community of at least 250 million Euro unless more than two-thirds of the sales of the participating firms pertain to a single Member State. If the conditions for EC merger control are satisfied, the authority for decisions regarding the merger lies exclusively with the EC Commission. The authority for other mergers remains with the respective national authorities. EC merger control is governed by a rule of reason. In addition, it is strongly influenced by objectives derived from industrial policy. Among the criteria to be observed for evaluating a merger proposal, the likelihood that it favors the development of technological and economic progress ranks high, albeit circumscribed by the provision that it has to serve consumers and must not inhibit competition.

The overriding goal of EC competition policy is stated in Article 3 lit g of the Treaty to consist of establishing a system which safeguards that competition must not be distorted, neither by private restraints nor by government interference. Therefore the competition policy of the EC encompasses monitoring subsidization of enterprises by the respective national governments (Art. 87 and 88 EC Treaty). Still, no unanimity exists regarding the ultimate goal of EC competition policy. As stated in Article 4 of the Treaty the economic policy of the Member States and the Community shall be conducted in 'accordance with the principle of an open market economy with free competition'. The logical connection between the goals to be pursued by the Community and competition, however, is unsettled. Article 98 says,

> The Member States and the Community shall act in accordance with the principle of an open market economy with free competition, favouring an efficient allocation of resources, ...

The last clause, beginning with 'favouring' may alternatively be interpreted as a statement of facts or as a normative statement in the spirit of a constructivistic industrial policy. Karel van Miert, the Commissioner in charge of EC competition policy until 1999, took side with the industrial policy stance by saying that competitions policy 'is not an end in itself to be pursued dogmatically; it is an instrument, albeit an important one, for achieving agreed Community objectives' (cited by Haid 1999, p. 167). Since the objectives are defined encompassingly they also include safeguarding freedom which is expected to enhance economic welfare.

United Kingdom

The development of competition policy in the UK followed similar lines to that of Germany. Prior to World War II cartels were not illegal; establishing and maintaining them was considered acceptable business practice. As far as a cartel contract entailed clauses which were deemed undue restraints of trade they were not enforceable. Hence activities of cartels were not inhibited by government interference. During the Great Depression of the 1930s they were even welcomed and encouraged. In the mid-1950s nearly half of the manufacturing sector was subject to agreements significantly restricting competition (Symeonidis 1999, p. 6, Utton 2000, p. 269).

The first step of competition policy occurred in 1948 with the passage of the Monopolies and Restrictive Practices Enquiry and Control Act which aimed at preventing private monopolies. The government of that time, led by the Labour Party, was far from intending to establish a competitive order, however. The dominant goal of the policy was the socialization of the economy. The remaining private sector was to be supervised and regulated by the government (Lever 1999). The legislation of 1948 opened an initial explorative phase during which 'The Monopolies and Restrictive Practices Commission', set up by the Act, produced 23 reports, 17 of which were concerned with restrictive agreements. As subsequent research indicated this emphasis was well received since, as already mentioned, in the mid-1950s between 50 and 60 per cent of UK manufacturing was regulated by cartels.

It was only in 1956 that the door was opened for an effective competition policy by a Conservative government passing the Restrictive Practices Act. The law established the principle that restraints of competition are against the public interest unless proved otherwise. The landmark decision by the Restrictive Practices Court, which paved the way for a consequent application of this principle, came in the case regarding a cartel set up by the Yarn Spinners' Association. The Registrar had rejected the admissibility of the cartel on the ground that it resulted in higher prices than would be the case under competition, and had allowed the survival of high-cost producers and the maintenance of excess capacity in the industry. Although some beneficial effects on employment may result they were considered to be outweighed by the detrimental effect to the public (Symeonidis 1998, p. 58).

The British cartel law of 1956 was amended in 1976 and 1996 and has finally been replaced by the Competition Act of 1998 by which UK competition law regarding cartels and other contractual restraints is brought into line with the law of the EC. Subject to some specified exemptions to be granted by the authorities, agreements between undertakings, practices which may affect trade within the UK and have as their object, or effect, the prevention, restriction or distortion of competition within the UK are prohibited. The same applies to any conduct on the part of one or more undertakings which amounts to the abuse of a dominant position. Since the British law parallels the EC law the practice of UK competition policy may rely on the jurisdiction of the European Court of Justice and the practice of the EC Commission.

Similarly to Germany and the EC, merger control guided by the goal of maintaining competition in a market economy was not introduced in the UK until 1965 by the Monopolies and Mergers Act, and the Fair Trading Act of 1973, amended in 1980, the validity of which has not been affected by the Competition Act of 1998. The decisive criterion for merger control has been the public interest, an encompassing notion of common weal which includes technical progress, employment and balanced trade. In the practice of merger control these aspects have originally been given substantial weight. A change occurred by the adoption of the 'Tebbit Doctrine'. Norman Tebbit, the Secretary of State responsible for competition policy, had emphasized in 1984 that mergers have to be evaluated, if not exclusively but primarily, with regard to their effect on competition (Veljanovski 1995, pp. 148ff). Still, the ultimate responsibility for merger control rests with the government. This assignment has recently been strongly defended: 'the Secretary of State is politically accountable for his decision-making and ultimately the decisions he has to make are ones of policy not of law. Therefore it is appropriate that they be taken by a politician' (Robertson 1996, p. 217). However, as noted by Utton (2000, p. 283), 'The current Government has recently indicated that it may now be prepared to address this anomaly.'

France

In France the Penal Code of 1810 prohibited price cartels. This ban was abandoned, however, in 1864, after cartels, even before that time, had been allowed by courts on the ground that they served to prevent ruinous competition. Similarly to Germany in the 1920s, in France after World War II cartels were judged as causing inflation and were therefore combated by price controls (Jenny 1995, p. 164). Primarily following pressures from the USA, a first competition law was passed in 1953. It aimed at supplementing government price controls. At that time in France competition policy was not believed to be suitable for enhancing economic efficiency. The French government and the economic establishment preferred to rely on industrial policy (Souam 1998, p. 207). This attitude found expression in the popular book by Servan-Schreiber (1967) about the American Challenge. The author pleaded for favoring big firms to become equal to US rivals. It was overlooked that the superiority of US competition did not follow from industrial policy but was caused, not least, by the existence of a competitive order enforced by antitrust.

The first step to adopt a modern competition policy was taken under Prime Minister Raymond Barre in 1977. Collusive conduct could be subjected to investigation and punished. These reforms were supported by results of research in industrial economics (Jenny 1995, p. 167) about excessive profits in concentrated industries and comparatively low efficiency in big firms, combined

> with obvious examples of industrial policy failures in industries in which the government had tried to increase concentration (such as the steel and computer industries) and the slowly emerging feeling that the lack of aggressiveness of French firms on international markets was partly a consequence of weak competition on their domestic market.

These insights led in 1986 to a regulation concerning freedom of pricing and competition which provided in principal for the prohibition of cartels and abusive conduct by dominant firms subject to submitting counter-evidence to the effect that the restrictive practices are conducive to increasing efficiency and economic progress of which consumers take an advantage. Merger control falls under the authority of the French Ministry of Economics which may ask the Conseil de la Concurrence to investigate a merger without being bound by the recommendation of the Conseil. Merger control in France therefore is completely under political control (Souam 1998, p. 226).

Convergence of Competition Policy

In retrospect, competition policy in the US and the development of competition policy in the European Community, in Germany, the United Kingdom and France appears to display a remarkable convergence. Starting from quite different political traditions, not least under the influence of economic theory, unified standards of evaluation have been developed. Despite differences in detail, to be discussed in Chapter 3, national competition policy in the various Member States of the EC has converged on EC law (Martin 1998). The convergence has been reinforced because community law takes precedence over national law if conflicts arise. If a restraint of competition extends national borders community law applies. The necessity to treat equal events equally within the EC creates a pressure on national legislation to harmonize national law with community law. In fact by now all Member States, with the notable exception of France, however, have passed national laws following the standards set by EC law.

1.5　CONCLUSION

Competition policy in a market economy serves a twofold purpose. Competition is the driving force for economic welfare to be attained by favoring an efficient allocation of resources and technical progress. It moreover provides for containing economic power. Competition policy aiming at maintaining a competitive order is thus a major pillar of economic policy in a market economy. Implemented during the last decade of the 19th century in the US, and after World War II in Europe, competition policy became a bulwark against socialism. This political impetus caused competition to prove resistant against ubiquitous tendencies for restraints of competition. On the other side, competition policy must be defended against the danger of degenerating into government regulation influenced by all kinds of particular interests.

In economics the understanding of the working of competition has grown only step by step. Since Adam Smith, the safeguarding of economic freedom used to be widely believed to enhance economic welfare. In detail, however, numerous misconceptions and diverging opinions prevailed. Hence the role of cartels has been the subject of heated controversies. Before World War II competition policy in a modern meaning only existed in the US. It came into existence in Europe in the 1950s. In the meantime, however, a far-reaching convergence regarding the guiding principles of competition policy has been achieved. As a rule, cartels are prohibited, merger control is applied with the goal of preventing monopolization of industries, and dominant firms are subject to government regulation to contain the abuse of economic power.

The convergence of guiding principles for competition policy has been enhanced by an improved theoretical understanding of the working of a market economy and the influence of monopolistic market power. First, insights can be gained by the basic models of perfect competition and monopoly, or monopsony, respectively. A deeper understanding, however, requires the use of more subtle models suitable for analyzing the strategic behavior of enterprises, how economic performance is related to market structures and contractual restraints of trade. These are the questions to be addressed in the next chapter.

2. Industrial Economics as the Foundation of Competition Policy

As mentioned in the previous chapter US antitrust originally met with mistrust and antipathy by professional economists. Politicians, most of them lawyers, were the ones to take side with public sentiments against trusts, and courts, albeit at first only hesitatingly, brought the law to life and effectiveness. In economics it was only in the 1930s that with the development of the theory of imperfect competition Robinson (1933) in England, Chamberlin (1933) in the US, and von Stackelberg (1934) in Germany laid the groundwork for economic theory to extend the boundaries of the polar cases of perfect competition and monopoly for an analysis of oligopolies and monopolistic competition. The foundation laid by the pioneers has been improved by game theory, in particular by the work of Nash (1951). In the present chapter the outstanding results of the major models of industrial economics will be discussed to prepare for the subsequent detailed analysis and evaluation of competition policy.

2.1 COMPETITION IN OLIGOPOLY

We shall first consider a market with a limited number of producers supplying an identical commodity or service. The market in this case is called homogeneous. We shall then turn to a heterogeneous market where differentiated products are supplied. In the first step of the analysis the number of firms is assumed to be exogenously given whilst in the following step the number of firms will be explained as the outcome of the competitive process, such that the market structure is endogenous.

Homogeneous Market: Cournot Equilibria

For an identical good the interaction of supply and demand yields a unique price which depends on the size of supply of all producers. Simplifying, a linear relationship between price p and the total supply of the respective good, $Q = \Sigma_{i=1}^{n} q_i$, shall be assumed,

$$p = a - bQ$$

where a denotes the vertical size of the market and b the horizontal size of the market. The vertical size of the market depends on the characteristics of the product, the preferences of buyers, their income and prices of other goods. The horizontal size depends inter alia on the number of buyers. If, with everything else kept unchanged, the number of buyers rises, the slope coefficient b will decrease and, in a graphical representation, the inverse demand curve becomes flatter.

Producers may fix the quantity to be supplied such that at an equilibrium some definite price p^* is determined. A model of this kind has been suggested by Cournot (1838). By contrast, Bertrand (1883) suggested that the price should be treated as the relevant control variable used by the individual supplier to gain an edge on competitors. Thus Cournot competition and Bertrand competition are distinguished. Although the two types of competition seem to be alternatives,[1] in reality they are not.

Usually a two-stage decision-making process is involved. At the first stage firms decide which productive capacity shall be established, and subsequently the firms fix the price to be charged. Under certain conditions such a two-stage decision-making process yields the outcome suggested by Cournot (Kreps and Scheinkman 1983, Tirole 1988, pp. 212ff). From the viewpoint of competition policy rivalry related to changes in productive capacities is much more important than price competition once capacities have been set up. Nevertheless changes in production engender price changes. Even though the dynamics of competition unfold primarily through investments to build up production facilities and to develop new processes and products, marketing then inevitably requires changes in price. We will come to this in due course when the effects of changes of costs are to be treated. However, since price changes are playing a secondary role, in the following analysis the perspective of the Cournot model will be adopted where firms are assumed to fix quantities (see also Sutton 1998, pp. 34ff).

Although in an oligopoly the individual producer, by choosing his output, can exert some influence on the market price it also depends on decisions taken by competitors which are beyond the control of the individual firm. The individual firm is assumed to maximize profits by choosing the level of its output, given the level of output chosen by the competitors. The simultaneous

---

[1] Whilst Cournot competition, given a limited number of competing firms, yields a price in excess of marginal costs, under Bertrand competition, if marginal costs are constant and identical among competitors, the price is driven down towards marginal costs irrespective of the number of competing firms. In the framework of the Bertrand model the observation that a price exceeds marginal cost cannot be explained other than by invoking collusion.

choice of output by all firms gives rise to an equilibrium which will be examined in what follows.

Given a cost function $C_i = F_i + c_i q_i$ of firm i where F_i denotes fixed costs, c_i are constant marginal costs, which equal average variable costs, profits are

$$\Pi_i = p(Q)q_i - c_i q_i - F_i$$

where $p(Q)$ is the linear demand function described above. Demand as seen by the individual seller can also be written

$$p = \left(a - b \sum_{\substack{j=1 \\ j \neq i}}^{n} q_j \right) - bq_i .$$

The equilibrium of an individual firm is depicted in Figure 2.1. It shows the inverse demand curve as seen by the seller, *dd,* and the associated marginal revenue curve, *MR,* the marginal cost curve, $MC = c$, and the average cost

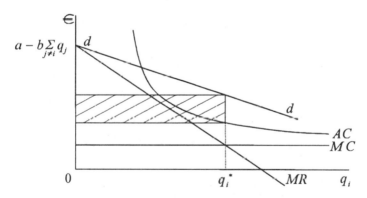

Figure 2.1   The equilibrium of an individual firm

curve, *AC.* The profit maximizing output q_i^* is determined by the intersection of the marginal revenue curve with the marginal cost curve. Total profits are given by the shaded area.

In the case of duopoly ($n = 2$) the Cournot equilibrium can be depicted by using two reaction curves. Maximizing profits

$$\Pi_i = [a - b(q_1 + q_2)]q_i - c_i q_i - F_i, \quad i = 1, 2,$$

requires

$$\partial \Pi_i / \partial q_i = a - b(q_1 + q_2) - bq_i - c_i = 0$$

which yields the equations

$$a - b(q_1 + q_2) - c_1 - bq_1 = 0$$

$$a - b(q_1 + q_2) - c_2 - bq_2 = 0.$$

They can be rewritten as follows to depict reaction curves. They show the individual output of firm i, given the output of the rival firm j,

Firm 1 $\qquad q_2 = \dfrac{a - c_1}{b} - 2q_1 \qquad (R_1)$

Firm 2 $\qquad q_2 = \dfrac{a - c_2}{2b} - \dfrac{1}{2}q_1. \qquad (R_2)$

The reaction curves, as shown in Figure 2.2 intersect at the Cournot equilibrium point C.

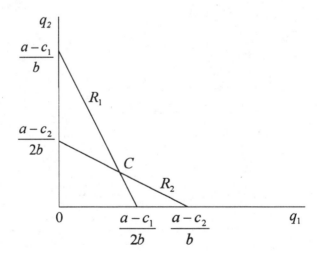

Figure 2.2   Reaction curves in Cournot equilibrium

For an arbitrary number of competitors with identical cost functions, such that $F_i = F$ and $c_i = c$, profit maximization in a Cournot setting yields an equilibrium where[2]

$$q = \frac{a-c}{b(n+1)} \tag{2.1}$$

$$Q = \frac{n}{n+1}\frac{a-c}{b} \tag{2.2}$$

$$p = \frac{a-c}{n+1}+c \tag{2.3}$$

$$\Pi_i = \frac{1}{b}\left(\frac{a-c}{n+1}\right)^2 - F = bq^2 - F. \tag{2.4}$$

The Cournot equilibrium is the focal point of the following analysis. Both perfect competition in the meaning of Knight and monopoly are special cases which apply if $n \to \infty$ or $n = 1$, respectively. The Cournot model thus opens the door to analyzing more realistic intermediate cases.

At a Cournot equilibrium competition has seemingly come to a standstill. For the individual firm there is no reason to change output or prices. As pointed out by Phlips (1995, pp. 10f), 'There is competition, and yet no firm actively fights its competitors, because it is in no firm's individual interest to engage in "active" competition!' In reality, though, an equilibrium will almost never be completely attained. Demand changes, costs change because input prices change, and producers adopt innovations which yield lower costs. Still, if producers seek to maximize profits they are constantly chasing a moving goal. Identifying this goal is an important achievement to understand what is going on in a competitive market. All this implies that distinguishing between the notion of perfect competition and Cournot competition on one hand, and the so-called competition of the real world on the other hand, is misleading. Even though John Bates Clark (1888, p. 6, as cited by DiLorenzo and High 1988, p. 426) was right in stating that 'actual competition consists invariably in an effort to undersell a rival producer' it is important to understand that the price of a given product will never permanently fall below average costs. Successfully underselling rivals inevitably requires the

---

[2] Maximizing individual profits $\Pi_i = \left[a - b\left(q_1 + q_2 + ... + q_n\right)\right]q_i - cq_i - F_i$ requires $\partial \Pi_i / \partial q_i = a - b(q_1 + q_2 ... + q_n) - bq_i - c = 0$. Since cost functions are assumed to be identical, individual output levels are also identical. Hence one obtains $a - c - b(n+1)q = 0$, from which $q, Q, p,$ and Π_i can be derived.

adoption of innovations by which costs are reduced. The eventual outcome then will be a Cournot equilibrium.

Cost Differences

Whilst identical marginal costs yield an identical output for all firms, different marginal costs give rise to different market shares. In fact, in Figure 2.2 the marginal costs of firm 1 have been assumed to be lower than those of firm 2. Hence $a - c_1$ exceeds $a - c_2$ and thus q_1 is larger than q_2.

If in a duopoly one of the competitors succeeds in reducing marginal costs such that $c_1 < c_2$, the necessary conditions for maximizing profits imply

$$\begin{pmatrix} 2b & b \\ b & 2b \end{pmatrix} \begin{pmatrix} q_1 \\ q_2 \end{pmatrix} = \begin{pmatrix} a - c_1 \\ a - c_2 \end{pmatrix}$$

and hence

$$q_1 = \frac{a - c_1 - (c_1 - c_2)}{3b}$$

$$q_2 = \frac{a - c_2 + (c_1 - c_2)}{3b}$$

$$Q = q_1 + q_2 = \frac{(a - c_1) + (a - c_2)}{3b} \ .$$

Thus, following the reduction of the marginal costs of firm 1, its market share increases.

Inserting the individual output levels into the profit equations, and assuming that fixed costs do not exist, one obtains

$$\Pi_1 = (p - c_1)\, q_1 = \frac{1}{b} \left[\frac{a - c_1 - (c_1 - c_2)}{3} \right]^2 ,$$

$$\Pi_2 = (p - c_2)\, q_2 = \frac{1}{b} \left[\frac{a - c_2 + (c_1 - c_2)}{3} \right]^2 .$$

Following a decrease in marginal costs of firm 1

$$\partial \Pi_1 / \partial c_1 = -4q_1/3 < 0$$

$$\partial \Pi_2 / \partial c_2 = 2q_2/3 > 0.$$

Hence the profits of firm 1 rise while the profits of firm 2 decline.

Process Innovations in Oligopoly

The increase in profitability following a cost reduction entailed by an innovation yields a powerful incentive to innovate. This result so far developed for the case of a duopoly can be generalized for an arbitrary number of competitors. Following Arrow (1962) drastic innovations may be distinguished from non-drastic ones.

In the case of drastic innovation the monopoly price of the innovator falls short of the marginal costs of all competitors. This case, where the innovator captures the entire market, can rarely be expected to occur. It is much more likely for the monopoly price of the innovator to still exceed the marginal costs of the competitors. To examine this case of a non-drastic innovation more closely, let one firm out of n adopt an innovation such that marginal costs are reduced from $c = 2$ to $c^* = 1$ whilst all other firms still operate at marginal costs $c = 2$. At a Cournot equilibrium firm 1 then achieves profits

$$\Pi_1^* = \frac{1}{b}\left[\frac{a - c^* - (n-1)(c^* - c)}{n+1}\right]^2$$

while all other firms obtain

$$\Pi_j = \frac{1}{b}\left[\frac{a - c + (c^* - c)}{n+1}\right]^2.$$

The market price is $p = [a + c^* + (n-1)c]/(n+1)$. Without the innovation of firm 1 the profits of all firms would have been

$$\Pi_i^c = \frac{1}{b}\left(\frac{a-c}{n+1}\right)^2.$$

The changes of profits of the innovator and the competitors following the adoption of the innovation are shown in Table 2.1, where $a = 10$, $b = 1$,

$c = 2$, and $c^* = 1$ have been assumed.

Table 2.1 Profitability following a pioneering innovation

n	Π_i^c	Π_1^*	Π_j
1	16.00	20.25	–
2	7.11	11.11	5.44
3	4.00	7.56	3.06
10	0.53	2.68	0.49

This example yields the following conclusions. First, the increase in profits is absolutely largest for a monopoly ($n = 1$). That facilitates financing of research and development (R&D). Hence costly and technologically indivisible R&D projects can be more easily undertaken by a monopoly than by firms in a less concentrated market. Second, the relative size of the incentive to innovate is larger the more competitors are around. Whereas, in the given example, the profits of a monopoly rise by 26.6 per cent, in the case of ten competitors the profits for the innovator increase by 406 per cent.

Following an innovation, total output coming to the market increases, and the price declines until a new equilibrium is attained, where the market share and profitability of the innovator have risen. In view of these facts it is indeed completely misleading to contrast price competition with competition by innovations. They are just like the two sides of a coin. Price competition and competition through innovating activity occur simultaneously.

Strategic Trade Policy

Internationally a country can win an edge on his trading partners by subsidizing domestic firms. Surprisingly the advantage attainable in this way may exceed the costs the government has to incur. The possibility of such a strategic trade policy has originally been suggested by Brander and Spencer (1985) by using a model in which a domestic and a foreign enterprise meet as rivals on the market of a third country. We will by contrast look at the case of intraindustrial trade where after the formation of a common market both firms meet in Cournot competition. Transport costs are disregarded as a matter of simplification. Furthermore, in contrast to the analysis of Brander and Spencer, we assume marginal costs to be constant and the demand curve to be linear. As with Brander and Spencer, subsidies yield marginal costs to decline by s.

As following from the analysis of the previous section, the market share and profits of the domestic producer 1 increase whilst the market share and profits of the foreign firm 2 decline. If $c_1 = c - s$ and $c_2 = c$ one obtains

$$q_1 = \frac{a - c + 2s}{3b}, \quad q_2 = \frac{a - c + s}{3b}$$

and

$$\Pi_1 = \frac{1}{b}\left(\frac{a - c + 2s}{3}\right)^2, \quad \Pi_2 = \frac{1}{b}\left(\frac{a - c - s}{3}\right)^2.$$

The domestic economy can be shown to gain even if the expenditures sq_1 are covered by a lump sum tax. The net gain of the domestic economy is

$$V(s) = \Pi_1 - sq_1,$$

and the incremental gain of the strategic trade policy is

$$V'(s) = \frac{\partial \Pi_1}{\partial s} - q_1 - s\frac{\partial q_1}{\partial s}$$

from which it follows that

$$V'(s) = \frac{a - c - 4s}{9b}.$$

Since initially $s = 0$, following the introduction of a subsidy, $V'(s) > 0$. Initially, as long as the subsidy is still low, the domestic economy clearly gains. The advantage arrives at a maximum if $V'(s) = 0$ and $V''(s) < 0$. This yields an optimal subsidy

$$s^* = \frac{a - c}{4}$$

at which $V''(s^*) = -4/9b < 0$, as required, and

$$V(s^*) = \frac{(a - c)^2}{8b} \quad \text{and} \quad \Pi_2^* = \frac{(a - c)^2}{16b}.$$

Thus the profits of the domestic duopolist is twice as large as the profit of the foreign firm.

The sum total of the gains of both duopolists amounts to

$$\Pi^* := V(s^*) + \Pi_2^* = \frac{3}{b}\left(\frac{a-c}{4}\right)^2 .$$

It falls short of total profits which could have been achieved in the absence of subsidies,

$$\Pi := \Pi_1 + \Pi_2 = \frac{2}{b}\left(\frac{a-c}{3}\right)^2$$

since

$$\Pi - \Pi^* = \frac{(a-c)^2}{b}\left(\frac{2}{9} - \frac{3}{16}\right) > 0 .$$

The decline in the sum total of profits is caused by an increase in total output, which amounts to

$$Q^* = q_1^* + q_2^* = \frac{2(a-c)+s}{3b} ,$$

and a lower market price in comparison to a situation without subsidies where

$$Q = \frac{2}{3}\frac{a-c}{b} .$$

Thus both domestic and foreign consumers gain. On the side of production, however, only domestic firms gain, whereas foreign producers are losing out. They can therefore hardly be expected to keep silent. Presumably they will start prodding their government to adopt defensive actions, for example, by introducing antidumping tariffs or import quotas.

Stackelberg Case

So far competitors have been assumed to behave symmetrically. If they are different, though, they may be presumed to adopt different strategies. This may in particular apply if firms have different cost functions. However, to isolate the influence of adopting different strategies we shall assume that cost functions are identical among firms. One firm takes the output of the rival as given, whereas the other firm assumes a leading position and maximizes profits by taking into account the adaptive behavior of the rival. As before marginal costs are assumed constant and the demand function to be linear. Insert the output of the follower, that is, firm 2,

$$q_2 = (a-c)/2b - (1/2)q_1$$

as entailed by adaptive behavior, into the profit function of the leader, that is, firm 1,

$$\Pi_1 = [a - b(q_1 + q_2)]q_1 - cq_1,$$

and then maximize Π_1 with respect to q_1 to arrive at

$$q_1 = (a-c)/2b$$

and consequently

$$q_2 = (a-c)/4b.$$

The leader thus produces as much as if he holds a monopoly, whilst the follower produces half of it. The total output of both firms amounts to 3/4 of the output which could be expected under perfect competition.

In contrast to Cournot competition where both duopolists decide on their respective output simultaneously and independently, the Stackelberg equilibrium can be interpreted as the outcome of sequential decision making. If firm 1 enters the market first, it holds a monopoly initially. Each firm to enter the market subsequently faces a *fait accompli* which may give rise to adaptive behavior as suggested by Cournot. An entrant supplying more than implied by adaptive behavior would cause the price to decline, possibly as far as average costs such that neither the entrant nor the incumbent would be profitable. Entry with non-adaptive output would thus be unattractive. By contrast, the adaptive behavior of the entrant would secure profitability for both firms, albeit at different rates. Asymmetry of behavior is easily understood in particular if entering the market requires fixed costs which are sunk. Under this condition an entrant can almost be sure that the incumbent maintains the previous level of output. If entry occurs and the price declines, the incumbent is able to remain in business as long as the price does not fall short of average variable costs, whereas the entrant incurs losses from the very beginning and cannot hope to improve the situation unless he reaches a collusive understanding with the incumbent. If the incumbent signals credibly that he will not give in, adaptive behavior is the best option for the entrant. An asymmetric choice of strategies in the sense of Stackelberg is particularly likely if cost functions differ such that the incumbent enjoys a cost advantage *vis-à-vis* entrants.

Monopolistic Competition

Competition does not only pertain if firms are offering identical products but also if similar products are supplied which are substitutable, as seen by the buyers. The heterogeneity of products may be entailed by the differing characteristics of the various commodities and services, by transport costs or different terms of delivery. Heterogeneity begs the question which products are sufficiently close to each other to be counted as belonging to the same relevant market.[3] Substitutability can be expressed approximately by the cross-price elasticity. With respect to two products, i and j, the cross-price elasticity gives the percentage change in demand for product i by a 1 per cent increase in the price of product j.[4] By virtue of substitutability the products of a relevant market and their suppliers are competing with each other despite their heterogeneity.

Chamberlin (1933) has baptized this situation as monopolistic competition. For each respective product, for example a particular type of motor car, first productive facilities must be set up, and second, the appropriate selling price has to be determined.

The inverse demand function governing the decision-making of the individual firm regarding a particular product k reads (Henderson and Quandt 1958, pp. 199ff),

$$p_k = a_k - \sum_{j \neq k}^{n} b_j q_j - b_k q_k$$

Using an appropriate unit of measurement allows the function to be written in the same way as in the case of homogeneous products. The individual equilibrium of profit maximization can be depicted just as in Figure 2.1 even though b_j and b_k are different by virtue of heterogeneity and limited sub-

[3] For details regarding delineating a relevant market see Chapter 3.
[4] Substitutability is measured approximately in this way because a price change also engenders an income effect. An unbiased measure of substitutability requires the income effect of a price change to be eliminated by using the Slutsky equation of demand theory. However, since the quantitative weight of the income effect is quite small for most goods the cross-price elasticity may in most cases serve as an approximately correct measure of substitutability.

stitutability.

Bertrand–Nash Equilibrium for Heterogeneous Products

Whereas decisions regarding the level of output pertain to the long run, in the short run the price must be determined. For analyzing short run phenomena, that is, decisions to be taken once some productive capacity is given, a Bertrand model is appropriate. For a duopoly assume demand functions

$$q_1 = \alpha_1 - \beta p_1 + \gamma p_2$$

$$q_2 = \alpha_2 - \beta p_2 + \gamma p_1$$

where the own-price effect is presumed to exceed the cross-price effect, thus $\beta > \gamma$. Disregarding fixed costs, the profits of firm i are

$$\Pi_i = (p_i - c_i)q_i.$$

For maximizing profits each firm fixes the price of its own product under the presumption that the competitors will not change their prices in response to the own move. The outcome is a Bertrand–Nash equilibrium.

The first order conditions for profit maximization of the two duopolists,

$$\partial \Pi_1 / \partial p_1 = \alpha_1 - 2\beta p_1 + \gamma p_2 + c_1 \beta = 0$$

$$\partial \Pi_2 / \partial p_2 = \alpha_2 - 2\beta p_2 + \gamma p_1 + c_2 \beta = 0$$

give rise to the reaction curves of both firms,

Firm 1: $\qquad p_2 = -\dfrac{\alpha_1 + c_1 \beta}{\gamma} + \dfrac{2\beta}{\gamma} p_1 \qquad (R_1)$

Firm 2: $\qquad p_2 = \dfrac{\alpha_2 + c_2 \beta}{2\beta} + \dfrac{\gamma}{2\beta} p_1 \qquad (R_2)$

which are depicted in Figure 2.3 for the case $\alpha_1 = \alpha_2$, $c_1 = c_2$. The curves are sloping upwards because the products are substitutes. If one firm raises the price the demand for its own product declines whilst the demand for the substitutable product of its rival increases, which allows the competitor to raise his price, too.

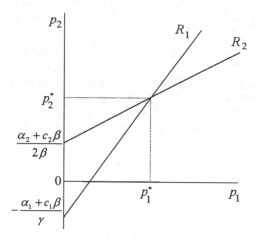

Figure 2.3 Reaction curves for the case $\alpha_1 = \alpha_2$, $c_1 = c_2$

The Bertrand–Nash equilibrium, determining the prices of both goods simultaneously, is given by the intersection of the reaction curves. A change in marginal costs and a change in demand of either good engenders a shift of the reaction curves and thus a change in both prices. By looking at Figure 2.3 the following conclusions are obvious.

(i) Following a decline in the marginal costs of firm 1 the reaction curve R_1 shifts upwards and gives rise to a new equilibrium where both prices are lower than before. Since the slopes of the reaction curves are different price p_1 declines more than price p_2.

(ii) Following a rise in demand for good 1 caused by an increase in α_1, this in turn causes the reaction curve R_1 to shift downwards which engenders both prices to rise, where p_1 is raised more than p_2.

(iii) Analogous results hold for a change in the costs of, and the demand for, good 2.[5]

---

[5] Quantitatively the effects of changes in marginal costs and demand can be derived from the necessary conditions for a profit maximum holding at a Bertrand–Nash equilibrium. They can be written

$$\begin{pmatrix} 2\beta & -\gamma \\ -\gamma & 2\beta \end{pmatrix} \begin{pmatrix} p_1 \\ p_2 \end{pmatrix} = \begin{pmatrix} \alpha_1 + c_1\beta \\ \alpha_2 + c_2\beta \end{pmatrix}$$

with solutions

$$p_1^* = \left[2\beta(\alpha_1 + c_1\beta) + \gamma(\alpha_2 + c_2\beta) \right]/D$$
$$p_2^* = \left[2\beta(\alpha_2 + c_2\beta) + \gamma(\alpha_1 + c_1\beta) \right]/D$$

where $D := 4\beta^2 - \gamma^2 > 0$ since $\beta > \gamma$ by assumption. This gives rise to the partial changes

If the marginal costs of a producer are reduced his profits increase, whereas the profits of his competitor decline.[6] Thus, in the short run too, cost-reducing innovations pay. For competitors the emerging disadvantage creates an incentive to close up with the pioneer. With regard to cost reducing innovations the Bertrand–Nash model, which pertains to the short run, thus qualitatively yields the same conclusions as the Cournot–Nash model does for the long run.

Free Entry in Cournot Competition

If free entry pertains, the profitability of the incumbents attracts new competitors. In the Cournot model the inverse demand function depicted in Figure 2.1 shifts downwards until it touches the average cost curve. Thus profits are driven to zero.[7] That allows the number of surviving firms to be determined. Assuming all producers to have identical cost functions of zero profits implies

$$\Pi_i = \frac{1}{b}\left(\frac{a-c}{n+1}\right)^2 - F = 0$$

from which it follows that[8]

$$\partial p_1^* / \partial \alpha_1 = 2\beta/D \qquad \partial p_2^* / \partial \alpha_1 = \gamma/D$$
$$\partial p_1^* / \partial \alpha_1 = 2\beta^2/D \qquad \partial p_2^* / \partial \alpha_1 = \gamma\beta/D.$$

[6] This can be shown as follows. Differentiate the profit function of firm i, $\Pi_i = (p_i - c_i)q_i$, with respect to marginal costs c_i which gives $\partial \Pi_i / \partial c_i = (p_i - c_i)\partial q_i / \partial c_i + (\partial p_i / \partial c_i - 1)q_i$. Then differentiate the demand function by using the chain rule first with respect to p_1 and p_2 and subsequently with respect to c_i. Insert the result into $\partial \Pi_i / \partial c_i$ and take account of the results given in footnote 5 to obtain

$$\partial \Pi_1 / \partial c_1 = [(p_1 - c_1)\beta + q_1](2\beta^2 - \gamma^2)/D < 0,$$

since $\beta > \gamma$ and $D > 0$, and

$$\partial \Pi_2 / \partial c_1 = (p_2 - c_2)\gamma\beta(1 + \beta)/D > 0.$$

[7] This tangential solution has been suggested by Chamberlin (1933) and Robinson (1933) for the case of monopolistic competition. Novshek (1980) has shown this equilibrium to apply also in the case of a Cournot model.

[8] Since n must be integer even under free entry profits will not always become exactly zero. Actually $\Pi_i \geq 0$ implies $n + 1 \leq (a - c)/\sqrt{bF}$. Still the zero profit condition may be considered as yielding an approximately correct solution for the equilibrium number of surviving firms under free entry.

$$n+1 = \frac{a-c}{\sqrt{bF}}.$$ (2.5)

Thus the number of surviving firms depends on the vertical size of the market, measured by a, the horizontal size of the market, measured by the slope coefficient b, marginal costs, and the level of fixed costs.

At a free entry equilibrium the price can be derived by inserting $n+1$ from equation (2.5) into $p = c + (a-c)/(n+1)$, as given by equation (2.3). It yields

$$p = c + \sqrt{bF}.$$ (2.6)

Obviously the equilibrium price does not depend on the vertical size of the market. An increase in the vertical size of the market gives rise to two opposing effects. On the one hand, higher demand is conducive to an increased price. This effect, however, is completely offset by an increase in the number of competitors. The price remains at a level which just covers average costs.[9] By contrast, the horizontal growth of the market, that is, a decrease of the absolute slope b of the inverse demand curve, yields the price to decline.

Since at a free entry equilibrium all producers operate on the declining branch of the average cost curve, free entry seems to entail excess capacity.[10] Thus a smaller number of firms, or at the extreme even a single firm, would be able to satisfy the given demand at lower average costs (Weizsäcker 1980, pp. 50ff). Seemingly a social optimum exists which is superior to the equilibrium attainable by competition. This argument, however, is misleading. It would only be valid if a benevolent dictator existed, being in command of perfect information such as to identify the optimum and to achieve it. These conditions are practically never satisfied. For a reasonable evaluation, the equilibrium attained by competition must be compared with the equilibrium which would arise in the case of a smaller number of firms or, at the extreme, under monopoly, where consumers are clearly worse off.[11]

---

[9] Average costs are $c + F/q = c + Fb(n+1)/(a-c) = c + bF/\sqrt{bF} = c + \sqrt{bF}$.

[10] For example, in a study published by the German Monopolkommission (1986, pp. 231ff) in quite a few industries the level of production of the three largest firms fell short of the cumulative production implied by the minimal efficient firm size.

[11] Let Q_C and Q_M denote total output arising under Cournot competition and in the case of monopoly, respectively. To simplify let $b = 1$. Under Cournot competition a zero profit equilibrium $Q_C^* = n(a-c)/(n+1)$ and $n+1 = (a-c)/\sqrt{F}$. Hence $Q_C^* = (a-c) - \sqrt{F}$. In the case of monopoly output is $Q_M^* = (a-c)/2$ and profits are $\Pi_M = (a-c)^2/4 - F$. Since profits are non-negative, $(a-c)/2 \geq \sqrt{F}$. A monopoly would entail output to be higher if $Q_M^* > Q_C^*$,

The foregoing analysis implies horizontal concentration and the ensuing monopolistic market power to be technologically determined as dependent on indivisibilities which give rise to fixed costs. From this observation it is frequently argued that increasing concentration is the inevitable consequence of technological laws (Piore and Sabel 1984). The truth of this claim is dubious, however. Until the mid 18th century crafts and industry were populated by small and medium-sized enterprises which ordinarily operated at constant average costs. By contrast, following the Industrial Revolution large-scale firms arose for which fixed costs played an important role. Since average costs decline with increasing output Karl Marx, as a keen observer of his time, came up with the forecast that 'the big capital would beat the small one' and concentration would continue to increase. Particularly the formation of trusts in the US and cartels in Germany and elsewhere were seen as supporting the validity of this forecast. With hindsight, however, it has become evident that the early emergence of big firms was not following from immovable laws of history. At the beginning of the Industrial Revolution the steam engine gave large enterprises an edge on their smaller rivals. This trend was broken, however, by the development of electricity and internal combustion for operating engines, which gave a new chance to small firms. A similar development has occurred recently in information processing. Giant installments have successively given way to micro computers and the PC. All this does not exclude economies to scale from existing in some industries. Their extent, though, appears to be limited. In most industries the minimal efficient size is attained at a moderate level of output (Scherer 1980, p. 87). In numerous industries large firms and smaller ones are existing side by side (Geroski 1989) which would be impossible if increasing returns to scale prevailed. Even though economies of scale are of overriding importance in some industries, and are thus crucial for the emergence of a concentrated market structure (Sutton 1991), it is not generally true that the technological development would with necessity give rise to ever increasing horizontal concentration.

Market Size, Fixed Costs and Horizontal Concentration

Mergers frequently used to be justified on the ground that larger markets, as entailed by the European Common Market and globalization in general, would necessitate larger firms. A similar reasoning has been advanced to justify trusts and mergers in the US towards the end of the 19th century. Railways had opened the vast areas west of the settled regions of the East and

---

which implies $(a-c)/2 > (a-c) - \sqrt{F}$ or $(a-c)/2 < \sqrt{F}$. Since the opposite is true, output in a Cournot equilibrium with free entry is higher than in the case of monopoly.

had brought together previously separated local markets.

An amalgamation of local markets yields a horizontal extension of the relevant market. Graphically the inverse demand curve, following a decline of the slope coefficient b, moves out anticlockwise because at a given price the larger market comprises a greater number of buyers. An extension of the market may also entail an increased division of labor, a rise in productivity and an ensuing increase in income per head. The increased ability to pay may then also yield a vertical increase of the market.

Obviously, following the growth of the market, competition becomes more vigorous. If, for example, two previously separated markets, each being controlled by a monopolist, are merged, a duopoly arises which entails a lower price and larger total supply. Understandably the firms will be tempted to reestablish the old situation by merger or collusion.[12]

By contrast, given free entry, regardless of whether a market grows horizontally or vertically, a larger market may accommodate a larger number of firms. For ascertaining to what extent restraints of competition might affect the market structures it is useful to investigate how the number of firms can be expected to develop under free entry if markets grow. For this purpose consider an oligopoly on a homogeneous market with identical producers. Individual profits are thus

$$\Pi_i = bq^2 - F = 0 . \tag{2.7}$$

Hence, as $q = \sqrt{F/b}$, vertical growth of the market does not affect the size of individual output q. This implies that the number of firms grow at the same rate as total output $Q = nq$.

By contrast, if the market grows horizontally the number of firms can be shown to grow less than proportionally. First note that (2.7) implies $\sqrt{bF} = bq$. Therefore,

$$(n+1) = (a-c)/bq \tag{2.8}$$

Differentiating (2.7) yields $\partial q/\partial b = -q/2b$. Differentiating (2.8) and recalling that q depends on b, leads to $\partial n/\partial b = -(n+1)/2b$. Hence, following horizontal growth of the market, that is, a decline of b, both individual output

---

[12] International comparisons conducted by Bain (1966) for the 1950s and by Pryor (1972) for the 1960s came up with the result that the horizontal concentration of larger markets was not significantly lower than for smaller markets. For the EC Sleuwaegen and Yamawaki (1988) found that from 1963 to 1978 horizontal concentration, as measured by $CR4$, had increased in West Germany, France, Italy, Belgium, and the Netherlands.

and the number of firms increase. The number of firms obviously grows less than proportionally. More explicitly, define

$$\frac{1}{B} := \frac{n}{Q} \frac{\partial Q/\partial b}{\partial n/\partial b}$$

and insert $\partial q/\partial b$ and $\partial n/\partial b$ to obtain

$$\frac{1}{B} = 1 + \frac{n}{n+1} > 1 .$$

Thus $B < 1$. Obviously $B = 0.5$ if n goes to infinity and $B = 2/3$ if $n = 1$. Within these bounds B rises with increasing concentration.

To illustrate the outcome entailed by horizontal growth of the market assume $a = 100$, $F = 100$, $c = 0$ and $b = 1$ for each one of two separate local markets, and hence $b = 1/2$ after the two markets have been merged. Free entry yields $n = 9$ and thus $n = n_1 + n_2 = 18$. Total output is $Q = Q_1 + Q_2$ $= 90$. After the two markets have been combined free entry gives rise to $n = 13$ and $Q = 92$. With respect to the number of surviving firms a shake-out has taken place. Concerning horizontal concentration two things have happened. On each local market the number of surviving firms is lower than before, but the total number of firms competing on the common market is larger than the number of firms previously existing on each local market. Hence competition has increased which leads to a higher level of total output and a lower price.

If the market grows both vertically and horizontally the B-coefficient is expected to fall into the range from 0.5 to 1. By contrast, blockaded entry would imply $B = 0$ and collusion may even yield $B < 0$.[13] These findings suggest that an empirical estimation of the B-coefficient may indicate to what extent barriers to entry exist.

In a study pertaining to a sample of about 300 four-digit lines of business in West Germany from 1978 to 1993 Neumann, Weigand, Gross and Münter (2001) found a B-coefficient of 0.5–0.6.[14] Hence, although substantial competition appears to prevail, restraints of competition cannot be ruled out to exist. For appraising their weight one can utilize the Mosteller model outlined

---

[13] Qualitatively the same results arise if marginal costs are assumed to be inversely related to the level of fixed costs (Neumann, Weigand, Gross and Münter 2001).

[14] The data have been published by the German Monopolkommission. The 300 lines of business can be considered as a representative selection of some 1000 lines of business data for which have come from the German Federal Statistical Office (Statistisches Bundesamt).

in Chapter 1.

Random effects alone may cause an unequal distribution of market shares to arise. As shown in Table 1.1 the variance of market shares declines with an increasing number of competitors. According to the Mosteller model a unique association between the number of firms and the variance of market shares

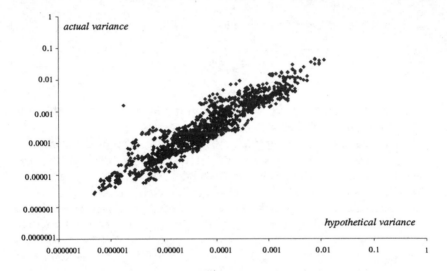

Figure 2.4   Actual vs hypothetical variances of market shares

can be expected to exist. The size distribution may of course also be affected by non-random causes such as strategic behavior associated with sunk costs or government subsidies. To assess the explanatory power of the Mosteller model and thus the extent to which competition is undistorted, in Figure 2.4, the actual variance of market shares is plotted against the theoretical one of the Mosteller model. The outcome displays a surprisingly close relationship. The logarithmic difference between the two may be interpreted as showing to what extent distortions of competition exist. Since they entail barriers to entry they can be expected to reduce the measured *B*-coefficient. Exactly this has been found to exist in the sample of West German business lines. Hence the conclusion can be drawn that for the sample of industries under consideration, even though the competitive process appears to be working fairly well, there are distortions of competition which are of concern for competition policy.

2.2   RESTRAINTS OF COMPETITION IN OLIGOPOLY

Various kinds of restraints of competition may be distinguished. All of them are based on collusion aiming at excess profits.

Maximizing Joint Profits

A cartel which may be considered as the prototype of collusion is assumed to behave like a monopolist to maximize joint profits,

$$\Pi = p(Q)Q - \sum_{i=1}^{n} c_i q_i - \sum_{i=1}^{n} F_i, \qquad Q := \sum_{i=1}^{n} q_i.$$

If the cost functions are identical among the participating firms total output will be

$$Q = (a - c)/2b.$$

In this case the output of each member of the cartel can be assumed to be the same. Different marginal costs, however, give rise to a divergence of interest among the members of a cartel. Firms with low marginal costs will prefer a higher level of output than firms with higher marginal costs. A possibility to compromise, for which some empirical evidence has been adduced by Choi, Menezes and Tressler (1985), would consist in maximizing profits predicated on the average value of individual marginal costs where agreed-upon market shares serve as weights. This strategy yields an output that falls short of the monopoly output based on the marginal costs of the most efficient firm. The result indicates that the strategy of cartels is conducive to setting a price which protects less-efficient producers.

Still, a cartel agreement does not remove rivalry altogether. Cartel members continue to be rivals guided by self-interest. Therefore, cartels are prone to decay. In fact, cartels would not pose a problem for competition policy if they were unstable such that producers would find it unattractive to join a cartel. Cartels would then be short-lived phenomena. Experience, however, shows that cartels do exist and have been maintained for a long time. Hence it is important to identify circumstances which are conducive to cartel stability.

Stability of Collusion

To achieve joint profit maximization the common interest of cartel members would require mutual mistrust to be removed. This may be attained by entering a contract which obliges the parties to a performance in accordance with the common goal. However, agreeing to a contract does not always ensure that the parties abide by their obligations. The history of cartels shows that in troubled times firms frequently believed themselves to be better off by cheating.[15] Even contractual penalties may be unable to enforce compliance with the contract if the advantage expected from cheating outweighs the punishment imposed by the cartel. Compliance is much more effectively enforced by the fear of retaliation by deceived partners to the agreement (Telser 1971, pp. 143ff). Therefore, for oligopolies secret price cutting has frequently been reported. However, since it is hardly possible to advertise the willingness to charge lower prices to a large number of customers, without communicating it also to competitors, secret rebates are usually granted to major customers only (Stigler 1964). They are of course interested in maintaining secrecy since once the rebates become common knowledge their privilege is gone.

The fragility of cartels is particularly severe if they are illegal and cannot be enforced by appeal to courts. That gives rise to the question under which conditions collusive agreements between competitors can be expected to arise and to hold. Game theory has contributed to understand what is involved.

Although joint profit maximization is in the common interest it is not always in the interest of the individual firm, too. That shall be illustrated for a duopoly where firms are competing only once. The output may be chosen according to the following strategies

- Cournot (Π^C)
- Collusion (Π^K)
- Cheating (Π^A) when the rival firm abides by the contract (Π^0).

The resulting profits are ranked as follows,

$$\Pi^A > \Pi^K > \Pi^C > \Pi^0.$$

For example, if the inverse demand function is $p = 10 - Q$ and marginal costs are $c = 1$ the alternative profits are listed in the pay-off matrix of Table 2.2.

The cells show the profits achieved by firm 1 and firm 2, respectively. Obviously collusion would yield the largest profit for both simultaneously. However, if one firms defects by supplying the Cournot quantity whilst the

---

[15] See the evaluation regarding cartel stability by Sombart (1921) and others as mentioned in Chapter 1.

other firm abides by the contract, cheating yields a higher profit for the
defector than colluding. By contrast, the deceived party receives a profit

Table 2.2   Pay-off matrix in a duopoly

| | | Firm 2 | |
		Cournot	Collusion
Firm 1	Cournot	9, 9	11, 8
	Collusion	8, 11	10, 10

which is even lower than in the case of a simultaneous Cournot equilibrium.
Hence, unless each firm can be sure of the partner to abide by the contract, it
is preferable to adopt the Cournot strategy.

In contrast to this case of the so-called prisoners' dilemma where the game
is played only once, the strategic character of the game is quite different if the
game is repeated indefinitely. Whilst in a one-shot game the Cournot–Nash
equilibrium dominates, in a repeated game with indefinite duration collusion
is much more likely. In a repeated game the individual firm may defect once
and achieve an extraordinarily high profit. The basis for future cooperation
will be undermined, however, and in the most unfavorable case it will be
completely destroyed forever, in which case in the future only Cournot equilibria are feasible. In this case the individual duopolist will find cheating
profitable only if

$$\Pi^A - \Pi^K > (\Pi^K - \Pi^C)/\rho$$

where ρ is the discount rate. For defection to pay, the excess profit obtainable by cheating once must exceed the present value of difference between
future profits attainable by collusion and future profits achievable under
Cournot competition. Defection is more likely the higher the discount rate. It
depends on the prevailing rate of interest and the likelihood of the market to
continue to exist in the future. The smaller the likelihood is, the larger is the
relevant discount rate and thus the smaller is the likelihood of collusion. If
defection pays the Cournot solution will come about from the very beginning.

This reasoning gives some hints regarding the likelihood of collusion as
depending on the state of development of a particular market. In the initial
phase of a market there is large uncertainty regarding its future existence and
much uncertainty with regard to the success of the individual enterprise. The
rate of discount will thus be high and the likelihood of collusion low. The
same applies presumably towards the end of the life cycle of a market when

the profitability of the respective products is threatened by emerging innovations. By contrast, during the heydays of a market, after most failing enterprises have been shaken out and the continuance of the market appears sure to the incumbent firms, the discount rate will be low and collusion is thus likely.[16]

The probability of collusion arising also depends on the number of competitors. The larger the number of rival firms the larger is the profit to be expected from defection and the greater therefore the incentive to cheat. This applies both to homogeneous and heterogeneous markets. However, both cases differ with regard to the attractiveness of collusion for individual firms.

Attractiveness of Collusion Depending on Participation

In the case of a homogeneous market, collusion is attractive only if almost all firms participate, as shown by Salant, Switzer and Reynolds (1983). Assume a linear inverse demand curve with $b = 1$ and identical cost functions of all firms with constant marginal costs. At a Cournot equilibrium profits of the individual enterprise are $\Pi_i = [(a-c)/(n+1)]^2$. If among n firms $m+1 < n$ cooperate, $n - (m+1) + 1 = n - m$ independent competitors remain, namely $n - (m+1)$ outsiders and the cartel, among which Cournot competition applies. Each member of the cartel thus earns profits

$$\Pi_k = \frac{1}{m+1} \left(\frac{a-c}{n-m+1} \right)^2 .$$

Participating in the collusion pays for the individual firm only if $\Pi_k > \Pi_i$, that is, if

$$\frac{1}{m+1} \frac{1}{(n-m+1)^2} > \frac{1}{(n+1)^2} .$$

For example, if $n = 5$, all of them must participate to render the cartel attractive, given $n = 6$ it requires 5 to join the cartel, with $n = 10$ at least 9 must participate, and it requires 17 if $n = 20$. Hence a great majority of firms operating in a market must join the cartel to render cooperation attractive. This conclusion is borne out by experience. Cartels on homogeneous markets, like

---

[16] This conclusion is supported by the finding of Symeonidis (1999, p. 21) that in the UK during the 1950s across industries a moderate growth rate has been more conducive to stable collusion than a stagnant or declining demand and that fast growth hinders collusion.

coal mining, steel and cement, have been stable only if a great majority of competitors did participate.

In contrast to a homogeneous market, on a heterogeneous market profits of firms joining a cartel are always higher than under Bertrand competition irrespective of the share of participating firms (Deneckere and Davidson 1985). To show this assume a demand function

$$q_i = \alpha - (1+\gamma)p_i + (\gamma/n)\sum_{j=1}^{n} p_j$$

where the direct price effect is given by $1+\gamma-\gamma/n = 1+\gamma(1-1/n)$ and the cross-price effect by $(\gamma/n)\sum_{j\neq i} p_j$, or $\gamma(1-1/n)p_j$ if the prices of all competing products are identical. Obviously the direct-price effect is larger than the cross-price effect. Let marginal costs of all firms be identical and zero.

Profits of an individual firm are

$$\Pi_i = p_i\left[\alpha - (1+\gamma)p_i + (\gamma/n)\sum_{j=1}^{n} p_j\right].$$

Profit maximization at a Bertrand–Nash equilibrium requires

$$\partial\Pi_i/\partial p_i = \alpha - (1+\gamma)p_i + (\gamma/n)\sum_{j=1}^{n} p_j + p_i\left[-(1+\gamma)+(\gamma/n)\right] = 0$$

to be satisfied. Since the demand functions and marginal costs are identical for all firms one obtains a symmetric solution where $p_i = p$ for all i. Hence $\sum_j p_j = np$. Inserting into the maximum conditions yields the price attained at a Bertrand–Nash equilibrium,

$$p^N = \frac{\alpha}{2+\gamma(1-1/n)}$$

and individual profits

$$\Pi_i^N = p^N(\alpha - p^N).$$

Now assume collusion among $m < n$ firms by setting up a cartel or by merger. Let p denote the price charged by the cartel and r the price of outsiders which is identical for all of them. The profits of the colluding firms are

$$\Pi_i^K = p\{\alpha - (1+\gamma)p + (\gamma/n)[mp + (n-m)r]\}.$$

Maximizing with respect to p yields

$$2\left(1 + \gamma\frac{n-m}{n}\right)p = \alpha + \gamma\frac{n-m}{n}r. \tag{2.9a}$$

The profits of an outsider are

$$\Pi_j^0 = r_j\left[\alpha - (1+\gamma)r_j + (\gamma/n)\left(mp + \sum_{j\neq i}r_j\right)\right].$$

Maximizing with respect to r_j requires

$$\partial\Pi_j^0/\partial r_j = \alpha - (1+\gamma)r_j + (\gamma/n)\left(mp + \sum_{j\neq i}r_j\right) + r_j[-(1+\gamma) + (\gamma/n)] = 0.$$

As $r_j = r$ for all j, $\sum r_j = (n-m)r$ which yields

$$\left(2 + \gamma\frac{n+m-1}{n}\right)r = \alpha + \gamma\frac{m}{n}p. \tag{2.9b}$$

Equations (2.9a) and (2.9b) depict reaction curves, the intersection of which determines prices p and r attained at a Bertrand–Nash equilibrium between the cartel and outsiders. Inserting these prices into the respective profit functions yields the profits of cartel members and outsiders, respectively. In the following table prices and profits for alternative numbers of competitors are given if $\alpha = 1$, $\gamma = 9$ and $m = 2$.

Table 2.3   Prices and profits at a Bertrand–Nash equilibrium and collusion among two firms ($m = 2$) out of n firms

n	p^N	p	r	Π_i^N	Π_i^K	Π_i^0
3	0.125	0.181	0.149	0.109	0.131	0.155
4	0.114	0.141	0.124	0.101	0.110	0.118
20	0.095	0.097	0.095	0.085	0.086	0.086

*Assumptions: $\alpha = 1, \gamma = 9$, marginal costs $c = 0$.

First of all note that prices and profits decline at the respective Bertrand–Nash equilibrium for an increasing number of competitors. Furthermore, collusive prices always exceed those entailed by a Bertrand–Nash equilibrium, and profits of cooperating firms are higher. Thus, in contrast to a homogeneous market, collusion is always attractive. It is noteworthy, however, that outsiders' profits rise even more. Hence there is a permanent temptation to defect.

Moreover, for a heterogeneous market contractual collusion is more difficult to monitor because demand does not depend on prices alone but also on advertising and product design. This is an additional reason for a cartel on a heterogeneous market to be prone to decay.

Collusion and Free Entry

High profits engendered by cartels entice entry of outsiders. The history of cartels in Germany abounds with evidence for this conclusion (Kestner and Lehnich 1927, pp. 40f). For example the potash syndicate was founded by four firms in 1879. By 1909 the number of firms had risen to 52. Another example is the rolling mill cartel in the steel industry which, as reported by Kestner and Lehnich (1927, p. 41), had to be dissolved under the pressure of competition from outsiders after wire drawing mills turned to supplying iron bars. Similar developments are reported from the iron tube industry and the cement industry. On the other hand there have been quite a few cases where cartels proved to be stable for long periods of time (see Chapter 1, and for more recent times Schwalbach and Schwerk 1999).

For a cartel to be maintained, outsiders must either be integrated or shunned. Integration yields an increasing number of cartel members. Each member thus has to reduce its output such that, if fixed costs exist, average costs increase. Eventually profits are driven to zero. As compared to a Cournot equilibrium, though, total output is lower and the price is higher.[17]

---

[17] The proof runs as follows (Neumann 1998, pp. 49f). Let n_K and n_C denote the number of firms in the case of a cartel and competition, respectively. For the inverse demand function $p = a - bQ$ assume $b = 1$. If profits are driven to zero following entry one obtains

$$n_K = \frac{1}{F}\left(\frac{a-c}{2}\right)^2$$

and

$$n_C = \frac{a-c}{\sqrt{F}} - 1$$

respectively. Hence

Cartelization thus makes consumers worse off without making producers better off. Understandably the cartel will attempt to fend off the emergence of outsiders. Evidence for this conclusion is reported in Chapter 3.

2.3 THE STRUCTURE–CONDUCT–PERFORMANCE PARADIGM

Following the theoretical analysis the question arises whether and to what extent theoretical predictions are borne out by empirical evidence. How useful is price theory for competition policy? This question has been raised by Mason (1939), and Bain (1951) was the first to investigate the relationship between profitability and horizontal concentration for a cross-section of US industries. He thus pioneered the Structure–Conduct–Performance paradigm. Utilizing this approach brought about a very large number of empirical studies (surveyed by Weiss 1971, Scherer 1980, Böbel 1984, Schmalensee 1989), pertaining to the relationship between market structure, in particular concentration, market shares, firm size and conduct on one hand, and profitability or the price–cost margin on the other hand.

Let p denote the price, v average variable costs, q output, and K the capital stock. The difference between the price and long-run total average costs, as related to the price, is

$$\frac{p - v - (i + \delta)(K/q)}{p} = \frac{pq - vq}{pq} - (i + \delta)\frac{K}{pq}$$

where i is the rate of interest, denoting the opportunity costs of capital, and δ is the rate of economic depreciation. If marginal costs are constant they equal average variable cost, hence $v = c$. Under perfect competition, at an

$$y := n_K - n_c = \frac{1}{F}\left(\frac{a-c}{2}\right)^2 - \frac{a-c}{\sqrt{F}} + 1.$$

Define $x := (a - c)/\sqrt{F}$ to obtain

$$y = \frac{1}{4}(x^2 - 4x + 4) = \frac{1}{4}(x - 2)^2.$$

Thus $y > 0$ unless $x = 2$. Since $n_c + 1 = (a-c)/\sqrt{F}$, $x = (a-c)/\sqrt{F} > 3$. Hence $n_c \geq 2$ implies $n_K \geq n_c$. As $p_c = c + (a-c)/(n_c + 1)$ and $p_K = (a-c)/2$, and $n_c + 1 > 2$, $p_K > p_C$, and consequently $Q_K < Q_C$.

equilibrium, the price–cost margin $(p-c)/p = (pq - vq)/pq$ then covers fixed costs per unit of output which depend on the rate of interest, depreciation and the capital stock. An excess of revenues over total costs, that is, an economic profit, may follow from collusion. It may also arise because the adjustment to a long-run equilibrium is not yet completed. It may finally be due to the fact that at a free-entry equilibrium, since the number of firms is integer, the entry of an additional supplier would render profits to become negative and therefore would not occur.

An empirical analysis within the framework of the Structure–Conduct–Performance paradigm may pertain to the relationship between market structure and conduct on one hand, and the price–cost margin or profitability, respectively, on the other hand.

Price-Cost Margin and Market Structure in a Homogeneous Oligopoly

For interpreting the results of empirical studies we return once more to the model of a homogeneous oligopoly. Maximizing the profits of firm i,

$$\Pi_i = p(Q)q_i - C(q_i), \quad Q := \sum_{i=1}^{n} q_i$$

by choosing the appropriate level of output, q_i, given some conjecture regarding the reaction of rivals, one obtains

$$p + qp'(Q)\left(1 + \sum_{\substack{j=1 \\ j\neq i}}^{n} dq_j/dq_i\right) = c_i, \quad c_i := C'(q_i)$$

which can be rearranged to derive a transparent measure of monopolistic market power (Cowling and Waterson 1976). Let $s_i = q_i/Q$ denote the individual market share, $\varepsilon = -(p/Q)\,dQ/dp = -p/Qp'(Q)$ the price elasticity of demand, and $z_j := (q_i/q_j)\,dq_j/dq_i$ the elasticity of conjectural variation which denotes the expected percentage change of the output of rival j following a change in the output of firm i under consideration. Simplifying we shall assume the elasticity of conjectural variation to be the same for all rivals, hence $z_j = z$. The monopolistic market power of firm i can then be depicted by[18]

---

[18] Profit maximization requires

$$m_i := \frac{p - c_i}{p} = \frac{s_i + z(1 - s_i)}{\varepsilon}.$$

In the Cournot case $z = 0$ and hence $m_i = s_i/\varepsilon$. Given perfect collusion, that is, parallel behavior of all firms, $z = 1$, and thus $m_i = 1/\varepsilon$. Incomplete collusion, that is, $1 > z > 0$, yields an individual price–cost margin which is larger than in the Cournot case but falls short of the one to be expected for a pure monopoly.

The individual price–cost margin can furthermore be shown to depend on horizontal concentration and relative marginal costs. First, one obtains the average price–cost margin of the market under consideration,

$$m := \frac{p - c}{p} = \frac{H + z(1 - H)}{\varepsilon}$$

which depends on the Herfindahl index of horizontal concentration, H, the elasticity of conjectural variation, and the price elasticity of demand.[19] These are the determinants of monopolistic market power, as suggested by Abba P. Lerner and discussed in Chapter 1. For an oligopoly the effective price elasticity turns out to be $E := \varepsilon/[H + z(1 - H)]$. The higher the horizontal concentration, the more tightly knit the collusion, and the lower the price elasticity of demand, the larger is monopolistic market power. The likelihood of collusion presumably increases with a rise in horizontal concentration, since a smaller number of competitors renders rivalness more perceptible and the firms to be more conscious of their oligopolistic interdependence. Collusion

$$p\left[1 + \frac{q_i}{Q}\frac{Qp'(Q)}{p}\left(1 + \sum_{j \neq i}\frac{q_i}{q_j}\frac{dq_j}{dq_i}\frac{q_j/Q}{q_i/Q}\right)\right] = c_i$$

Inserting s_i, ε, and z yields

$$p\left[1 - \frac{s_i}{\varepsilon}\left(1 + \sum_{j \neq i} z\frac{s_j}{s_i}\right)\right] = c_i.$$

Since $\sum_{j \neq i} s_j = 1 - s_i$ one obtains m_i, as shown above.

[19] For each firm $m_i = (p - c_i)/p$ can be rewritten as $(1 - m_i)p = c_i$. Multiplying with the market share s_i yields $(s_i - s_i m_i)p = s_i c_i$. Summing over all i and noting that $\sum_i s_i = 1$ gives $(1 - \sum_i s_i m_i)p = \sum_i s_i c_i = c$. Rearranging leads to $(p - c)/p = \sum_i s_i m_i$. Inserting m_i, as given above, and using $H = \sum_i s_i^2$ yields m, as shown in the main text.

is more easily monitored and is thus more likely to arise (Stigler 1964).

For an individual firm, from $(1-m_i)p = c_i$ and $(1-m)p = c$ by eliminating p, one obtains the individual price–cost margin

$$m_i = 1-(1-m)c_i/c$$

which thus depends first on the average price–cost margin of the market and individual marginal costs c_i, as related to the average of marginal costs of all competing firms. Given some market power as being revealed in the average price–cost margin, the individual price–cost margin is higher than the average if marginal costs are relatively low.

Price–Cost Margin and Market Structure for a Heterogeneous Market

A relationship between the price–cost margin and the market structure also exists in the case of differentiated products. The demand for a particular product i depends on the set of all n prices belonging to a relevant market, as shown by the demand function

$$q_i = q_i(p_1, p_2,..., p_n).$$

Given constant marginal costs c_i and fixed costs F_i profits of firm i are

$$\Pi_i = (p_i - c_i)q_i - F_i.$$

Maximizing profits by choosing the appropriate price p_i and taking into account the conjectural variation of prices by rival firms requires

$$\partial\Pi_i/\partial p_i = q_i + (p_i - c_i)\left[\partial q_i/\partial p_i + \sum_{j\neq i}(\partial q_2/\partial p_j)(\partial p_j/\partial p_i)\right] = 0$$

to be satisfied. Multiply by p_i/q_i and use the following definitions,

$$e_i = -(p_i/q_i)(\partial q_i/\partial p_i)$$
$$e_{ij} = (p_j/q_i)(\partial q_i/\partial p_j)$$
$$\mu_{ij} = (p_i/p_j)(\partial p_j/\partial p_i)$$

where e_i is the direct price elasticity, e_{ij} the cross-price elasticity of demand and μ_{ij} the elasticity of conjectural variation, to obtain

$$\frac{p_i - c_i}{p_i} = \frac{1}{e_i - \sum_{j \neq i} \mu_{ij} e_{ij}} .$$

If no reaction of competitors is expected, that is, in the Bertrand case, $\mu_{ij} = 0$, and the price–cost margin depends only on the direct price elasticity of demand for the product under consideration. This elasticity e_i can be shown to increase with the number of substitutable products and to decrease with the size of the market share. Collusion, as measured by the elasticity of conjectural variation, causes the price–cost margins to rise.

Empirical Evidence: Price–Cost Margin and Market Structure

The theory of oligopoly, as outlined above, suggests a positive association between the price–cost margin and the Herfindahl index of concentration to exist across industries. Across individual firms one would also expect the price–cost margin to be positively associated with their respective market shares or the Herfindahl index of concentration and the relative level of marginal costs. If individual market shares are used as explanatory variables horizontal concentration does not come into play immediately. It would only be relevant insofar as a high level of horizontal concentration is conducive to collusion, as suggested by Stigler (1964).

These relationships are derived from the necessary conditions for maximizing profits. They are functional relationships which can hardly be interpreted as depicting causation running from market shares or concentration, respectively, to price–cost margins. Actually, as shown in the previous section, horizontal concentration is endogenous depending on technological conditions prevailing in the industry and the existence or non-existence, respectively, of freedom of entry. Nevertheless, the relationship between price–cost margins and horizontal concentration can be taken as a refutable empirical hypothesis. It is certainly important to know whether firms do behave as predicted by the theory of industrial organization, and in particular whether their behavior can be understood by assuming them to maximize profits. Unless they are guided by profit maximization the predicted relationships would not hold. The frequently raised objection against the Structure–Conduct–Performance approach as being void of empirical content is thus misleading.[20]

---

[20] In addition it is sometimes objected that the price–cost margin also depends on the price elasticity of demand and relative marginal costs. These variables, in most empirical studies, are captured by using fixed effects or by using other firm-specific or industry-specific variables.

Regarding causality, although in principle it may run in either direction, for the empirical studies there are good reasons to believe that increasing concentration does cause the price–cost margin to rise. In principle large firms may enjoy comparatively low marginal costs because bigness allows them to apply more efficient techniques. Since their market shares are large, horizontal concentration is high. Both horizontal concentration and the price–cost margins are thus determined by a third factor, namely the higher cost-efficiency of large firms. However, it is misleading to use this observation to dismiss the hypotheses of causation running from concentration to price–cost margins. First, concentration changes only slowly whilst the price–cost margin is more volatile, because it is affected by changes in demand and input prices. Concentration thus displays some exogeneity. Therefore a positive association between the price–cost margin and concentration is at least partly a causal one. Second, no convincing evidence exists for large firms to be always superior to small firms with regard to efficiency and technical change, as will be discussed in more detail below in Section 2.4. Third, concentration is conducive to collusion as suggested by Stigler (1964) and may follow from mergers undertaken with the intent to raise monopolistic market power.

In fact, in a great number of studies pertaining to the US, England and Germany, a positive association between the price–cost margin and horizontal concentration, as measured either by the combined market share of the leading firms or the Herfindahl index has been found.[21]

A representative example is a study conducted by Rhoades and Cleaver (1973) for 352 US manufacturing industries. The price–cost margin (*PCM*) as of 1967 was regressed on 4-firm concentration (*CR*4), the growth of industry sales from 1963 to 1967 (*G*), the capital–output ratio, defined as gross book

---

[21] Some irritation has been caused by a study conducted by Ravenscraft (1983) pertaining to Line of Business data of the US. The regression coefficient associated with the individual market share was significantly positive whereas horizontal concentration apparently exerted an adverse influence. Three objections must be raised against the claim that this finding disproves the existence of a positive association between the price–cost margin and horizontal concentration. First, as mentioned above, it is dubious to use both concentration and market shares as explanatory variables unless concentration is presumed to enhance collusion (see Cowling and Waterson 1976, Kwoka and Ravenscraft 1986). Second, since the market share and concentration are positively associated, for purely statistical reasons, multicollinearity may cause biased estimates. Third, Ravenscraft's study pertains to 'operating income divided by sales' as dependent variable, where operating income is defined as revenue less expenditures for materials input, wages, expenses for marketing and R&D, administrative expenditures and depreciation (see Ravenscraft 1983, p. 22). This variable clearly is not the price–cost margin but some kind of profitability. He thus investigated the relationship between concentration and so on and profitability rather than the price–cost margin. Likewise for his regression pertaining to a cross-section of industries he deducted expenditures for advertising and R&D as well as depreciation per unit of revenue from the price–cost margin, such that this regression, too, pertained to profitability rather than the price–cost margin.

value of assets over sales (*C/O*), a dummy variable (*P − C*), introduced to capture entry barriers, with one for consumer industries and zero otherwise, and the geographic size of the market (*GM*). The results were as follows

$$PCM = 5.698 + 0.097CR4 + 0.053G + 0.110C/O + 4.927(P - C) + 0.001GM$$
$$\quad\quad (5.04)\quad\quad (3.314)\quad (6.73)\quad\quad\quad (5.31)\quad\quad\quad\quad (0.051)$$

$$\overline{R}^2 = 0.234 .$$

The *t*-ratios, given in parentheses, indicate that all variables, with the exception of *GM*, are statistically significant.

As shown by Salinger (1990) the relationship between the price–cost margin and *CR4* has remained remarkably stable for the US from 1971 to 1984. Horizontal concentration, corrected for imports, turned out to be a statistically significant explanatory variable in all years without showing a trend regarding the strength of the association. Moreover, regressing the price–cost margin of 1982 on the concentration of 1982 and 1972 did not show a difference. This supports the presumption that concentration does determine the price–cost margin and that reverse causality does not exist. The question 'What happened to the concentration–margin relationship?' has been answered by Salinger with the clear-cut answer 'Nothing!'

For 94 British industries Cowling and Waterson (1976) estimated the following regression equation

$$\log\left[PCM(68)/PCM(63)\right] = 0.333 + 0.2957\log\left[H(63)/H(58)\right]$$
$$\quad\quad\quad\quad\quad\quad\quad\quad (0.683)\ (2.942)$$

$$\quad\quad\quad\quad + 0.4985\log\left[TU(63)/TU(58)\right] + 0.0344DG$$
$$\quad\quad\quad\quad\quad (1.480)\quad\quad\quad\quad\quad\quad\quad\quad (0.619)$$

$$\overline{R}^2 = 0.096 \quad\quad\quad\quad\quad \text{t-ratios in parentheses,}$$

where

PCM	=	value added less wages divided by sales
H	=	Herfindahl index of horizontal concentration
TU	=	number of trade union members/total number of employees
DG	=	dummy variable: 1 for durable good industries, 0 otherwise.

Again, the particularly interesting relationship between the price–cost margin and concentration turned out to be positive and statistically significant.

For West Germany, in various studies pertaining to joint stock companies

(Neumann, Böbel and Haid 1979, 1983, 1985) and industries (Neumann and Haid 1985), a positive and statistically significant relationship between the price–cost margin and horizontal concentration has been found. A more recent panel estimation pertaining to 240 German joint stock companies from 1965 to 1986 yields a relationship between the price–cost margin (*PCM*), as defined by sales minus expenditures for input materials and wages, divided by sales, and the 6-firm concentration ratio (*CR6*) of 2-digit industries[22]

$$\Delta PCM = 0.4090 \, \Delta CR6, \qquad t = 2.37$$

according to which the price–cost margin was positively and statistically significantly associated with horizontal concentration.

Given exports and imports, domestic concentration does not provide a reliable picture of competitive conditions. In the above mentioned studies pertaining to the relationship between the price–cost margin and concentration in Germany, Neumann, Böbel and Haid used the ratios of exports and imports to sales for the respective industries as additional explanatory variables. The export ratio was shown to exert an adverse effect on the price–cost margin. The import ratio had a negative influence only during recessions, being insignificant during booms (Neumann, Böbel and Haid 1983). The adverse effect associated with exports can be interpreted as follows. The price–cost margin averaged for domestic and export sales is $m = xm(F)$ $+(1-x)m(D)$, where x is the share of exports in total sales, $m(F)$ and $m(D)$ being the price–cost margins existing for exports and domestic sales, respectively. Empirically $\partial m/\partial x = m(F) - m(D) < 0$ was found to hold. Hence the price–cost margin attained on foreign markets was lower than the one prevailing on the domestic market. On foreign markets domestic firms thus face more vigorous competition than on their home markets, where foreign firms have to overcome impediments which do not exist for domestic firms.[23]

It is furthermore noteworthy that the positive association between concentration and the price–cost margin from 1965 to 1977 was more highly significant in business cycle booms than in recessions. This finding confirms the theoretical prediction that, except under perfect competition, a vertical increase in demand gives rise to an increase in monopoly power which engenders a higher price–cost margin.

---

[22] I am indebted to Jürgen Weigand. The *CR6* ratio was used because data of the Herfindahl index were not available for all industries. Including additional explanatory variables into the regression did not affect the relationship between *PCM* and *CR6*.

[23] A similar result has been reported by Bourlakis (1997) for Greece. Sleuwaegen and Yamawaki (1988) found a significantly positive association between the price–cost margin and EC-wide concentration (*CR3*) for Germany, France and Italy.

Profitability and Market Structure

Whilst Bain and many others of his followers focused on the relationship between profitability and horizontal concentration, Shepherd (1972) demonstrated for 231 US firms from 1960 to 1969 that a positive and statistically significant relationship existed between profitability, as measured by net income after tax as per cent of equity, and the market share of the individual firm. Horizontal concentration was disregarded because of collinearity with the market share. It remained an open question whether and to what extent higher profitability follows from the exercise of monopolistic market power or from lower costs. Whether firms do earn above-normal profits due to monopolistic market power depends primarily on the existence or absence of barriers to entry. Given free entry, profits become zero in the long run, irrespective of concentration and the individual market share, irrespective, too, of whether collusion obtains or not. It is not unlikely that high concentration and barriers to entry are to be observed simultaneously. How they are related, whether barriers give rise to concentration or whether firms in a concentrated industry adopt strategies to fend off the entry of newcomers must be examined in each case. Thus Tirole (1988) has presumably been right in stating that the relationship between profitability and market structure cannot be interpreted off-hand as a causal one but as a case of 'descriptive statistics'.

Consequently the theoretical foundation for an association between profitability and market structure to hold has been questioned. Brozen (1971) argued that firms using a superior technique would grow faster than competitors such that concentration would rise. For profitability to be positively related to concentration should therefore be explained by reference to lower costs instead by invoking monopoly power. If this were true, however, comparatively high profitability should be a firm-specific phenomenon. If, by contrast, it were caused by monopolistic market power, all firms in an industry should enjoy higher profits. These alternative hypotheses have been examined by McGahan and Porter (1999) for a large sample of US industries during the time from 1981 to 1994. They found industry-specific effects to clearly dominate firm-specific effects.

Brozen (1974) argued in addition that the competitive process would entail imitation which would level down initial differences in profitability and market shares. Under effective competition a positive relationship between profitability and concentration thus appears as purely transitory. Still, it would be important to know how persistent initially achieved differences in profitability are. Initial differences are leveled off fast if barriers to entry are low or even completely absent. Hence, as suggested by Bain (1956) barriers to entry may cause excessive profits to persist for a long time. It is true that the persistence of profitability of incumbent firms and the entry of newcomers is theoretically so far only incompletely understood. There can be no doubts, however, that barriers to entry weaken the effectiveness of competition, regardless of whether barriers to entry are caused technologically, depend on privileges granted by the government, or if they are set up by the strategic behavior of incumbents. Brozen (1974), presuming a purely transitory relationship between profitability and concentration, criticized the fact that profits and concentration for only a single year used to be compared by previous studies.

> None had looked at the profitability of the same industry at a later time to determine whether the above average rates of return in concentrated industries had persisted.

Exactly this has been done in the meantime. Both conceptionally and empirically the relationship has been examined in an international study edited by Mueller (1990). The basic idea underlying the empirical investigation can be expounded as follows (Mueller 1990a, p. 36). Transitory differences in profitability can be depicted by the equation

$$\Pi_{it} = \alpha_i + \lambda_i \Pi_{it-1} + u_{it}, \quad i = 1,2,...,n.$$

Profits of firm i in period t thus depend on a constant α_i, on profits of the previous period and on a random variable. The velocity for profits to be eroded is measured by the adjustment parameter λ_i. Once an equilibrium has been attained $\Pi_{it} = \Pi_{it-1}$, and permanent profits are

$$\Pi_{ip} = \frac{\alpha_i}{1 - \lambda_i}.$$

In empirical studies pertaining to the US, Canada, West Germany, France, the UK and Japan, the adjustment parameter λ_i was found to fall into the range 0.3 to 0.7 (Odagiri and Yamawaki 1990, pp. 179ff). Hence an initial profit difference melts down to about 1/10 of its original size after two to four years.

In a second step permanent profits, Π_{ip}, could be shown to depend on market structure and advertising expenditures (Mueller 1990a, p. 43). Likewise the velocity of erosion, as measured by the adjustment parameter λ_i, turned out to be lower the higher the market share and horizontal concentration.

Beyond these conceptional questions the use of profitability as a dependent variable gives rise to measurement problems because accounting profits, taken from published balance sheet data, need not be identical with economic

profits. Econometric studies which nevertheless came up with statistically
significant results should therefore be treated cautiously (Fisher and
McGowan 1983).[24] Problems of this kind do not arise for studies pertaining
to the relationship between the price–cost margin and market structure even
though some inaccuracies are inevitable, too, because marginal costs cannot
be reconstructed reliably from published accounting data. Still, the usual
assumption that marginal costs and average variable costs are equal is presumably nearly correct. To avoid all these problems Leonard Weiss suggested investigating the association between prices and the market structure.
In fact, for a large number of markets a positive relationship has been found
(Schmalensee 1989, p. 987).

Questions also arise as to whether the combined market share of the largest
firms in an industry is a reliable indicator of monopolistic market power. In
fact, as shown by Davies and Geroski (1997) for the US, and by Baldwin and
Gorecki (1994) for Canada, industries display a substantial degree of mobility
of individual market shares. This observation may lead to the conclusion that
high mobility of market shares is an indicator of effective competition and
that therefore high concentration does not tell the truth regarding the tough-
ness of competition. Thus a high level of concentration as such is not sufficient proof that competition is weak. This has already been discussed in
Chapter 1. Nevertheless, taking into account the whole body of available
knowledge, mobility of market shares does not disqualify concentration as a
prima facie indicator of existing monopolistic market power. According to
comparative studies pertaining to the dynamics of market structure (Mueller
1991) the group of leading firms of an industry is hardly ever threatened by
the encroachment of a powerful newcomer. Davies and Geroski (1997, p.
384) observed that in the US 'entry and exit into the top five was relatively
infrequent; the typical industry had just one entrant or exitor'. Even though
the average price–cost margin of the leading firm group of an industry is
affected by competition within the group, the degree of monopolistic market
power of the group itself does presumably crucially depend on the level of
concentration and to what extent incumbency is endangered by the potential
entry of newcomers.

From all this may be concluded that although the empirical studies conducted within the framework of the Structure–Conduct–Performance paradigm are not without problems, with hindsight an unequivocal result appears
to stand out. Price–cost margins and horizontal concentration are positively
associated reflecting a functional relationship implied by oligopoly theory. It
is somewhat doubtful whether a positive association between profitability and

---

[24] For example, no sensible results could be found for the relationship between accounting
profits and market structure for West German firms in Neumann, Böbel and Haid (1979).

market structure exists. As far as such a relationship has been found, various reasons may account for this finding. First, it may be caused by collusion which is facilitated by a high level of horizontal concentration. Second, it may follow from incomplete adjustment. Following an exogenous increase in demand or a decrease in costs due to technological progress profits arise which, because of sluggish entry and imitation, are only gradually eroded. Third, profits may follow from indivisibilities. As the number of firms entailed by free entry is an integer, profits may arise without inducing entry since setting up new facilities would render profits to become negative. Profits may in fact become negative if entrants misjudge their prospects.

For these reasons observing a positive relationship between profitability and concentration does not yield compelling evidence for collusion to prevail. On the other hand, the non-existence of such a relationship does not prove monopolistic market power to be absent. A positive association between the price–cost margin and concentration is an unequivocal indicator of monopolistic market power to be present even if profits are zero. It would, however, be premature to explain the equality of price and average costs by only invoking technological necessities. The choice of technique, and for that matter the level of fixed costs to be attained, follows from economic decisions of firms. Barriers to entry may entail the choice of high fixed costs which are accompanied by relatively low marginal costs which entails a high price–cost margin. Under free entry without collusion a technique characterized by lower fixed costs might be chosen.

Therefore, the thrust of competition policy must be directed at inhibiting barriers to entry and thus leave little chance for the emergence of collusion. Although collusion can neither be inferred from observing a high price–cost margin nor from profitability alone, excessive profits and persistence of profitability should alert the responsible authorities to examine the case carefully.

2.4   MONOPOLY WELFARE LOSS

Monopolistic market power yields higher prices and a lower level of output and thus entails a welfare loss. On the other hand mergers, which cause horizontal concentration to rise, or even a cartel may yield cost reductions which tend to lower prices and to increase output. This trade-off gives rise to applying a rule of reason for the evaluation of mergers. In European competition law it is also used to justify exemption from the general rule against cartels. The theoretical reasons for this kind of trade-off to apply are now to be discussed.

Static Welfare Loss

In a partial framework the monopoly welfare loss can be quantified by invoking the notion of consumer surplus. A more thorough understanding can
be gained, however, by a general equilibrium approach. That will be demonstrated by the simple example of an economy where two goods are produced
along a production possibility curve TT', as depicted in Figure 2.5. The strict
concavity of the curve implies that marginal costs rise following an increase
in output.[25] The figure also shows social indifference curves which reflect the
preferences prevailing in the society.[26] Indifference curves farther to the right
represent a higher level of social welfare. Point Q, where a social indifference

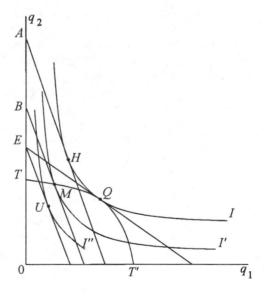

Figure 2.5   A general equilibrium approach to monopoly welfare loss

curve touches the production possibility curve, denotes a competitive equilibrium which is the social optimum. At this point relative prices are equal to
relative marginal costs. If monopoly power arises for good 1 its relative price
increases and a new equilibrium will initially be attained at point U. Since at
this point the available resources, in this case labor and capital, are less than

---

[25] If marginal costs are constant the production possibility curve is a straight line. See Bergson
(1973).

[26] For deriving social indifference curves see Mishan (1964, pp. 43ff).

fully employed, both wages and interest rates decline until at point M full employment is re-established. Since factor rewards are lower than before a monopoly rent has been created. Measured in units of good 2 monopoly profits are given by EB on the vertical axis. Since point M is located on a lower level of the social welfare curve than point Q monopoly gives rise to a welfare loss. To compensate for the loss income, measured in units of good 2, would have to rise. Therefore the monopoly welfare loss can be quantified as a part of the (hypothetical) compensating income change $AE = BE + AB$ where BE depicts monopoly profits and AB denotes the monopoly welfare loss. The difference AE can be shown to equal an area below the compensated demand curve. [27]

In a partial analysis the monopoly welfare loss can be depicted, as shown in Figure 2.6, as an area below the compensated demand curve DD'. The compensated demand curve describes the relationship between the price and quantity demanded of a commodity after the income effect of the price change has been eliminated. Since the income effect depends on the share of income expended on the product in question, which ordinarily is quite small,

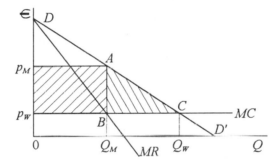

Figure 2.6   A partial analysis of monopoly welfare loss

it does not make much of a difference if instead of using the compensated demand curve the ordinary, that is, the Marshallian, demand curve is used to

---

[27] Denote utility given by indifference curve I by u^0. The variation of income AE can then be shown as

$$E(p_1^1, p_2^0, u^0) - E(p_1^0, p_2^0, u^0) = \int_{p_1^0}^{p_1^1} \frac{\partial E(p_1, p_2^0, u^0)}{\partial p_1} dp_1 = \int_{p_1^0}^{p_1^1} q_1(p_1, p_2^0, u^0) dp_1$$

The first equation follows from the definition of a definite integral. The second equation follows from Shephard's lemma (see Varian 1984, p. 54). Hence the compensating income change is an area below the compensated demand curve $q_1(p_1, p_2^0, u^0)$.

quantify the monopoly welfare loss (Willig 1976).

In Figure 2.6, under perfect competition, the price p_W would equal marginal costs which, as a matter of simplification, have been assumed to be constant and thus to be identical with average variable costs.[28] Consumers' surplus is thus given by the area DCp_W.

If the good under consideration were to be supplied by a monopoly, the price would be higher, giving rise to a monopoly profit depicted by the area $p_M AB\, p_W$. Whereas some of the consumer surplus enjoyed by consumers under perfect competition is turned into monopoly rent another part, given by the triangle ABC, is definitely lost. In Figure 2.5 this loss has been shown by the line AB.

The area of the triangle ABC is

$$WL = (1/2)\Delta p(-\Delta Q).$$

Using an approximation for the price elasticity of demand,

$$\varepsilon = -\frac{p}{Q}\frac{\Delta Q}{\Delta p}$$

one obtains

$$WL = (1/2)(\Delta p/p)^2 \,\varepsilon\, pQ.$$

For an oligopoly the welfare loss can be depicted as follows (Cowling and Mueller 1978). Given a linear inverse demand curve of the market, $p = a - bQ$, and constant marginal costs, c, the welfare loss amounts to $WL = (1/2)(p - c)(Q_W - Q_C)$ where Q_C is total output at a Cournot equilibrium and Q_W applies under perfect competition. Inserting $Q_W = (a - c)/b$ and $Q_C = (n/n+1)(a - c)/b$ one obtains

$$WL = \frac{1}{2}\frac{1}{b}\left(\frac{a-c}{n+1}\right)^2 = \frac{1}{2}\Pi_i\,.$$

The monopoly welfare loss thus equals half the profits of one of the identical firms.

---

[28] By contrast, the general equilibrium approach of Figure 2.5 implies marginal costs to rise which, in a partial equilibrium approach would require to take into account the producers' surplus in addition to the consumers' surplus (see Aiginger and Pfaffermayr 1997).

The result is depicted in Figure 2.7 where DD' shows the demand of the market. For a Cournot oligopoly with three firms p_C is the equilibrium price. The welfare loss is shown by the area of the shaded triangle which is one half of the profits of an individual firm.[29]

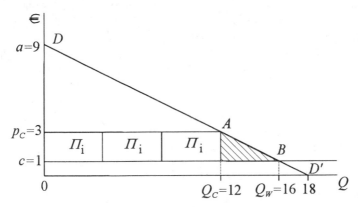

Figure 2.7   The welfare loss in an oligopoly

A first attempt to quantify the welfare loss caused by monopoly power has been undertaken by Harberger (1954). He utilized data for US manufacturing industries from 1924 to 1928 and, assuming unitary price elasticity of demand, came up with an estimate of the welfare loss of about 1/10 of value added. This result, of course, was predicated on considering only a section of the US economy and using a price elasticity of demand which was presumably too low. In subsequent studies (surveyed by Needham 1978, p. 243, and Böbel 1984, pp. 177ff) under alternative assumptions substantially higher estimates for the monopoly welfare loss have been found.

Higher Costs Following Rent Seeking

An important aspect to be taken account of is the fact that in addition to efficiency losses, as given by the static deadweight loss, welfare losses may be caused by wasting resources and dissipating rents. Monopoly profits are an income in excess of opportunity costs, that is, exceeding the income which could be earned in the next best use of the resources, and can thus be classified as a rent. Rents may accrue for two reasons. Their accrual may be caused

---

[29] Assume the inverse demand function $p = 9 - 0.5Q$, and $c = 1$. For $n = 3$ one obtains $p = 3$. The respective output levels are $Q_c = 12$ and $Q_w = 16$. Profits of firms i are $\Pi_i = 8$, and the welfare loss is thus $WL = 4$ and amounts to $WL / pQ = 4/36 = 1/9$.

by natural or by artificial scarcity. Natural scarcity exists for natural resources, which are in limited supply, and human abilities. Artificial scarcities depend on fiat, such as, for instance, government protection against foreign competition, the necessity to obtain a government license for entering a certain business or profession, patent protection and so on. Furthermore, monopoly rents arise insofar as competition policy, or the absence of competition policy, allows collusion to arise and to be maintained.

As far as artificial scarcity is concerned rent-seeking behavior from beneficiaries can be expected to arise. Firms and trade associations may attempt to influence law makers or government executives to grant special favors. Taking into account that numerous people may participate in rent-seeking activities a competitive process arises, as suggested by Tullock (1967) and Posner (1975). Eventually resources may be expended to such an extent that the entire monopoly profit is dissipated. Hence, besides the deadweight loss of monopoly, monopoly rents created by rent seeking are suggested to be counted as a welfare loss.

In the same vein Cowling and Mueller (1978) pointed out that marketing expenditures can be used to acquire monopolistic market power and that thus those expenses, too, should be counted as a welfare loss. From this point of view they estimated welfare losses for the US and the UK amounting to 4–13 per cent of gross income of enterprises.

For costs under monopoly to exceed costs under competition has furthermore been attributed to X-inefficiency (Leibenstein 1966). For a monopoly there is no competitive pressure to apply the most efficient technique or organizational form. Moreover trade unions are likely to cut into monopoly rents by forcing firms to pay higher wages.[30]

However, classifying rent-seeking expenditures as monopoly welfare loss appears somewhat dubious in light of the general equilibrium approach. In the framework of the general equilibrium approach, for a welfare loss to arise requires the actual income to fall short of the income which would be attainable under perfect competition. By contrast, expenditures incurred by firms to obtain monopoly power, for example expenses for lobbying or advertising, give rise to income for somebody else. In contrast to the efficiency loss due to monopoly, as measured by the loss of consumer surplus, it is not income foregone but income spent on commodities and services along the production possibility frontier of the economy. Hence counting rent-seeking expenditures

---

[30] In fact, empirical studies have shown that higher concentration is conducive to higher wages. In the studies of Neumann, Böbel and Haid cited above an adverse influence of firm size on the price–cost margin has regularly been found. Since large firms can hardly be expected to charge lower prices than their smaller rivals, nor to pay more dearly for material inputs, they presumably pay higher wages or are subject to diseconomies of scale or both.

as a social loss due to monopoly is on quite a different footing from the welfare loss evaluated by a compensated variation of income, that is, by a loss of consumer surplus. Classifying it as a loss inevitably involves a value judgement by which income earned in consequence of rent seeking is considered to be less worthy than income earned by any other activity. The same argument applies as far as monopolists seeking a quiet life is concerned. Leisure chosen by managers of big companies, which are not subject to the pressure of tough competition, is part of their income and as such it is contained within the possibility set of the economy. The distributive outcome entailed by those managers indulging in a quiet life may arouse dislike by others but it is very different from an efficiency loss like the one measured by foregone consumer surplus. As will be shown below, only by adopting a value judgement, which may be appealing if the long run is taken into account, can behavior of that kind be classified as a social welfare loss due to monopoly.

Static Efficiency Trade-off

Despite the X-inefficiency of large-size monopoly power, held by large firms, may be accompanied by lower average and marginal costs. That gives rise to a trade-off between a monopoly welfare loss and cost savings which has been emphasized by Williamson (1968, 1969) and has come to play some role in merger control.

The trade-off can be illustrated by Figure 2.8. Assume initially perfect competition to exist, which is subsequently replaced by a monopoly which

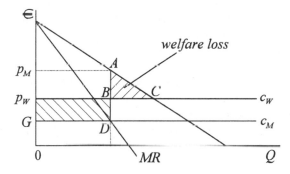

Figure 2.8 Static efficiency trade-off.

entails marginal costs to decrease from c_W to c_M. The price rises from p_W to p_M which causes a monopoly welfare loss depicted by the area of the triangle ABC and, simultaneously, to an increase in monopoly profit, shown by the area of the rectangle $p_W BDG$. Invoking examples with iso-elastic demand functions, Williamson was able to demonstrate that monopolistic market power must be substantial for the monopoly welfare loss to exceed the increase in profits following the cost reduction. For example, given a price elasticity of demand of two requires the monopoly price to exceed average costs by 10 per cent for a net welfare loss to arise. These calculations do not, however, take into account that reducing marginal costs ordinarily requires expenditures for research and development, and for education and training of employees. These expenditures, which usually come in the form of fixed costs, lessen the advantage following from lowering marginal costs and thus increase the weight attributable to the monopoly welfare loss.

Long-Run Effects of a Static Loss

Furthermore, long-run effects must be taken into account. On one hand Schumpeter (1942) suggested that technological change is primarily driven by research and development undertaken in large firms. A competitive structure of industry is thus claimed to inhibit progress. This argument entails a trade-off between a static welfare loss of monopoly and a long-run welfare gain caused by technical change (Nelson and Winter 1982). This claim turns out to be dubious, however, following a more detailed examination.

First, along the lines suggested by Arrow (1962) and elaborated in various directions in a voluminous literature (reviewed by Reinganum 1989) monopoly power changes incentives and in that way may either enhance or inhibit innovations depending on specific conditions. The theoretical debate therefore has remained largely inconclusive. Looking at empirical studies one finds, first, that small and medium-sized firms are playing a much more important role than presumed by Schumpeter in 1942 (Jewkes, Sawers and Stillerman 1958, Acs and Audretsch 1990, Audretsch 1995), and, second, that horizontal concentration is conducive to impeding innovative activity (Geroski 1990 and 1994 for the UK, Neumann, Böbel and Haid 1982 and Weigand 1996 for Germany). In view of this evidence, contrary to Williamson's suggestion, monopolistic market power, as captured by high market shares, can be expected to generate reduced levels of productivity and comparatively high costs of production. This presumption has been shown to be borne out empirically by investigations pertaining to British (Nickell 1996) and Norwegian (Klette 1999) manufacturing industries.

Second, from a macroeconomic point of view a static welfare loss can be shown to yield a lower rate of growth of income and thus causes actual income to fall short of potential income which could have been achieved if competition had been obtained. Hence the basis from which savings can be drawn to cover investments in tangible and intangible capital is reduced. Given the preferences prevailing in the economy, investments will then be lower. As will be shown below, the growth rate of the economy will then be lower, too. Individual decision makers will ordinarily be unaware of this macroeconomic effect. From their point of view they may claim to be reasonably innovative but still monopolistic market power exerts a drawback on innovative activity across the board.

Third, as argued above, a change in income distribution in the wake of rent seeking can hardly be criticized on efficiency grounds. Nevertheless, it may entail losses for third parties which quantitatively go far beyond the change in distribution alone. As Adam Smith ([1776] 1950, vol. 2, p. 278) observed,

> By a perpetual monopoly, all the other subjects of the state are taxed very absurdly in two different ways; first, by the high price of goods, which, in the case of free trade, they could buy much cheaper; and secondly, by their total exclusion from a branch of business, which it might be both convenient and profitable for many of them to carry on. It is for the most worthless of all purposes too that they are taxed in this manner. It is merely to enable the company to support negligence, profusion, and malversion of their own servants, whose disorderly conduct seldom allows the dividend of the company to exceed the ordinary rate of profit in trades which are altogether free, and very frequently makes it fall even a good deal short of that rate.

Still, as is quite clear from this statement, it remains true that a value judgement is involved. It might be justified by adopting the following principle with regard to tolerating monopolies. They must not be allowed unless they entail positive externalities, and they should be disallowed if external diseconomies prevail. This seems to be the underlying value judgement adopted by Adam Smith. In his view, allowing a perpetual monopoly causes the total savings of the economy to be reduced and thus economic growth to be slowed down. Hence the behavior criticized by Adam Smith does not just change the distribution of income between different groups of people such that the gain of some of them matches the loss of others. It additionally causes a net loss for society in that the rate of growth of income is lower, making everybody worse off compared to what might be achieved. If one is prepared to subscribe to this judgement of actual income falling short of potential income as to be expected in the long run following rent seeking, this may in fact be classified as a social loss due to monopoly.

On all three counts a static loss yields a lower rate of growth and thus causes a permanent loss which is much larger than the static loss itself. This appears to be a remarkable insight.

Let the shortfall of actual income $y(m)$ from potential income y be depicted by $y(m) = (1 - \tau)y$, where τ is the rate of welfare loss due to monopoly. Furthermore, let $g(m)$ denote the rate of growth of income as depending on the rate of loss, g the potential rate of growth, and i the rate of interest, which can safely be assumed to exceed g. Then the present value of the total welfare loss arising from now until infinity is

$$V = \frac{y}{i-g} - \frac{y(m)}{i-g(m)}.$$

Since $V = v/(i-g)$, where v is the annualized welfare loss of income per year, the welfare loss per unit of actual income is

$$\lambda := \frac{v}{y(m)} = \frac{1}{1-\tau} - \frac{i-g}{i-g(m)}.$$

Clearly, if the rate of growth of income were not to be affected by the degree of monopoly and the static loss of welfare involved, the annualized welfare loss would be $v/y(m) = \tau/(1-\tau)$ and $v/y = \tau$.

To demonstrate the effect of the static welfare loss on the rate of growth various combinations of the interest rate, the static loss and the ensuing annualized loss are given in Table 2.4 where it is assumed that $g - g(m) = -0.2\tau$.

Table 2.4   Annualized welfare loss as depending on interest rate, growth rates and the static welfare loss

	i	g	τ	$g(m)$	λ
A	0.04	0.02	0.001	0.0198	0.011
B	0.04	0.02	0.01	0.018	0.101
C	0.04	0.02	0.03	0.014	0.262
D	0.03	0.02	0.01	0.018	0.177

At an interest rate $i = 0.04$, a potential growth rate $g = 0.02$, a static welfare loss of $\tau = 0.001$, as suggested by Harberger, and an actual growth rate $g(m) = 0.0198$, one obtains an annualized welfare loss per unit of income which amounts to 0.01. It is thus ten times the value found by Harberger. If the static loss is $\tau = 0.01$ (line B) one obtains $\lambda = 0.101$, hence once more about ten-fold of the static loss. A static loss of 3 per cent yields an annualized loss of even 26 per cent. A lower rate of interest obviously yields a higher loss, as can be seen from line D, where at an interest rate $i = 0.03$ the annualized loss per unit of income amounts to 0.177, which is almost double the value applying in the case of $i = 0.04$. It can thus be concluded that even a static welfare loss which at face value seems to be innocuous may in the long run turn out be seriously large.

Growth Depending on the Rate of a Static Welfare Loss

To assess the order of magnitude of the effect of a static welfare loss on the rate of growth of income, a simple growth model will be outlined in which technical change is endogenous, depending on expenditures for research and development (Neumann 1997). Such a model may be interpreted as a short-cut depicting the outcome of an evolutionary process. In this view the market appears as an equilibrating mechanism which yields a survival of the supreme technique and the best organizational form of economic activity which gives rise to maximum utility of consumers, subject to a given institutional environment. Thus the evolutionary process operating through markets can be interpreted as a maximization calculus. The equilibrium derived from such a calculus is a focal point towards which the evolutionary process develops. Although an equilibrium will almost never be actually attained because evolution is open-ended, unfolding in the search for new methods, the concept of an equilibrium to be understood as a focal point for the analysis is extremely helpful in investigating the long-term consequences of alternative institutional environments which entail monopoly power and ensuing welfare loss.

Irrespective of the source of distortion, in each period income per head is assumed to fall short of potential income by τy. Capital accumulation can then be depicted by the equation

$$\dot{x} = (1-\tau)f(x) - r(a) - \tilde{c} - (n+a)x \qquad (2.10)$$

where, measured in efficiency units of labor, x is capital, and $\tilde{c}$ is consumption. Furthermore, $f(x)$ is a well-behaved neoclassical production function, $a = \dot{A}/A$ is the rate of purely labor-augmenting technical change, n is the growth rate of labor input, and $r(a)$ denotes R&D expenditures per efficiency unit of labor, where $r'(a) > 0$, $r''(a) > 0$, $r(0) = 0$, and $r'(0) = 0$. Technical change is thus generated by expenditures for R&D which are subject to diminishing returns. If utility

$$\int_0^\infty Lu(c)e^{-\rho t}dt$$

with instantaneous utility $u(c) - c^{1-\eta}/(1-\eta)$, and ρ being time preference, is maximized by choosing c and a, subject to equation (2.10) and $\dot{A} = aA$, one obtains a steady state depicted by the following set of equations,

$$(1-\tau)f(x) - r(a) - \tilde{c} - (n+a)x = 0 \qquad (2.11)$$

$$(1-\tau)f'(x) - \eta a = \rho \qquad (2.12)$$

$$[(1-\tau)f'(x)-n-a]r'(a)+r(a)-(1-\tau)[f(x)-xf'(x)]=0 \qquad (2.13)$$

Equations (2.12) and (2.13) are depicted in Figure 2.9 by the schedules XX' and AA', respectively. They are thus sufficient to determine x^* and a^*. Equation (2.11) can then be used to find $\tilde{c}^*$.

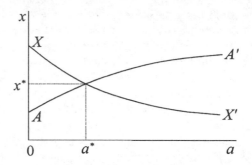

Figure 2.9   Optimal technical change

Following an increase in τ both curves shift to the left such that a^* is decreased. Differentiating equations (2.12) and (2.13) yields

$$\frac{\partial a^*}{\partial \tau} = \frac{-1}{[(1-\tau)f'-n-a]r''/f + \eta(r'+x)/f}.$$

Provided η is close to unity,[31] the denominator clearly is dominated quantitatively by x/f, that is, the capital–output ratio which can be taken to amount to 4–5. Hence, $\partial a^*/\partial \tau$ should be expected to be around -0.2. Hence. the rate of growth of income per head to be expected under competitive conditions would be reduced by about 0.2 times the rate of the static welfare loss per unit of income, as has been assumed in Table 2.4.

As suggested by Adam Smith, the shortfall of actual income from potential income bears some similarity with income tax which also reduces the basis from which savings can be drawn. In contrast to income tax, the proceeds of which could be used for public investment, the shortfall of income from potential income due to monopoly power is a definite loss. Hence the effect of income tax on productivity growth can be taken as a conservative estimate of what a static welfare monopoly welfare loss would do. In fact across OECD

---

[31] As argued in Neumann (1997, p. 44), it can in fact be shown to fall short of one.

countries for the period from 1964 to 1984, Neumann (1997, p. 104) found a regression coefficient of -0.17 ($t = 4.61$) for the impact of taxes on income and profits on the rate of growth of labor productivity.[32] This is a magnitude which is close to the value that could have been expected from the theoretical model outlined above.

Second-Best Theory in Defense of Restraints of Competition?

A fundamental theorem of welfare economics holds that perfect competition gives rise to a Paretian welfare optimum. The conclusion derived therefrom that economic policy should aim at establishing perfect competition throughout the entire economy has been questioned by Lipsey and Lancaster (1956). They advanced the theory of second best which says that, if perfect competition is infeasible in one sector of the economy, it is optimal for competition to be restrained in the rest of the economy, too.

The validity of this theorem can be demonstrated by using a model of an economy composed of two sectors, as depicted in Figure 2.5. Since for the monopoly in sector 1 marginal costs MC_1 equal marginal revenue $p_1(1-1/\varepsilon_1)$, whereas in sector 2 marginal costs MC_2 equal the price p_2 at the equilibrium attained at point M, the output of good 1 falls short of, and the output of good 2 exceeds, the output which would be optimal. An outcome approaching the optimum at point Q could be achieved by allowing monopoly power to arise also in sector 2. If the price elasticities in both sectors were equal monopoly power in both sectors would exactly render the equilibrium to be attained at the optimum point Q, because the ratio of marginal revenues would equal the ratio of prices, $p_1(1-1/\varepsilon_1)/p_2(1-1/\varepsilon_2)$ $= p_1/p_2$. Conversely, if competition policy would inhibit monopoly power in sector 2 welfare would be lower.

However, this theoretically unassailable reasoning should not be accepted as a guideline for competition policy. First, aiming at a second-best solution requires information which ordinarily is not available. Allowing restraints of competition to combat restraints amounts to 'driving out the Devil by Beel-

---

[32] Using data for overlapping decades 1964–73, 1969–78 and 1974–83, as published by OECD (1987, 1989), across sixteen industrialized countries the following equation has been estimated

$$\hat{a} = 6.84 - 0.59n - 0.17\tau - 1.21D1 - 2.41D2, \quad \bar{R}^2 = 0.70$$
$$\quad\quad (15.08) \quad (3.23) \quad (4.61) \quad (3.05) \quad (5.94)$$

where t-statistics are given in brackets, and $\hat{a}$ = rate of growth of labor productivity, n = rate of growth of employment, τ = taxes on income and profits per unit of GDP, $D1$, $D2$ = dummies for decades which may be taken to represent differing rates of time preference.

zebub'. Massive government intervention would be invited and particular interests would come forward and could succeed. Second, the theory of second best suffers from being static in character. The recommendation to allow restraints of competition to be established depends on the conclusion that competition is infeasible because of economies of scale and fixed costs. Technology, however, is following from economic decisions which are subject to change. Numerous examples exist where during the history of an industry initially prevailing indivisibilities and ensuing economies of scale have been overcome by miniaturizing. This could hardly have been expected if restraints of competition had been allowed to arise or such restraints had even been encouraged to emerge. The static character of the theory of second-best blinds to competition being seen as a process of discovery which has to be supported by an appropriate competition policy. As far as unavoidable restraints of competition exist, that is, in the case of a so-called natural monopoly, and in the case where the government grants monopoly rights to pursue specified objectives, the conduct of the monopolies must be regulated to inhibit the abuse of monopolistic power.

2.5   CONCLUSION

In industrial economics market performance is explained by invoking the conduct of enterprises depending on market structure and technology. The Cournot model and the notion of a Nash equilibrium have proved a useful framework of analysis to understand how alternative modes of conduct and market structure affect economic performance. The predictions derived therefrom are amenable to empirical testing and in fact have overwhelmingly been supported by empirical evidence. Persistently excessive profits of incumbent firms and the price–cost margin rising with increasing horizontal concentration are proof of prevailing monopolistic market power and underline that freedom of entry is crucial.

Monopoly welfare losses can be quantified. Even though in the short run mergers may be justifiable by cost savings, which outweigh static welfare losses, in the long run monopoly is likely to inhibit innovations and thus to reduce economic growth and welfare.

The next chapter will be devoted to translating the insights gained by theory and evidence to devise competition policy such as to contain restraints of competition. Invoking examples for the US, Germany and the EC, the practice of competition policy will be discussed and evaluated.

3. Containing Restraints of Competition

Since restraints of competition ordinarily exert an adverse influence on economic welfare, competition policy should aim at containing them. In view of a pervasive 'propensity to monopolize' there is hardly any reason for suspecting competition to be too tough. Moreover, since future developments cannot be anticipated with any degree of reliability it is impossible for an optimal state of competition to be conceived of. Therefore, as already discussed in Chapter 1, competition policy should refrain from seeking to establish a particular structure of the economy rather than adopting a defensive attitude aiming at inhibiting restraints of competition. However, looking at particular cases only a few of them will turn out to be exclusively harmful. In most cases there are both advantages and disadvantages which must be evaluated to arrive at a definite judgement. However, recognizing that generally a trade-off exists does not imply that an evaluation of benefits and damages has to be undertaken in each case. By contrast, it is feasible to identify categories of cases where harmful effects can be expected to outweigh any imaginable advantages to such an extent that a *per se* prohibition is justified. For the rest, a case-by-case decision invoking a rule of reason is required. Still, if the favorable effects are presumed to outweigh any harmful effects, monitoring the conduct of enterprises may be necessary for an abuse of monopolistic market power to be forestalled.

As outlined already in Chapter 1, cartels are outlawed both in the US and in the EC whilst the admissibility of mergers and most vertical restraints is subject to applying a rule of reason. Cartels which are admitted under certain conditions, as well as dominant firms, are subject to abuse control. Hence the present chapter will be concerned first with collusion, and second with mergers. The third and fourth sections will be devoted to abuse control exercised by the government with respect to cartels and dominant firms.

3.1 COLLUSION

Collusion between firms with regard to prices and output are generally prohibited. However, both in the US and Europe a few sectors of the economy are exempted. For the rest, cartels are prohibited *per se* in the US, whereas in the EC as well as in Germany cartels are prohibited subject to specific exemptions.

Per se Prohibition of Cartels in the US

The *per se* prohibition of cartels in the US has been derived from the Sherman Act by various court decisions. It is grounded on the presumption that cartels, by violating the prohibition of monopolizing, aim at fixing prices – and output – in such a way as to favor producers at the expense of consumers. Any favorable side effects which might be possible are considered to be negligible and are therefore disregarded. Hence, a case-by-case treatment appears superfluous. This evaluation of cartels was first adopted in the Addyston Pipe case of 1898 where a cartel concerning cast iron pipes for water and gas with a combined market share of two-thirds in the Middle West and the West of the US was declared illegal (Scherer and Ross 1990, p. 318).[1] Doubts as to the validity of the *per se* rule arose when Chief Justice White in 1911 had proposed a rule of reason to apply in the cases of Standard Oil of New Jersey and the American Tobacco Company. It was difficult to understand why a merger undertaken with the intent to monopolize should be treated differently from a cartel which aimed at the same outcome. The rationale for the differential treatment was delivered in 1927 in the Trenton Potteries case and 1940 in the Socony Vacuum case where the *per se* rule was confirmed. The decision in the Trenton Potteries case referred to 'The Sanitary Potters' Association', a cartel of manufacturers of vitreous pottery for bathrooms and lavatories, which held a combined market share of 80 per cent. The defense claimed that the prices fixed were reasonable and did no injury to the public. The defense was rebutted by the court stating that (Neale 1966, p. 36)

> The aim and result of every price-fixing agreement, if effective, is the elimination of one form of competition. The power to fix prices, whether reasonably exercised or not, involves power to control the market and to fix arbitrary and unreasonable prices. The reasonable price fixed today may through economic and business changes become the unreasonable price of tomorrow. Once established, it may be maintained unchanged because of the absence of competition.

[1] This decision has been criticized by Bittlingmayer (1982) on the ground that in the industry concerned increasing returns to scale prevail, such that a competitive equilibrium where marginal costs equal the price is not feasible because marginal costs fall short of average costs and marginal cost pricing would entail losses. Moreover, given a high volatility of demand a cartel would recommend itself as a superior solution to overcome the non-existence of a competitive equilibrium. This reasoning is fallacious, however, because in the case of declining average costs an equilibrium does exist where the average cost curve becomes tangential to the demand curve as seen by the seller, as shown in Chapter 2. Although changes in demand may yield losses during recessions they are offset by profits during business cycle upswings.

The rebuttal of the defense was thus grounded on a forecast regarding the long-run consequences of a cartel which, according to economic theory, are expected to be different from those entailed by a merger. As Bork (1965, p. 830) correctly noted,

> The only difference between the two forms of elimination of competition which suggests a more lenient attitude toward mergers (is) that cartels contain no possibility of the creation of efficiencies, their sole purpose and effect being the restriction of output, while mergers may or may not enable the achievement of efficiencies.

This assessment is supported by the following reasoning. As suggested by Hayek (1968), competition is a most effective method of discovery, which gives rise to a flow of cost-reducing innovations. Insofar as costs are sunk and equipment lasts for many years, in each industry at any time various kinds of equipment with differing efficiency exist side by side. Usually more recent investments entail lower marginal costs and average variable costs whereas fixed costs are higher. Once demand declines during a business cycle recession, firms with more recent technology are better able to survive if prices decline, whereas firms with a higher level of average variable costs are forced to exit. This process is accelerated if firms with modern technology are inclined to increase their output to exploit economies of large scale. By contrast, less efficient firms were able to survive under the protective umbrella of a cartel if all its members would curtail their output and thus ensure that prices drop less. Firms of a cartelized industry therefore enter the subsequent business cycle upswing with excess capacity. They will only reluctantly invest to extend production and thereby adopt new techniques. Hence economic progress is slowed down just as suggested by the court in the Trenton Potteries case.

This assessment of cartels has been supported by the Supreme Court 1940 in the Socony Vacuum case. The Court dealt explicitly with the argument that cartels are defensive arrangements intended to remedy ruinous competition. Mr Justice Douglas then continued to state (Neale 1966, p. 38),

> Ruinous competition, financial disaster, evils of price-cutting and the like appear throughout our history as sensible justifications for price-fixing. If the so-called competitive abuses were to be appraised here, the reasonableness of prices would necessarily become an issue in every price-fixing case. In that event the Sherman Act would soon be emasculated; its philosophy would be supplanted by one which is wholly alien to a system of free competition.

Instead of installing price control competition policy should aim at maintaining a competitive structure of industry. Admitting cartels would undermine this goal as becomes clear by the following reasoning. For a cartel to achieve its objective it must fend off outsiders to avoid the collusive arrangement to be undermined. Observing a cartel to exist for a long time thus suggests that the cartel in fact adopts defensive strategies against potential and actual outsiders which will be discussed in the third section of this chapter in more detail. In principle those practices could be inhibited by an appropriate abuse control. It is more effective, however, to avoid them in the incipiency by an outright prohibition of cartels.

Exemptions from the Prohibition of Cartels

In the US as well as in Germany, a few sectors of the economy are legally exempted from the *per se* rule against cartels, namely agriculture, banking and insurance, and companies utilizing patent rights.

In Germany previously existing exemptions pertaining to transportation (§ 99 GWB), and public utilities (§§ 103ff GWB) have been repealed in 1999. Utilizing television rights for professional sports have been introduced as a new exempted field (§ 31 KartellG). Following a *rule of reason* specific exemptions apply to agreements concerning standards and terms of business, specialization and rationalization, cooperative arrangements among small business firms intended to improve their competitiveness, cartels set up to cope with a structural crisis, and cartels deemed to serve the public interest. In the case of specialization and rationalization cartels, collusion with respect to prices may be permitted as an ancillary restraint if the objective of the agreement is not attainable otherwise and if the agreement serves the public interest.[2]

Similar regulations apply in the EC. Although the EC Treaty does not specifically name exempted sectors,[3] Article 81 contains a general clause which authorizes the EC Commission to grant exemptions. This authorization has been used to grant block exemptions applying to exclusive dealing, cooperative R&D, terms of delivery and rebates, subject to limitation in time, and the provision that the combined market share of participating firms must not exceed some specified level.

For evaluating these provisions it should be taken into account that so-called lower order cartels are not completely innocuous. If competition with terms of delivery, rebates, product characteristics and R&D is eliminated by

---

[2] The legal device of an 'ancillary restraint' has been discussed in the US by Judge Taft in the Addyston Pipe case as a possible exemption from the *per se* rule against cartels 'but remained undeveloped and its possibilities unexploited' (Bork 1965, p. 800).

[3] Nevertheless agriculture is an exempted sector. According to Article 36 EC Treaty the regulations regarding competition apply to agriculture only insofar as stipulated by the Council of Ministers. Even though this occurred in 1962 the agricultural sector is in fact exempted insofar as the market is regulated. See also Chapter 4.

collusion, only prices are left to compete with. Allegedly, market transparency is improved thereby, which is claimed to make consumers better off. Although transparency in fact increases it does not necessarily make competition more tough. The opposite is the truth. Transparency facilitates monitoring tacit collusion. Thus lower order cartels may serve to support more encompassing clandestine agreements.

Structural Crisis Cartels

Cartels are frequently defended as being indispensable for coping with declining demand. To evaluate the merit of this argument cyclical changes in demand must be distinguished from structural changes. Given sunk costs it is not always possible to cut down productive capacity immediately, following a business cycle downturn. Hence firms incur losses. On the other hand, during a business cycle upswing profitability rises because demand is outpacing the increase in output. Unavoidable losses incurred during recessions are thus likely to be offset by profits enjoyed during booms. Thus cartels aiming at compensating for changes in profitability during the business cycle can hardly be justified (see also Martin 1999). By contrast, for a structural crisis which requires dismantling sunk investments, cartels may be evaluated more favorably. Still, in the US, cartels aiming to cope with a structural crisis are also subject to the *per se* verdict of the Sherman Act.[4] Structural crisis cartels are permissible, however, both according to EC law and German law.

In Europe, within the European Community for Steel and Coal (ECSC), structural crisis cartels have been repeatedly permitted. In Germany a structural crisis cartel has been allowed for synthetic fibers. In the European iron and steel industry excess capacities which caused structural crises to emerge arose primarily because some Member States, as part of their industrial policy, defended their national iron and steel industries by generous subsidies and thus impeded the dismantling of excess capacities. Eventually the problem was solved when mergers gave rise to larger firms which then cut down on productive facilities.

Concerted Practices

Prohibiting cartels by law does not forestall illegal collusion from existing.

---

[4] During the 1930s cartels had initially been permitted by the 'National Industrial Recovery Act' to cope with the disastrous consequences of the Great Depression. This abandonment of antitrust was, however, declared unconstitutional by the Supreme Court (see Martin 1999, p. 37). In fact, in the above mentioned Socony Vacuum case a structural crisis cartel founded in the 1930s was ruled to be subject to the *per se* verdict by the Supreme Court in 1940.

Although illegal cartels are less stable than legal ones, since abiding by an illegal contract cannot be enforced, the prospect of above-normal profits attainable through collusion is conducive for concerted practices to arise. For two reasons this presumption applies in particular to mature industries at the height of their life cycle. First, since they can be expected to last, collusion is more likely, as suggested by game theory (see Chapter 2). Second, in mature industries usually high fixed costs prevail which frequently are sunk. They constitute a barrier to entry which provides for a defense against competition from outsiders.

For competition policy it is necessary to identify illegal collusion. Certainly collusion entails parallel business behavior. The reverse does not hold, however. Therefore, parallel business behavior in itself does not constitute proof of illegal collusion. Nor is it sufficient to show awareness of mutual interdependence as typical for oligopoly. For establishing proof of illegal collusion it must be shown that parallel business behavior follows from a meeting of the minds. This principle applies both to US antitrust law and European law. US law requires a conspiracy against the public to be proved. European law requires concertation to be proved. Since an expressive agreement in written form frequently does not exist, or cannot be proved to exist, the authorities in charge of administrating competition policy must rely on circumstantial evidence. In practice two lines of reasoning are available.

Rules of conduct established and observed within a common organization, like a trade association, may provide a piece of evidence for the existence of collusion. A case in point has been the US Sugar Institute. As to be discussed in more detail in the next section, the 'Code of Ethics' established by the Institute has been identified as a case of illegal collusion by the US Supreme Court in 1936.

An alternative line of reasoning starts from observing that price competition is absent and infers therefrom that such a state would be impossible without collusion. It is incumbent on the authority to show that parallel pricing is observed, although under competition one would expect pricing behavior to differ. On theoretical grounds one might object that in the case of oligopoly a change in demand yields an identical response of output even if marginal costs differ. For example, for a duopoly at a Cournot equilibrium, $q_i^* = (a - 2c_i + c_j)/3b$. Hence, following a change in demand, as $\partial q_i / \partial a = 1/3b$ the output of both firms changes at the same rate. Thus parallelism of behavior cannot be accepted as irrefutable evidence of collusion. Still, contrary to the assumption underlying the given example, in reality the demand functions are not known with certainty. Individual firms presumably hold diverging expectations regarding the development of demand. Therefore their decisions with respect to output and prices are likely to diverge unless collusion exists. A case in point has been the decision of the European Court of

Justice (1972) against European producers of dyestuffs.

The leading European dyestuff producers used to meet regularly for an exchange of information and experience. At a meeting on August 8, 1967 the representative of a Swiss firm announced that his company intended to raise prices by 8 per cent effective from October 16, 1967. The four German participants of the meeting which together held an 80 per cent market share in Germany raised their prices also by 8 per cent effective from October 16, 1967. Similar sequences of events had been observed in 1964 and 1965. The Federal Cartel Office in Germany charged the German firms with illegally practicing a cartel. On appeal this charge was subsequently turned down by the Federal Court of Justice because the existence of an explicit agreement, which at that time was required according to § 1 GWB, could not be proved. By contrast, the participating firms were found guilty by the European Court of Justice of a concerted practice in the meaning of Article 81 (then Article 85) of the EC Treaty. The Court stated that by the announcement of the increase in prices any uncertainty regarding future behavior had been removed. The Court found that the market for dyestuffs was fragmented and divided along national border lines. The similarity of the rates of change and the timing of the price increases could not be explained away as a result of parallel yet independent behavior prompted by market forces. The Court said (Bellamy and Child 1993, pp. 53f),

> Although every producer is free to change his prices, taking into account in so doing the present or foreseeable conduct of his competitors, nevertheless it is contrary to the rules on competition contained in the Treaty for a producer to co-operate with his competitors, in any way whatsoever, in order to determine a coordinated course of action relating to a price increase and to ensure its success by prior elimination of all uncertainty as to each other's conduct regarding the essential elements of that action, such as the amount, subject-matter, date and place of the increases.

Obviously the previous German law which required the existence of an explicit agreement was too restrictive. Consequently in 1973 the GWB was amended as to outlaw concerted practices in line with the EC Treaty.

Information Exchange

Organizing an exchange of market information among producers may provide circumstantial evidence for collusion to exist. Information exchange, in particular so-called open price systems, have originally been propagated in the US by Eddy (1912) as an alternative to the tough and allegedly ruinous competition of his time. Thus the underlying motive had been the same as that which used to be advanced for justifying cartels. In fact, after the prohibition of cartels became effective in the US, following Eddy's proposal, a large number of 'Open Price Associations' came into existence. A similar development could be observed in Germany and the UK. After the enactment of the 'Law Against Restraints of Competition' (GWB) 1957 in Germany, numerous 'Preismeldestellen' were founded (Röper and Erlinghagen 1974, p. 27). In the UK, after the prohibition of cartels by the Restrictive Trade Practices Act in 1956, about 150 information exchange agreements emerged (Röper and Erlinghagen 1974, p. 27, Symeonidis 1998, p. 64). This sequence of events strongly suggests that those agreements were intended to substitute for cartels which could no longer be maintained legally. However, whether joining an information exchange can be counted as illegal collusion depends on the particular circumstances of the case. This may be illustrated by considering some examples of market information exchanges which came under scrutiny by courts in the US, Germany and the EC.

In the case of the American Column and Lumber Company, which in 1921 came to be examined by the Supreme Court, 365 member firms representing 90 per cent of the market (Röper and Erlinghagen 1974, p. 28) had committed themselves to report prices on a monthly basis. The stated aim was 'to keep prices at reasonably stable and normal levels' (Neale 1966, p. 44). Whilst in this case, and likewise in the case of the Linseed Oil Company (1923), the agreement was found illegal, the Supreme Court found no fault in the case of the Maple Flooring Manufacturers' Association. According to the Court, in other cases circumstantial evidence had led to the conclusion 'that concerted action had resulted or would necessarily result in tending arbitrarily to lessen production or increase prices'. In the case under consideration, however, persuasive evidence pointing to collusion was not found, because the prices of participating firms were not uniform and on the whole they were lower than prices of firms which did not belong to the association (Neale 1966, p. 46). A further remarkable case, finally decided by the Supreme Court in 1936, was concerned with the US sugar industry. During a time of weak demand 'The Sugar Institute' propagated and tried to enforce a 'Code of Ethics' (Neale 1966, p. 47). The Institute circulated to members statistics of production, stocks and deliveries in elaborate detail. Producers used to announce price changes in advance such that any proposal to change the price could be withdrawn unless all the refiners were ready to follow suit. Furthermore, members committed themselves to the announced prices and to refrain from granting secret price reductions. Although each firm was free to announce price changes as often as it liked, the Supreme Court in particular condemned the agreement not to deviate from a once announced price. It also took into account that the frequency of price changes had declined and the margins and profitability had increased despite a concededly large excess capacity.

In Germany the Kammergericht, which is the court of appeal against decisions taken by the Federal Cartel Office, upheld a decision of the Federal Cartel Office to disallow an information exchange among 17 producers of aluminum tubes who accounted for 70 per cent of the market. Participants were obliged to notify within four days all offers in detail to a central office which had to disseminate the information to all participants on demand. The Court considered uncertainty with regard to reactions of rival firms as a salient feature of competition which was removed by the information exchange. The same principle has been applied by the EC Commission in similar cases (see Schmidt 1999, pp. 267ff).

An information exchange pertaining to sales figures of agricultural tractors in the UK (Albach 1996) has been held to be illegal by the EC Commission. The agreement provided for detailed and timely information regarding sales and market shares of members and non-members to be disseminated among the participating firms. Regular meetings offered opportunities to discuss problems of common interest. The adverse decision of the EC Commission was upheld by the Court of First Instance and finally by the European Court of Justice 1998. The EC Commission will not object to an exchange of sales figures if a time lag of twelve months is observed and if only aggregate data are exchanged (Tsoraklidis 1999, p. 33).

Likewise an information exchange scheme initiated by the German association of the iron and steel industry was disallowed by the EC Commission. The exchange was planned to comprise the major German producers and to pertain to information regarding deliveries of some 40 products into all member states of the EC. According to the EC Commission such an exchange of information would constitute a grave restraint of competition on a mature and highly concentrated market. It would increase market transparency to such an extent that any attempt at independent competitive moves would elicit countermoves of rival firms which would discourage competitive behavior in the first place (EC Commission 1998, p. 25).

These examples are well suited to illustrate the problem which more recently gave rise to some discussion in the economics literature. There are quite a few studies dealing with the question how, through information exchange, uncertainty regarding demand, as depicted by the inverse demand function $p = a - bQ$, can be reduced and how such an exchange affects pricing on oligopolistic markets.[5] These inquiries, although interesting as a

---

[5] Novshek and Sonnenschein (1982), Clarke (1983a and b), Vives (1984), Phlips (1995, pp. 81ff), Raith (1996). For a Cournot oligopoly it has been shown that an exchange of information regarding the location parameter a is desirable for the individual firm only in the case of cooperation, that is, collusion. By contrast, in the case of Bertrand competition information exchange is always profitable. In an experimental study Cason and Mason (1999) found that

piece of economic theory are entirely beside the point as far as competition policy is at stake. Information exchange schemes have hardly ever pertained to exchanging knowledge regarding the demand function rather than with information about prices and sales, that is, with information regarding the behavior of competitors. The consequences of exchanging informations about sales have been studied by Jin (1994). For the case of substitutable commodities he concludes (p. 331) that 'In a Cournot industry, sales reports benefit firms but hurt the society, while in a Bertrand industry, they lower profits but raise the social welfare.' Thus for competition policy the following conclusion can be drawn. If the exchange in the case of Cournot competition is profitable it should be prohibited since it causes a welfare loss. In the case of Bertrand competition, although beneficial for the society, it will not arise because it is individually disadvantageous.[6] This finding clearly supports the decision of the EC Commission and the European Court of Justice in the UK tractor case.

In the cases mentioned above exchange schemes did not pertain to information about demand functions rather than to information regarding the behavior of competitors. Recipients of such information cannot draw inferences regarding the state of knowledge of the informant unless they are also informed about his cost function. This, however, is hardly ever true. The exchange scheme then constitutes circumstantial evidence for collusion. The exchange may provide information as to whether competitors did abide by a collusive agreement or whether they undersold their partners. This is immediately evident where price information is exchanged, but it also applies to a heterogeneous market where information regarding sales is exchanged. Where products are differentiated prices are not immediately comparable since price differences may be attributable to differences in quality. In this case sales are a more reliable indicator of success in the market. If the market share of a rival increases buyers obviously switched between competing sellers. Since detailed information about the characteristics of the various products is easily available from advertisements of the respective sellers the

---

sellers in repeated laboratory markets generally shared information and restricted output below the static Nash equilibrium level.

6   The same result has been derived by Huck, Normann and Oechsler (2000) in a study of experimental oligopoly markets. Their conclusion, however, that 'Our findings clearly reject the hypothesis that more information about competitors yields a tendency towards collusion' (pp. 42–3) is misleading. Information exchange does occur in the real world. For a rational enterprise, motivated by profit maximization, it would be out of the question to enter an agreement conducive to lower profitability. Hence it is not the question whether information exchange would yield a tendency towards collusion. It is rather the question, whether collusion, once it occurs, is facilitated by information exchange. From this perspective an information exchange scheme operated by firms can serve as circumstantial evidence for collusion to obtain. As in the cases cited above, the suspicion must be corroborated by additional evidence.

recipient of information regarding the change in market shares can draw inferences as to whether a gain in market shares has been caused by defecting from a collusive agreement.

Information regarding the behavior of rivals opens chances for retaliation. This applies in particular to timely information.[7] Sometimes transparency regarding prices has been claimed to invigorate competition. This allegation, however, is entirely misleading in particular if transparency derives from information exchange among competitors. Since more vigorous competition reduces profitability, it is hardly believable for a firm to join an exchange scheme voluntarily which would cause profits to decrease. On the contrary, transparency is conducive to stabilizing collusion. Hence, timely exchange of information is circumstantial evidence for tacit collusion. This is reminiscent of Adam Smith' remark concerning the pervasiveness of collusion among businessmen even if they meet for merriment and diversion. He continues (A. Smith [1776] 1950, vol. 1, p. 144),

> It is impossible indeed to prevent such meetings, by any law which either could be executed, or would be consistent with liberty and justice. But though the law cannot hinder people of the same trade from sometimes assembling together, it ought to do nothing to facilitate such assemblies; much less to render them necessary.

The misunderstanding that transparency would be conducive to competition lies also at the bottom of regulations imposed on producers in the European Community of Steel and Coal (ECSC). Producers are committed to published price lists from which deviations are only allowed for aligning to competing offers from countries outside the ECSC. Moreover, to enhance transparency pricing is subject to a basis point system where prices are calculated to include transportation costs from some common basis point (see Phlips 1995, pp. 119ff). In the US such a scheme would be illegal. The ECSC regulation is obviously based on the notion that an announcement by a firm to align to any competing offer is an indication of tough competition. The opposite is the truth, however. The announcement, if credible, removes any incentive for a competitor's attempt to gain market share by reducing prices.

---

[7] Up to six months ahead of actual production, US automakers announce plans for their monthly domestic production of cars. Following an investigation conducted by Doyle and Snyder (1999) for the years 1965–95, they came to the conclusion that automakers' announcements did affect market outcomes and that the results do not allow the rejection of the hypothesis of a collusive auto industry (p. 1359).

3.2 MERGER CONTROL

The size and size distribution of firms may change through internal growth or
by mergers and acquisitions. Actually mergers did play a prominent role
(Mueller 1995, p. 32). For the UK, George (1990, p. 73) observes that more
than 50 per cent of the increase in horizontal concentration was attributable to
mergers and acquisitions. In the US merger waves which occurred around
1900 and in the 1920s had similar effects. In the 1950s and 1960s, however,
the number of horizontal mergers declined following a strict antitrust policy.
Whereas horizontal concentration remained largely unchanged, aggregate
concentration rose following conglomerate mergers.

Kinds of Mergers

A merger may take various forms. Two or more firms may merge into a
single unit. A firm may acquire another firms or a majority of its stock. For
the US by the Clayton Act of 1914 and the Celler–Kefauver Antimerger Act
of 1950, for Germany by § 37 KartellG and for the EC by Article 3 of the
Merger Control Regulation the notion of a merger is exhaustively defined.
The crucial question is whether a new economic unit emerges or whether, in
the case of an acquisition, the acquiring firm obtains a dominant influence on
the acquired firm.

Regarding firm size three dimensions may be distinguished, horizontal size
as measured by the market share, vertical size as measured by the relationship
between value added and total revenue, and finally conglomerate size as
measured by the extent and diversification of lines of business within a single
enterprise.

An illustration of how the various kinds of mergers developed in the US,
Germany and the UK is provided in Tables 3.1–3.3. In the US the share of
horizontal mergers declined whereas the share of conglomerate mergers increased. A similar but somewhat less pronounced development can be observed in the UK. By contrast, in Germany the share of horizontal mergers

Table 3.1   Kinds of mergers in the US 1950–77 (in per cent)

	Horizontal	Vertical	Conglomerate
1950–55	70.1	12.3	24.4
1956–63	49.1	15.8	45.3
1964–72	38.2	9.0	59.9
1973–77	39.4	11.6	56.1

Source: Smiley (1995, p. 50).

hardly declined and conglomerate mergers increased only slightly.

Table 3.2   Kinds of mergers in Germany 1974–90

| | Horizontal | | Vertical | | Conglomerate | | Total |
	Number	per cent	Number	per cent	Number	per cent	number
1974/75	571	74.5	103	13.4	92	12.0	766
1985/86	1020	67.5	151	10.0	340	22.5	1511
1989/90	2167	73.2	314	10.6	481	16.2	2962

Sources: Monopolkommission, Hauptgutachten 1982/83, p. 213, Berichte des Bundeskartell-amtes 1985/86 (Bundestags-Drucksache 11/554, p.119), and 1989/90 (Bundestags-Drucksache 12/847, p. 137).

Table 3.3   Kinds of mergers in the UK 1965–89

	Number	Horizontal in per cent	Vertical in per cent	Conglomerate in per cent
1965–69	466	82	6	13
1970–74	579	73	5	23
1975–79	1003	62	9	29
1980–84	987	65	5	30
1985–89	1413	62	2	35
1989	281	60	2	37

Source: Hughes (1993, p. 27).

Natural Selection or Restraints of Competition?

On one hand mergers and acquisitions reflect the evolutionary process of markets. Process and product innovations create opportunities for success and give rise to reorganizing existing structures of industry. As far as economies to scale exist, given a sufficient extent of the market, large firms enjoy advantages *vis-à-vis* smaller competitors. Which size of firm succeeds in surviving is determined in the competitive process. Admittedly, firms frequently grow driven by the ambitions of individuals striving to build an empire which entails influence and power. Thus the emergence of giant firms has sometimes been attributed to the hubris of ambitious tycoons. However, if competition is not restrained they would not succeed unless the organization created by them is more profitable than rival organizational forms.

As a matter of illustration recall the message of the Mosteller model of undistorted competition as depicted in Figure 1.1. If any two firms merge their combined market share may initially increase. It will, however, eventually fall short of the sum of previous shares if unimpeded competition obtains. This is particularly true if the previous distribution of market shares is restored by the entry of a new firm.[8]

Whilst in a competitive economy with freedom of entry the survival of organizational forms depends exclusively on cost advantages and the superiority of product and services supplied, barriers to entry may cause the emergence and survival of organizations which cannot be justified by comparative advantages alone. Even though in this case survival, too, depends on superior profitability, profits do not depend solely on superior efficiency rather than on exploiting monopolistic market power. Mergers and acquisitions are thus Janus-faced. Many mergers are the outgrowth of the evolutionary process of a market economy, others are primarily driven by the ambition to acquire monopolistic market power. For many mergers both explanations apply.

Merger control must thus be guided by a *rule of reason* aiming at curbing the emergence of undue monopolistic market power. The focus lies primarily on horizontal mergers. Vertical and conglomerate mergers must be examined as to what extent they are conducive to enhance horizontal concentration. On top of this, vertical and conglomerate mergers may be problematic beyond economic reasons. The sheer size may become a political nuisance. Decisions of giant firms concerning the location of production, setting up or closing down factories may assume political weight and influence the government. Firms may become 'too big to fail' This may have far-reaching ramifications, as small and medium-sized firms are adversely affected. The government, arbitrating between conflicting interests, may grant subsidies to maintain social peace and thereby distort competition.

Mergers, and in particular acquisitions of small firms by large ones, are investments which are subject to the same determinants as investments in general, that is, expected returns, the rate of interest, and the costs of acquisition. Just as investments in general increase during business cycle upswings and decline in recessions so does merger activity. In fact merger waves can be shown to parallel the ups and downs of the business cycle. In this context, too, the movement is driven both by expectations regarding improvements of efficiency and the enhancement of monopolistic market power. Low interest rates which are typical for the beginning of a business cycle upswing are

---

[8]   Assume initially five firms exist. If the two largest firms with a combined market share of 72 per cent merge to become the leading firm, even if no entry occurs, its market share drops to 52 per cent. The outcome is even worse in the case of entry which causes the market share of the leading firm to fall back to 46 per cent. Unless the merger yields lower costs or improved quality of products, free entry eventually removes any advantages initially achieved.

conducive to increased investment. They also favor the emergence of collusion, as demonstrated in Chapter 2 for the case of a repeated game with indefinite duration. Mergers and investments to establish collusive organization may thus be elicited.

In fact mergers and cartels can be shown to be substitutable. In the US, after cartels were declared illegal by the Sherman Act, they were replaced by mergers which could more effectively be defended by invoking the *rule of reason*. Substitutability between cartels and horizontal concentration can also be observed in Germany (Neumann 1995, p. 106). The largest number of legal cartels with the stated purpose of rationalization and specialization are to be found in industries where horizontal concentration is low, for example cement, building trades, machine building industry and food processing. For example in 1983 for 30 (2-digit) industries the simple correlation coefficient between $CR3$ concentration and the number of cartels registered with the Federal Cartel Office and all kinds of legal and registered recommendations issued by trade associations was -0.36 ($t = 1.95$) where the cement industry has been excluded as an outliner because of extremely low concentration and an excessively large number of registered recommendations. This finding suggests strongly that, whenever a high level of horizontal concentration had been achieved through merger, the firms need not rely on the less stable method of cartelization to obtain monopolistic market power. Substitutability between cartels and horizontal concentration has also been shown to hold in the UK (Symeonidis 1998). Whilst until the 1950s a permissive policy regarding cartels caused the industrial structure to be fragmented, the enactment of the Restrictive Trade Practices Act in 1956 gave rise to a merger wave which caused horizontal concentration to increase substantially.[9]

Preventive Merger Control

For undesirable mergers to be inhibited, in its incipiency merger control requires an obligation on the part of participating firms to notify their intention to the appropriate authorities. Notification is mandatory if the turnover of the participating firms or their assets involved exceed some stipulated level. In the US, intended mergers, according to the Hart–Rodino–Scott Pre Merger Notification Act of 1976, must be notified to the US Department of Justice and the Federal Trade Commission. In Germany the Federal Cartel Office

---

[9] 'For example, the average change in the 5-firm sales concentration ratio $C5$ between 1958 and 1975 in industries affected by the Act, and for which observations are available for both these years, was 14.9 percentage points. This compares to 7.4 percentage points for industries which were not cartelized and were therefore not affected by the legislation' (Symeonidis 1998, pp. 68f).

must be notified and in the EC the Commission. Following notification the authorities must decide whether the merger can be permitted or is to be prohibited because a restraint of competition is involved. The authorities must take their decision within a stipulated time. Preventive merger control avoids the necessity to unravel a once consummated merger when, with hindsight, it turns out to be anticompetitive. For the authorities it is also possible to allow a merger subject to certain undertakings, that is, certain conditions to be satisfied by the firms. Usually, before official notification of a merger, firms planning a merger approach the authorities to inquire whether they can expect the merger to be approved of. They can abandon their plan if the authority indicates that the decision will be negative, and if appealing to the courts is not expected to be successful. Notification will therefore only occur if an approval can be expected or if, in the case of a difference of opinion, the notifying firms resolve to seek a court decision.

The Relevant Market

For horizontal concentration and a horizontal merger to be defined it is necessary to identify the relevant market. Relevancy pertains to commodities or services and to the geographic extent of the market. This appears simple in the case of homogeneous products. It is less easy if products are differentiated.

To define the relevant market frequently both demand and supply is taken into account. On the side of demand the crucial criterion is substitutability. Those products are counted as belonging to a particular market which buyers consider as substitutable because, given their characteristics, their intended use and their prices, they serve the same demand. On the side of supply those products might be assigned as belonging to a particular market which are produced using the same productive facilities. For example in the steel industry iron bars for reinforcing concrete and wire rods, which serve quite different demands, may be manufactured by the same rolling mill. Accordingly, Kaysen and Turner (1959, p. 295) invoked both aspects to define the relevant market.

> The market is then defined in terms of the buyers' substitution of one product for another and in terms of producers' substitution of one product for another. In order to define a market we attempt to obtain information on cross-elasticities of both demand and supply. Such an information is rarely available directly, but must be approximated by evidence on consumer behavior (is poultry considered a substitute for meat?) and on the degree of specialisation of equipment (can cotton looms easily be shifted to rayon weaving?).

Invoking substitutability both of demand and supply is logically flawed because the relevant supply cannot be identified unless the market to which it pertains is defined in the first place. Therefore it is preferable to focus only on demand to assign only those products to a particular market which are close substitutes in demand. In a second step of the analysis the structure of supply serving this market may be examined to identify actual and potential competitors. Obviously the second step can only be taken once the market to which the respective supply pertains has been defined. Substitutability of supply is only invoked for determining whether a merger gives rise to a dominant position.

In the practice of competition policy the relevant market is primarily defined by invoking demand substitutability. In Germany, according to the Kammergericht in a ruling upheld by the Federal Court of Justice, the relevant market has been defined as comprising 'all products which in view of their characteristics, their intended use and price are similar such that a reasonable consumer would consider them to be substitutable' (my translation).

A few examples may serve to illustrate the principle of substitutability as applied to define the relevant market. In the US the Supreme Court 1956 in the case US v. E.I. Du Pont de Nemours & Co. counted all flexible packaging materials as belonging to the relevant market and not only those made from cellophane (Kintner 1980b, p. 328). In the case of Diamond International Corporation v. Waltershoefer (1968) all egg cartons rather than only paperboard egg cartons were assigned to the same market because they all perform the same function (Kintner 1980b, p. 331). Whether products do serve the same function must be decided from the point of view of the buyer. In the case of Reynolds Metals Co. v. FTC (1962) (Kintner 1980b, p. 337) the question arose whether all decorative aluminum foil, which appears to be reasonably interchangeable, should be counted as belonging to the relevant market or only that sold to the florist trade. Invoking buyers' revealed behavior led to the conclusion that the narrow definition of the relevant market was the appropriate one. Since foil was sold to florists at prices of $0.75 to $0.85 per unit whilst similar decorative foil cost $1.15 to $1.22 per unit, such a difference in prices could not have persisted if buyers considered the foils as interchangeable.

Regarding supply substitutability in US antitrust, with some reluctance, an 'immediate entrant' has been taken into account. In Germany the Federal Cartel Office counts those productive facilities as belonging to the relevant market which are available on short notice, that is, in effect 'immediately' (Traugott 1998, p. 931). The same practice is adopted by the EC Commission (1997). The logic of this practice is flawed, however, as has already been pointed out above. For an immediate entrant to be identified the relevant market must be defined in the first place. This, however, can only be achieved with reference to demand substitutability.

How questionable it is to invoke supply becomes clear by looking at the German case of the intended merger between two leading building firms, Holzmann and Hochtief. The Federal Cartel Office, in its decision against this merger, had defined the relevant market to comprise large building projects exceeding DM 50 Mio. in value, based on the presumption that only the largest firms would command sufficient expertise to realize those kinds of projects. The Kammergericht, on appeal, annulled the decision primarily on procedural grounds, but it also expressed some doubts regarding the definition of the relevant market. The Federal Cartel Office was certainly right to dismiss the notion that the entire building market, extending from single family houses to skyscrapers, from airports to railway tracks, from bridges to harbors would constitute a single market. Still, referring to the value of projects appears equally misleading. Looking at the demand side, in fact, allows separate markets to be distinguished. Between single family houses and skyscrapers, or between them and airports or railway tracks, hardly any substitutability exists. They clearly do not belong to the same relevant market. Having defined the relevant market by invoking demand, in a second step, the supply side may be brought in. Here certainly asymmetry is involved. For ordinary buildings which require no specialized expertise, small and large building firms are equally able to compete. On the other hand, for some projects specialized expertise and a sufficiently large productive capacity is required. Hence in those cases only a few firms are active on the respective market.

In the 1984 Merger Guidelines of the US Justice Department the relevant market has been defined as comprising those commodities for which a hypothetical monopolist would profitably impose a small but significant and nontransitory increase in price – say of 5 per cent – lasting for a year. The relevant market is properly defined if such a price increase would not be thwarted by consumer substitution or entry of another producer into the market (George 1990, pp. 91ff). In the more recent Guidelines of 1992, and likewise in the practice of the Federal Cartel Office in Germany and the EC Commission, only demand substitution has been taken account of (Neven, Nutall and Seabright 1993, p. 50). Thus in the case of Coca Cola Enterprises/Amalgamated Beverages GB the EC Commission concluded that Coca Cola drinks in the UK belong to a separate market. Most competitors and traders, when asked what they expected consumers were likely to do in the case of a rise in price of 5–10 per cent, replied that the likelihood for consumers to switch to other drinks was low or even nil (EC Commission 1998, p. 35).

For defining the relevant market one may use the formula for the price–cost margin applying for differentiated products (see Chapter 2) which is

$$\frac{p_i - c_i}{p_i} = \frac{1}{e_i - \sum_{j \neq i} \mu_{ij} e_{ij}}.$$

In this formula μ_{ij} is the conjectural elasticity denoting the percentage change in p_j expected by firm i if it raises its price by 1 per cent. Perfect collusion and thus concerted behavior implies $\mu_{ij} = 1$.

Then look for the narrowest market where some degree of monopolistic market power can be exercised. As proposed in the US Merger Guidelines, assume that the price is raised above marginal costs, that is, beyond the price which would apply under perfect competition, and determine the own price elasticity of demand as seen by the seller, that is, e_i which applies if the price–cost margin is raised by 5 per cent. This price elasticity could be expected if competitors' reactions are ignored. If this elasticity falls short of 20, that is, if it is smaller than the reciprocal of a price–cost margin of 5 per cent, the product i under consideration is the relevant market. If the elasticity exceeds 20, cross–price elasticities of substitute goods must be included. Given a hypothetical monopolist the conjectural elasticities are unity. Then subtract the cross–price elasticities consecutively following their order of magnitude, beginning with the largest one, until $e_i - \sum_{j \neq i} e_{ij}$ falls short of, or becomes equal to, 20. That defines the relevant market.

The extent of the relevant market depends on the, arbitrarily chosen, price increase of 5 per cent. At a higher rate of increase the relevant market is larger, because the product under consideration has become too expensive and consumers prefer to switch to substitutes which, although less suited for the given demand, are relatively cheaper and can thus be afforded. Formally, if the price is raised by 10 per cent, given a direct price elasticity of $e_i = 20$, for the price–cost margin to be reduced to 1/10, additional cross–price elasticities must be invoked. The extent of the relevant market also depends on whether one chooses as the point of reference the level of marginal costs or a price which, in consequence of existing market power, exceeds marginal costs. If the 5 per cent rule is applied the hypothetical price–cost margin is higher and the relevant market would be larger since additional products would qualify as relevant substitutes. The failure to recognize that the presence of competitors and thus relevant substitutes is the consequence of market power (that is, the maintenance of price above the competitive level) has frequently been termed the 'cellophane fallacy' (White 2000, p. 140).[10]

---

[10] As reported above, in the US v. E.I. Du Pont de Nemours and Co. the Supreme Court had ruled that the relevant market did comprise all flexible wrapping materials and not only those made from cellophane. It thus ignored that Du Pont's elevated price had caused other wrapping materials to be competitive with cellophane.

Proceeding in the depicted way leaves no room for separately accounting for supply elasticity. All substitutable products, actual and potential ones, have been included. For the hypothetical argument, whilst the price of product i is assumed to be raised, the prices of all other products are kept unchanged. That implies an infinitely large supply elasticity for substitutable products. Since this is presumably not true in practice the extent of the relevant market is normally exaggerated.

The proposed procedure pertains to all substitutable products regardless of their geographic origin. It therefore simultaneously copes with the geographic extent of the relevant market. Taking this into account makes the implicit assumption of infinitely large supply elasticities particularly questionable. First, international barriers to trade exist in the form of transport cost, tariffs and taxes, import quotas and other non-tariff barriers. Even within the EC, Member States have retained some barriers justified for health reasons, in particular applying to pharmaceutical products and food. Second, there are collusive barriers. Firms may try, and achieve, to protect their markets through vertical constraints which enable them to charge geographically differentiated prices. The market for agricultural tractors may serve as an example. From 1970 to 1990 Ford and Massey-Ferguson were leading firms in the UK market whilst their market shares in Germany were extremely low. By contrast, Deutz and Fendt were the leading firms in Germany but were practically absent from the UK market. Likewise the distribution of market shares for motor cars in the EC, as illustrated in Chapter 1, gives rise to the suspicion that restrictive arrangements, particularly in the form of exclusive dealing contracts, exist and reduce the supply elasticity across national borderlines. The formation of the internal market within the EC and the dismantling of trade barriers within GATT and WTO have enabled the geographic extent of markets to increase, yet there are still substantial barriers which remain internationally.

Presumptions: United States

Whilst cartels generally fall under the *per se* verdict, subject to some exemptions, mergers are evaluated according to a rule of reason. Even a high level of horizontal concentration is not condemned *per se* because it may follow from ordinary business practice being caused by superior efficiency. That applies both to horizontal concentration following from internal growth of firms and to mergers and acquisitions. However, mergers may also be motivated by the desire to increase profits by exercising monopolistic market power. Therefore, mergers must be examined whether they are the outcome of the normal course of business or whether they are driven by the intent to monopolize.

As on homogeneous markets setting up a cartel is attractive only if a great majority of suppliers join it (Salant, Switzer and Reynolds 1983). For a merger a collusive intent can be presumed only if an overriding market share is at stake. Otherwise a merger pays if cost savings can be expected to improve profitability. A merger with collusive intent which would only entail a small combined market share is doomed to failure. Things are different, however, in the case of product differentiation (Deneckere and Davidson 1985). In this case a merger with collusive intent may improve profitability even if the involved market share is low.

To distinguish between a merger with collusive intent and a merger motivated by the desire to improve efficiency, Baxter (1980) proposed to watch the development of the quotation of shares at the stock exchange. If cost reductions are expected, profitability of the merging firms will rise whereas profitability of rival firms is adversely affected and the quotation of their shares at the stock exchange will decline accordingly. That applies both to homogeneous and heterogeneous markets (see Chapter 2). By contrast, in the case of collusive intent the profitability of rival firms is favorably affected, and even more so than the profitability of the merging firms themselves. However, it is also possible that mergers with collusive intent give rise to the anticipation of predatory behavior towards outsiders which would yield their share prices to decline.[11]

In the practice of merger control the authorities start from a priori presumptions regarding market dominance. In a further step the authority may then assess any efficiency gains against the welfare loss entailed by a merger with monopolizing intent.

In the US the Sherman Act distinguishes two cases, the offense of monopolization and the intent and conspiracy to monopolize. Monopolization means holding a monopoly in combination with defending this position by unfair means. The offense of monopolization thus requires a conduct which is likely to yield a monopoly or to reinforce monopoly power (general intent). An attempt or a conspiracy to monopolize (specific intent) must be proved by documents or by showing that practices have been adopted which lead to the exclusion of competitors. In contrast to the first case of general intent, in the case of specific intent it is not necessary to define a relevant market because monopolizing aims at a different market from the one on which the accused enterprise is active at the moment.

---

[11] Smiley (1995, p. 55). In a study pertaining to mega mergers around the turn of the 19th to the 20th century in the US, Banerjee and Eckard (1998, p. 815) report that the quotation of shares of non-participating firms declined in most of the cases. The likelihood that this was caused by the expectation of aggressive pricing of the merging firms was assessed to be low. They thus came to the conclusion that anticipated efficiency gains were the driving forces for the majority of mergers.

The prohibition of the Sherman Act becomes effective only if either a general or a specific intent can be proved to exist. A monopoly is not illegal if it can be shown to be thrust upon the firm. In the Alcoa case this question became the crucial point in the argumentation of the court. Alcoa had in anticipation of future demand created additional capacities and thus had left no chances for competitors. Judge Hand[12] ruled (Kintner 1980b, p. 377) that 'It was not inevitable that it should always anticipate increases in demand for ingot and be prepared to supply them' and hence dismissed the allegation that monopoly was thrust upon Alcoa. Nevertheless some doubts remain regarding the justification of this assessment. Generally, as put by Kintner (1980b, p. 378),

> It is one thing to compete fairly and aggressively regardless of the consequences of one's rivals; it is another to surround one's manor with moat and wall to keep out new competition or to deprive others of fair and reasonable access to supplies and markets by recognizable exclusionary devices.

By contrast to the Standard Oil case (1911) and the Tobacco case exclusionary and predatory devices could not be proved to have been adopted in the Alcoa case. The situation has been more obvious in the case of US v. United Shoe Machinery Corp. (1953). This firm, too, in defense had recourse to the thrust-upon doctrine by arguing that success was the result of superior skill, foresight and industry. The court, however, replied that the practice of providing its machinery to manufacturers only through long-term leases and not by outright sale created artificial barriers to entry such that success was not solely the result of fair competition (Kintner 1980b, p. 378).

Applying the Sherman Act requires proving that a dominant position is held by the firm involved. A first indicator is the market share. In the Alcoa case the market share amounted to more than 90 per cent. Frequently the statement of Judge Hand is cited that this market share is sufficient to constitute a monopoly, it is doubtful whether 60 or 64 per cent would be enough; and certainly 33 per cent is not (Kintner 1980b, p. 358).[13] By contrast, in merger control based on the Clayton Act the crucial question is whether com-

---

[12] The 2nd Circuit Court in this case adopted the role of the Supreme Court as court of last resort because some judges had previously been working for the prosecution and were thus disqualified such that the required number of six judges was not available at the Supreme Court.

[13] In the Alcoa case the additional question arose whether only virgin ingot should be counted as belonging to the relevant market or whether also secondary or scrap aluminum should be added, in which case the market share of Alcoa would have been substantially lower. The court, however, argued that Alcoa controlled the competition of secondary ingot because of its dominance in producing the primary ingot from which the secondary ingot was derived (Kintner 1980b, p. 327). This opinion has much later been supported by theoretical reasoning (Gaskins 1974).

petition may be substantially lessened. This can be assumed to hold if mergers or acquisitions give rise to an increased market share of leading oligopolists which yield an increase in monopolistic market power. This view can be justified by economic theory and empirical evidence about the relationship between the price–cost margin and horizontal concentration (see Chapter 2).

In the US the Department of Justice has issued Merger Guidelines to inform the public under what circumstances it considers competition to be substantially lessened in the meaning of the Clayton Act. Since 1984 criteria are stipulated in terms of the Herfindahl index of concentration. Before that time criteria were given in terms of combined market shares like $CR4$. In the 1950s and 1960s very tough standards used to be applied. The extreme case has been the merger between Brown Shoe Company and Kinney Shoe Company in 1955, which would have led to a combined market share of 4.5 per cent in the United States. The decisive reason for disallowing the merger, however, was that the respective geographic market was much smaller. In about 30 cities the merger would have resulted in a market share exceeding 20 per cent. In addition, the decision was motivated by the aim to protect small business. The court said (Kinne 1998, p. 15),

> But we cannot fail to recognize Congress' desire to promote competition through the protection of viable, small, locally owned business. ... Congress appreciated that occasional higher costs and prices might result from the maintenance of fragmented industries and markets. It resolved these competing considerations in favor of decentralization. We must give effect to that decision.

This reasoning has been supported by the Supreme Court 1966 in the case of Von's Grocery Company which held a market share of 4.7 per cent in the Los Angeles region. The firm to be acquired, Shopping Bay Food Stores, had a market share of 2.8 per cent. The court's ruling was decisively determined by the observation that the combined market share of the 20 largest retail stores increased from 44 per cent in 1948 to 57 per cent in 1958. Following this stance of antitrust enforcement horizontal mergers were deemed illegal in most cases. Not least for this reason merger activity in the US shifted toward conglomerate acquisitions, as documented in Table 3.1.

A dramatic change in antitrust enforcement occurred during the administration of President Ronald Reagan. Antitrust following from the Clayton Act came to be considered as undesirable government regulation. The presumptive criteria, as defined by certain levels of the Herfindahl index, were softened, and, under the intellectual influence of the contestability doctrine, potential entry was assigned much more weight. Consequently, a great many horizontal mergers were left uncontested and even mega mergers, like the one between Boeing and McDonnell-Douglas, went through.

Two different objections may be raised against this stance of competition policy. First, it is highly questionable to what extent potential entry suffices to counteract the damaging effects of an increase in horizontal concentration. As has been forcefully argued by Shepherd (1984), actual competition is much more effective than potential competition. Second, the very use of the Herfindahl index as a presumptive criterion may be misleading. Reference to the Herfindahl index is based on the assumption that a lower index implies better performance. This assumption is not always justified, as can be shown by comparing a symmetric duopoly with the Stackelberg case. In a symmetric duopoly each firm offers 1/3 of the output which would result under perfect competition, such that the Herfindahl index is $H = 0.5$. By contrast, in the Stackelberg case the leader has an output of 1/2 of the competitive output, and the follower supplies 1/4. Since market shares are 2/3 and 1/3, respectively, the Herfindahl index is $H = 0.5555$. It exceeds the one following in the case of a symmetric duopoly and prima facie would indicate a worse market performance. In fact, the opposite is true. Total output is higher and the price is lower in the Stackelberg case than for the symmetric duopoly. This is a similar phenomenon to the one which arose in the case where market shares are determined by random effects, as shown by the Mosteller model (see Chapter 1). For example, in the European automobile industry the Herfindahl index implied by undistorted competition turned out to exceed the actual one, although substantial restraints of competition presumably exist.

Presumptions: Europe

The decisive criterion governing merger control in Germany and the EC is the notion of market dominance. In Germany, according to § 19 KartellG, an enterprise is deemed to be dominant, either with respect to supply or demand, insofar as on the relevant market it has no competitors or is not subject to substantial competition, or if it holds an overriding market position. The assessment whether a dominant position exists has to rely on taking into account the market share, financial resources, access to supplies or markets, shareholding with other firms, legal and actual barriers to entry, feasibility of switching between lines of business and the elasticity of demand. Market dominance is equivalently defined in Article 2 of the EC Merger Control Regulation. In Germany, according to § 19 KartellG market dominance is presumed to exist at a market share of 1/3. It is also presumed to exist if three, or less than three, firms are holding a combined market share of at least 50 per cent or if five, or less than five, firms are holding a combined market share of at least 2/3. In EC merger control a market share in the Common Market exceeding 25 per cent is presumed to constitute a dominant position (Preamble No. 15 to the EC Merger Control Regulation). Both in Germany and the EC, market dominance may apply to a single firm or to a group of firms. Initially it was questionable whether a presumption of oligopolistic dominance did apply within the EC. The issue was clarified by the decisions of the EC Commission in the case Nestlé/Perrier in 1992 and a ruling of the European Court of Justice 1998 in the case Kali + Salz AG (González 1998) according to which oligopolistic dominance applies in the EC as well.

In the practice of merger control in Germany a merger by which smaller firms achieve a size which brings them more closely to the market leader (so-called 'Aufholfusion'), has frequently been approved of even if horizontal concentration rose. Possibly, the Herfindahl index may thereby be reduced. Whether this engenders an improvement of market performance appears doubtful, however, in particular because increased homogeneity in size among the leading firms of a market may be conducive to collusion.

Conglomerate and Vertical Mergers

A dominant position may be strengthened by upstream or downstream vertical integration or by using financial resources to intimidate and discourage potential entrants such that the own position is entrenched.

In the US the entrenchment doctrine was recognized in the case of a conglomerate and vertical merger in the case of Procter & Gamble/Clorox (Hermann 1986, pp. 255f). Procter & Gamble, a large enterprise supplying chemicals for cleaning and bleaching and sundry household articles, acquired Clorox Chemical Company, the leading firm on the market for household bleaching articles. The prohibition of this merger was upheld by the Supreme Court 1967 on the ground that the leadership of Clorox would be reinforced through the merger, because the superior financial power of Procter & Gamble would enable Clorox to displace competitors.

The same reasoning was advanced in Germany for prohibiting the acquisition of a majority holding in WMF (Württembergische Metallwarenfabriken) by Rheinmetall. WMF holds a dominant position in the fields of high quality table cutlery and large coffee machines. Rheinmetall is a leading supplier in the field of military equipment. The proposed merger was thus purely conglomerate in character. It was intended by Rheinmetall to reduce its dependence on the high risk field of military equipment. The proposal was turned down by the Federal Cartel Office, subsequently upheld by the Federal Court of Justice, on the ground that a leading firm acquisition by an enterprise like Rheinmetall, with command of ample financial resources would strengthen the dominant position of WMF. In contrast to a leading firm acquisition, a foothold acquisition, where a large firm acquires a small firm of another highly concentrated market, may render competition in that market to become more vigorous. However, if the market entered by a large firm has been primarily populated by small and middle-sized firms the move of the large firm should be disallowed.[14]

Potential Competition

Among the presumptive criteria potential entry plays a controversial role. Under the influence of the contestability doctrine it came to be assigned considerable weight. Hence the presumptions following from the Herfindahl index of concentration, listed in the US Merger Guidelines, lose some of their force. In fact, the Guidelines say that, 'if entry into a market is so easy that existing competitors would not succeed in raising price for a significant period of time, the Department is unlikely to challenge mergers in that market' (cited by Smiley 1995, p. 70). This principle is without fault. The question, however, is under what circumstances entry is in fact 'easy'. The Merger Guidelines suggest that entry is easy if it occurs timely, that is, within two years, and that it is likely and sufficient to enforce a rise in price to be revoked. In view of studies discussed in Chapter 2 regarding the persistence of profits, the development of concentration following the growth of markets, and the influence of foreign trade on price–cost margins, substantial barriers to entry appear to abound which raises considerable doubts as to whether entry is easy in general. Although merger control pertains to individual cases, the evaluation will be influenced by taking into account the general evidence.

In Germany the Federal Cartel Office, during the 1970s, hardly ever accounted for potential entry. This changed during the 1980s. A case in point has been the acquisition of Werner & Pfleiderer, the largest German producer of equipment for bakeries, by Fried. Krupp GmbH. The Federal Cartel Office did not object to the acquisition since potential competition by Britain's Baker Perkins, with its worldwide operations, was considered to prevent market dominance. On the other hand, doubts arise regarding the effectiveness of potential competition if an entry has not occurred for a long time, particularly because entry is unlikely due to barriers to international trade. Thus it is not the present market structure that really counts. The dynamics of markets must be taken into account as well. For example, the acquisition of a majority holding of Triumph–Adler by Olivetti was left uncontested by the Federal Cartel Office despite large market shares involved because the market for typewriters, supplied by Triumph–Adler, was undergoing dramatic changes under the influence of the PC and related equipment.

In EC merger control, recently potential entry has apparently been assigned increasing weight. In 1979 the European Court of Justice held that 'very large

---

[14] This arguments remains valid even though the related legal presumption of § 23a Sec. 1 GWB has been abandoned by the latest piece of legislation.

market shares are in themselves, save in exceptional circumstances, evidence of the existence of a dominant position'. Accordingly, the EC Commission, in the AKZO case, considered a market share of 50 per cent as sufficient to assume market dominance to exist (Haid 1999, p. 170). By contrast, the acquisition of Kässbohrer by Mercedes Benz in 1995 was approved of by the EC Commission although the acquisition led to very large market shares in Germany, namely 74 per cent for inter-city buses and 54 per cent for touring buses (Monopolkommission 1996, p. 340). A somewhat different picture emerges by recognizing the European Community as the geographically relevant market. In the EC the market shares amounted to 41 per cent for inter-city buses and 35 per cent for touring buses (EC Commission 14 February 1995, WuW 1995, p. 385). According to German law these market shares would be sufficient to presume a dominant position to exist. The EC Commission, however, considered potential competition, in particular from outside the EC, to suffice. As the market shares of actual competition from outside were extremely low, this decision by the EC Commission met with substantial criticism. The German Monopolkommission (1996, p. 341) pointed out that for inter-city buses all foreign competitors held but a tiny share of 1.1 per cent in Germany and for touring buses 10.3 per cent. The only integrated domestic competitor, that is, MAN, held a market share of 4.3 per cent for touring buses, and Neoplan had a market share of 26 per cent but bought the engines from Mercedes Benz. The Monopolkommission therefore considered the evaluation of the effectiveness of potential competition adopted by the EC Commission as hardly understandable.

Efficiency Defense

The rule of reason implies that mergers should be tolerated if they are following from ordinary business activity rather than the intent to monopolize. Hence mergers may be justified on the ground of efficiency, even though in the US neither the Sherman Act nor the Clayton Act provides specifically for an efficiency defense. In fact until recently the Supreme Court did not accept an efficiency defense. Hence in the case of the proposed acquisition of Clorox Chemical Company by Procter & Gamble the Supreme Court dismissed an efficiency defense stating that 'possible economies cannot be used as a defense to illegality. Congress was aware that some mergers which lessen competition may also result in economies but struck the balance in favor of protecting competition' (Kinne 1998, p. 16). A turning point occurred when the Supreme Court 1973, in the case of US v. General Dynamics took issue with a purely structural approach and emphasized the necessity of careful scrutiny. Accordingly, the Merger Guidelines of 1984 provided explicitly for an efficiency defense (Mueller 1996, p. 235) by stating (cited after Smiley

1995, p. 70),

> If the parties to the merger establish by clear and convincing evidence that a
> merger will achieve such efficiencies, the Department will consider those efficien-
> cies in deciding whether to challenge the merger. Cognizable efficiencies include,
> but are not limited to, achieving economies of scale, better integration of produc-
> tion facilities, plant specialization, lower transportation cost, and similar efficien-
> cies relating to specific manufacturing, servicing, or distribution operations of the
> merging firms. The Department may also consider claimed efficiencies resulting
> from reductions in general selling, administrative, and overhead expenses, ... the
> Department will reject claims of efficiencies if equivalent or comparable savings
> can reasonably be achieved by the parties through other means. The parties must
> establish a greater level of expected net efficiencies the more significant are the
> competitive risks.

The final sentence, in particular, alludes to a trade-off reasoning as propagated by Williamson (1968). The practice suggested by the Guidelines have
been supported by some decisions by lower courts (Kinne 1998, pp. 17ff).
The parties to a proposed merger were requested to prove that cost reductions
would yield an improvement for consumers. On the whole, however, an efficiency defense has only very reluctantly been admitted.[15]

According to German law (§ 36 KartellG) it is incumbent on the parties to
a proposed merger to prove that the merger yields an improvement of competitive conditions which outweigh disadvantages entailed by creating a
dominant position. The wording of the law leaves it open whether it involves
an efficiency defense.[16] In addition the German law provides (§ 41 KartellG)
for the Minister of Economics to grant permission of a merger in exceptional
cases if the restraint of competition is offset by economic advantages at large
such that the public interest justifies the merger. So far only very few cases of
this kind came up in Germany. In two cases, that is, VEBA/Gelsenberg
(1974) and BP/Gelsenberg (1979), the merger was deemed to be justified on
the ground that it would contribute to ensure an undisturbed supply of oil.
Another, more spectacular case, Daimler Benz/Messerschmidt-Bölkow-
Blohm (MBB) was motivated by industrial policy considerations. In a few

---

[15] Although the Merger Guidelines provide for an efficiency defense, according to a study by
Coates and McChesney (1992), invoking an efficiency defense, when controlled for by other
guidelines factors, was practically without influence on the decision of the Federal Trade
Commission during the time from 1982 to 1986.

[16] One might argue that the merger should yield lower costs which favor consumers. By contrast,
Herrmann (1989, p. 1217) claimed that the weighting clause requiring an improvement of
'competitive conditions' does not involve an efficiency defense. However, such an improvement cannot be measured but by referring to market performance. For advantages to outweigh
disadvantages certainly requires quantifying counteracting effects which clearly implies an
efficiency defense.

other cases granting an exception was driven by the desire to save jobs. However, with hindsight in none of these cases were expectations borne out by the subsequent development. Likewise, given the abundant supply of oil subsequently, the hope to secure the supply of oil turned out to be absurd. Similarly, the premises on which permitting the Daimler Benz/MBB merger were predicated turned out to be hardly realistic. These cases thus demonstrate how questionable the interference of industrial policy with competition policy is.

In the EC the 'Regulation on the control of concentrations between undertakings', that is, the Merger Control Regulation of 1989, declares as incompatible with the common market a merger which 'creates or strengthens a dominant position as a result of which effective competition would be significantly impeded in the common market or in a substantial part of it'. In the appraisal of mergers the EC Commission has to take into account, among other things, 'the development of technical and economic progress provided that it is to consumers' advantage and does not form an obstacle to competition' (Article 7, 1(b)). It is controversial whether this amounts to an efficiency defense. The wording alone does not justify this assumption (Jacquemin 1999, p. 217). Still, as admitted by Jacquemin and demonstrated by Haid (1999) by analyzing quite a few cases, industrial policy did play a role in merger control as exercised by the EC Commission. The Commission takes a one shot decision by which both considerations of competition policy and industrial policy are applied simultaneously. By contrast, in Germany a two-step procedure applies. At the first step the Federal Cartel Office examines whether a merger is tolerable from the viewpoint of competition policy. In the case of an adverse decision, unless the parties prefer to seek a court decision, they may try to have the merger admitted by Ministerial decree on the ground of public interest. In the EC both aspects enter the decision simultaneously. Hence, by necessity, the political traditions of the various Member States are brought to bear on the Commission's decision. Whilst in Germany competition policy has the longest tradition in Europe, and arguments derived therefrom clearly outweigh considerations of industrial policy, the situation is quite different in other Member States. Some of them have no tradition in competition policy at all, in other Member States both aspects are taken into account by weighing them differently. In Britain, for example, until quite recently merger control was dominated by reference to the public interest, which led Veljanovski (1995, p. 140) to state that the 'The UK stands out in Western Europe as having the most permissive and conducive environment for merger and acquisition activity'. Only in the later 1980s did the emphasis shift in favor of competition policy (Veljanovski 1995, pp. 148ff). In France traditionally industrial policy dominated economic policy with respect to mergers. Although a merger control has been in place since 1977, Jenny (1995, p. 172) observed that 'there is still a lingering feeling among French bureaucrats in charge of industrial policy that economic concentration is necessary to ensure the competitiveness of French firms and that the government should play an active role in the area of industrial structures'. For these reasons considerations derived from industrial policy can be expected to shape merger control in the EC. Hence the impression arises that in the EC merger and acquisitions are more liberally tolerated than they used to be in Germany (Haid 1999). Although some outstanding cases like Mercedes Benz/Kässbohrer might give rise to this conclusion it is not borne out quantitatively. From 1973 to 1991, that is, before EC merger control took effect, the Federal Cartel Office in Germany registered 14,403 mergers of which 98 were disallowed (Monopolkommission 1992, p. 2512). That amounts to 0.68 per cent. In the EC, from 1990 to 1997, 701 mergers were notified from which 8 were disallowed, hence 1.1 per cent.

Actually, overwhelming empirical evidence has been accumulated which shows that in most cases mergers and acquisitions do not yield efficiency gains. Even where immediately following a merger efficiency gains arise, in the long run they are offset by losses resulting from a slowdown of technical progress and X-inefficiency. This has been documented in some detail both theoretically and empirically in Chapter 2 and has by now been widely acknowledged (Jacquemin 1995, p. 87).[17]

Despite different traditions of competition policy in the US and Europe the evaluation of merger cases can be expected to converge. For one, in all countries economic theory is gaining increasing weight. Moreover, in the EC competition policy, both at the EC level and at the respective national level, is increasingly shaped by EC law. For major cases, particularly those which transcend national borders, EC law applies. As mergers within national border lines cannot eventually be treated differently from major ones, a convergence of standards of evaluation will necessarily arise. A convergence between US antitrust policy and EC competition policy can be expected to emerge because competition policy entails exterritorial effects. Since numerous large firms maintain productive facilities both in Europe and the US, a merger in the US regularly implies a merger of the corresponding European subsidiaries and conversely. A merger among US firms thus requires the

---

[17] In a large number of studies, reviewed by Mueller (1995), in the US and the UK initial expectations regarding increased profitability were not borne out. To a large extent this was due to a very large share of mergers and acquisitions being conglomerate ones. These results of studies conducted by economists are supported by the observation that numerous diversified companies tend to focus on their core activities and thus sell off non-core fields of business. As opposed to the US and UK conglomerate mergers played a less prominent role in Germany. Accordingly, the picture regarding profitability engendered by mergers is somewhat ambiguous. But also in Germany conglomerate mergers were less successful than horizontal mergers (Bühner 1994, pp. 30ff).

permission of the European authorities and a merger among European firms must be tolerated by the US authorities. This applies in particular to mergers extending US and EC borderlines like the merger between Daimler and Chrysler. Globalization of economic activities thus necessitates a globalization of competition policy.

Prohibition, Divestiture, and Undertakings

Both in the EC and the US merger control is exercised preventively. In the US it is, moreover, possible to break up an enterprise which came into existence by merger. The first spectacular cases were Standard Oil of New Jersey (1911), The American Tobacco Company (1911) and Dupont (1912). In an interesting study Comanor and Scherer (1995) have shown that the dissolution of the dominant firms gave rise to a competitive environment in which the successors eventually prospered. By contrast, US Steel, which was able to defend itself successfully in court from being dissolved, was much less successful afterwards. More recently the telecommunications monopoly AT&T was broken up. In combination with deregulation intensive competition arose. Similarly far-reaching possibilities for divestiture exist neither in Germany nor in the EC.[18] German law as well EC law only provides for the possibility to allow a merger subject to specific undertakings. The participating firms may be obligated to sell off some shareholdings or to observe specific rules of conduct. In principle the EC Commission may revoke a once granted permission of a merger if the respective firms commit a breach of an obligation attached to the prior decision of the EC Commission (Article 8, No. 5 lit(b) EC Merger Control Regulation). US authorities, too, are entitled to let a merger pass subject to undertakings.

Some undertakings are the outcome from bargaining between the firms planning a merger and the authorities, other ones are imposed by the authorities. Imposing undertakings aims at the enhancement of competitiveness of existing or potential competitors by reducing the market share of the merging firms in other markets. For example, in the EC Nestlé/Perrier was obligated to sell off some of its springs and trade marks. In addition firms may be forced to open access to markets by giving up vertical commitments and exclusive dealing contracts. In the case of Alcatel/Telettra the Spanish telecommunication firm Telefónica had to sell off its shareholding in Alcatel/Telettra because it was deemed as a barrier to entry for new competitors (Kerber 1994, p. 125).

---

[18] However, according to § 41, 3 KartellG, a consummated merger which has been declared illegal by the Federal Cartel Office or whose permission has been revoked must be broken up unless the Federal Minister of Economics grants permission by exception.

The practice of undertakings is problematic for two reasons. First, an undertaking frequently could not be carried out because a buyer was not found. From an economic point of view one might suspect that the price demanded was too high which indeed amounts to sabotaging the undertaking. A second aspect it still more important, however. Permitting a merger subject to undertakings is presumptuous because it amounts to the pretense of knowledge which in a competitive economy the authority cannot possibly have. The authority pretends to know what the market structure would be under undistorted competition and how a restraint of competition in one place can be offset with regard to economic welfare by increased competition in another place. In a competitive economy where competition itself is the method of discovery this is impossible to know a priori. Thus imposing undertakings necessarily yields a distortion of competition.

Joint Ventures

Most joint ventures are operated by large firms. Many of them participate in several joint ventures simultaneously (Monopolkommission 1996, pp. 275ff). That is easily understood. Although cooperation between them is profitable in some fields of activity, a full-blown merger need not be attractive for large firms which are active in various and differing fields.

A joint venture comprises features of both, collusion and merger. In competition policy it is to be treated according to which characteristics are dominant. As a matter of illustration two cooperative joint ventures in Germany shall be considered. In 1975 the Federal Court of Justice upheld a decision of the Federal Cartel Office disallowing four cement producers from selling their output through a jointly owned though legally independent sales organization. In 1980 the Federal Cartel Office prohibited HFGE (Handelsgesellschaft freier Groß- und Einzelhandelsbetriebe GmbH) set up by four trading groups who previously had purchased separately to obtain better terms by concentrated buying, as an illegal buyers' cartel. The decision was upheld in court. On the other hand, a joint venture created for exploration and exploitation of manganese nodules from the seabed was regarded as a pure merger by the Federal Cartel Office in 1976. No restraint of competition was found and the cooperation was deemed necessary since each of the participating enterprises alone was short of the required financial and technological capacity. In 1984 the Federal Cartel Office turned down a proposal by five leading cable manufacturers in Germany (Siemens, Philips, AEG, SEL (ITT), and Kabelmetall (Cables de Lyon)) to establish a joint venture for the production and distribution of optical fibers. This proposal was prohibited on the ground that it would strengthen the participating firms' dominant oligopoly, continue the former telecommunications cable cartel in a new shape, block the entry to the market, and impair technological competition in the production of optical fibers. The Federal Cartel Office, in this case of a joint venture comprising both cooperative and concentrative elements, found the anticompetitive effects to outweigh advantages to the public.

In EC competition policy a joint venture qualifies as a pure merger and is thus subject to merger control if it gives rise to a viable enterprise with all essential enterprise functions, and if it renders market-related services rather than only acting exclusively or predominantly for the parent companies. The revised merger control regulation of 1998 introduced the notion of full function cooperative joint ventures. It includes those joint ventures where more than one of the parent companies remains in a market which is that of the joint venture or neighboring that of the joint venture, irrespective of whether downstream or upstream markets are concerned (Denness 1998, p. 30). By contrast, a joint venture is treated as a purely cooperative organization if it serves to align the conduct of the parent companies.

For two reasons, in EC competition policy joint ventures have increasingly been treated as mergers. First, it is in the interest of firms since in merger control swift decisions can be expected and, given the present practice of EC merger control, a favorable decision is assumed to be likely. By contrast, in the case of cooperative joint ventures procedures according to Article 81 EC Treaty may be drawn out with uncertain outcomes. In particular the introduction of the notion of full-function cooperative joint ventures has led to a considerable simplification of the procedure because they are treated as mergers. However, if the parent companies use the joint venture as a vehicle of mutual coordination it is examined according to Article 81 EC Treaty (EC Commission 1998, p. 14).

Cooperation in R&D

An important role has been assigned to cooperation in R&D because technical progress and economic growth is expected to be enhanced. Two arguments stand out.

First, it is argued that joint R&D avoids a duplication of projects. The result is thus claimed to be achievable with less effort. The validity of this argument, however, is questionable. The success of research is subject to substantially higher uncertainty than most ordinary investments. R&D projects are to be considered as experiments with random outcome. The likelihood for at least one success among a number of simultaneously and independently conducted experiments increases with the number of experiments undertaken. For the entire economy the likelihood of success, following R&D conducted competitively, therefore exceeds the probability of success if all resources were to be invested in a single project.

The second argument in favor of cooperative R&D holds that by cooperation positive externalities arising from research can be internalized. Hence
incentives for research are greater, and R&D expenditures are increased
(D'Aspremont and Jacquemin 1988, Jacquemin 1988). This aspect certainly
carries some weight. It must not be exaggerated, however. Provided the invention arising from R&D is patented the crucial information regarding the
invention is publicly available. For quite a few inventions, particularly those
arising in small and medium-sized firms, patents are not applied for given the
costs of patenting, the time consumed, a preference for secrecy or little confi-
dence regarding protection provided by a patent (Simon 1996, p. 106). Where
a patent would not be applied for the associated knowledge it cannot be expected to be revealed to competitors in cooperative R&D.

For competition policy joint ventures in R&D are problematic if they extend to the marketing of results. Accordingly, in the EC White Paper on the
Internal Market (EC 1985) R&D cooperations are deemed innocuous if they
are confined to the pre-competitive stage and thus do not extend to marketing. Drawing the dividing line between legal and illegal cooperation in this
way is unrealistic, however. Firms can hardly be expected to cooperate in
R&D without taking account of their prospective competitive relationship
(Wissenschaftlicher Beirat beim BMWi 1987, p. 1345). This has emphati-
cally been underscored by Jorde and Teece (1990). They pointed out that
R&D and marketing, rather than being sequentially related, occur simultaneously in an interactive process. However, this observation alone does not
justify their proposition that cooperative R&D should be more leniently
treated in competition policy. Their characterization of R&D as a serial process applies primarily to the relationship between manufacturing enterprises
and their suppliers rather than to cooperation between competitors. Their
additional argument that R&D cooperation would not be conducive to restraints of competition in technologically fast moving industries does not
hold water either. Technical change is not an exogenous process. It is decisively influenced by competition. Therefore the dividing line between harmful and harmless cooperation in R&D must be, and in fact has been, drawn
differently.

In competition policy cooperative R&D is deemed potentially harmful if
participating firms are holding a dominant position. This applies both to the
US and the EC. In the US a simplified notification procedure has been introduced by the National Cooperative Research Act (NCRA) to subject cooperative R&D to a rule of reason. Moreover, if, following private litigation, the
respective court finds an illegal restraint of trade only simple rather than
treble damages are due. In the past cooperative R&D extending to marketing
has only been attacked by US antitrust authorities if horizontal concentration
was high (Brodley 1990, p. 101). A similar stance has been adopted by the

EC Commission. By block exemption issued in 1984 R&D cooperation among non-competing firms is always permitted. As far as competitors are concerned the exemption applies for firms with a market share falling short of 20 per cent, or 10 per cent respectively, if cooperation pertains to marketing as well. In practice, cooperative R&D has been leniently treated by the EC Commission even if big firms were participating. According to German law (§ 5 KartellG), rationalization cartels must be notified to the Federal Cartel Office and may be permitted if the outcome of rationalization outweighs the restraint of competition involved unless a dominant position is likely to emerge.

Vertical Mergers

The vertical extent of a firm depends on whether it pays to integrate upstream or downstream or whether it is more profitable to rely on market transactions. This principle, as propounded by Coase (1937), explains the vertical scope of an enterprise primarily by the assumption that transactions costs within the firm are weighed against transactions costs entailed by relying on the market. Costs associated with market transactions, the avoidance of which may cause vertical integration of upstream and downstream operations, may arise for technological reasons, they may also be caused by uncertainty and risks involved by market transactions, or they may be engendered by the exercise of monopolistic power of buyers or sellers. Vertical integration is advantageous to both participating firms and consumers (see pp. 141ff.) unless barriers to entry are set up, which are conducive to a dominant position to emerge.

An entry barrier may be caused by capital requirements. Frequently an innovation which would justify entry at a particular stage of production will not lead to an entry because the newly created enterprise which is not vertically integrated must buy from, or sell to, vertically integrated competitors. They may charge prices in such a way that an entry is not profitable. An example can be found in the Alcoa case in the US. Alcoa produced and sold an alloy called duralumin. Competitors willing to produce this alloy had to buy raw aluminum from Alcoa. As reported by Kintner (1980b, p. 401), 'Alcoa set the price of the ingot just below the price at which it would sell its own duralumin thereby putting a price "squeeze" on all competitors in the duralumin market'. It is therefore doubtful whether a firm operating at a single stage can be expected to wind up sufficiently profitable for being able to attract capital. Capitalists will moreover doubt whether somebody with proven expertise at just a single stage will be able to run a full line of a vertically integrated enterprise.

Entry may also be hindered by foreclosure practices exercised by incumbents. Foreclosure means that an incumbent, by upstream and downstream activities, reduces the scope of transactions which can be conducted profitably on an open market. In the case of limited resources of raw materials backward integration to control an essential resource may obstruct or even completely block access to the resource for newcomers. Since the incumbent monopolizes access to the resource, the price of the resource is raised, rendering entry at the downstream stage unprofitable.[19] How foreclosure by upstream integration and the following 'raising of rivals' costs' (Salop and Scheffman 1983) affects market shares, output and price of the final product depends on the circumstances of the particular case.[20] In the case of Cournot competition, if marginal costs at the manufacturing stage for non-integrated firms rise, the market share and profitability of integrated firms increase and total output in manufacturing is reduced whilst the price rises such that economic welfare declines in consequence of vertical integration.[21] This effect may be offset by an increase in welfare if vertical integration causes marginal costs of the integrated enterprise to decrease.

A barrier to entry may also arise by downstream integration if the integrated firm brings a large share of the market under its control such that no room is left for a competitor who has to incur fixed costs to set up a viable enterprise.[22]

3.3   ABUSE OF MONOPOLISTIC MARKET POWER

Two cases of abusing monopolistic market power are to be distinguished, namely the exploitation of buyers or sellers and interference with the freedom of competitors. According to German law exploitation is assumed to exist if a dominant firm or a cartel charges prices in excess of those which under effective competition are likely to obtain (§ 19, 4 No. 2 KartellG). Interference

---

[19] An example can be found in the history of the German iron and steel industry. When, following the German–French war of 1870–71, Lorraine came to the German empire leading firms of the German iron and steel industry acquired control over the iron ores of the region (Neumann 1966). Another example is the acquisition of iron ores at Lake Superior by US Steel shortly after its foundation in 1901 (Parsons and Ray 1975, Riordan 1998, p. 1234).

[20] See Salinger (1988), Ordover, Saloner and Salop (1990), Hart and Tirole (1990), Riordan and Salop (1994), Riordan (1998). These contributions refute criticisms previously advanced by Bork (1978, pp. 222–45), Posner (1976, pp. 171–84), Posner and Easterbrook (1981, pp. 869–76).

[21] According to the Cournot model of Chapter 2 one finds that

$$\partial q_1/\partial c_2 = 1/3b, \quad \partial q_2/\partial c_2 = -2/3b, \quad \partial Q/\partial c_2 = -1/3b$$
$$\text{and} \qquad \partial \Pi_1/\partial c_2 = q_1/3 \quad \text{and} \quad \partial \Pi_2/\partial c_2 = -2q_2/3.$$

[22] According to a study by Areeda and Turner (1980), the foreclosure doctrine applied to a great many cases in the US where horizontal concentration was high and foreclosing was not negligible.

with the freedom of competitors, as defined in § 19, 4 KartellG, occurs if a dominant firm or a cartel prejudices the opportunities of competitors substantially and without sufficient justification. This applies in particular if a dominant position is abused by hindering new competitors from entering the market or impeding their chances otherwise, in short, in a case of 'monopolizing conduct' in the meaning of the Sherman Act. In the EC, in addition to the cases mentioned, an abuse is also deemed to exist if conduct is conducive to obstructing trade between the Member States (Article 82 EC Treaty).

Monopolistic Exploitation

Abusive exploitation is a dubious notion, and it is not least for this reason that abuse control exercised with respect to dominant firms and cartels has turned out as a failure. The logical problems become evident by recalling the above mentioned reference to the German law (§ 19, 4, No. 2 KartellG). A dominant firm in a market economy tries to maximize the shareholder value and, following this principle, charge prices in excess of marginal costs. Unless the managers of the firm disregard the interests of the owners of the enterprise, for a dominant firm the price will exceed the price to be expected under perfect, and for that matter effective, competition. Reference to effective competition must be equivalent to refer to a situation without market dominance held by any firm. This is either a fictitious market or a market in another country. In both cases obviously effective competition is assumed to be viable for the given product. Hence the emergence of a dominant position could have been prevented by an appropriate competition policy. Once market dominance has arisen the leading enterprise will with necessity 'exploit' its customers. That is inevitable if a dominant position has been allowed to emerge. If exploitation is to be avoided the emergence of market dominance must be prevented in its incipiency. If that is not feasible for technological reasons in the case of a so-called natural monopoly, pricing has to be regulated by the government. Natural monopolies, however, are the exception rather than the normal case to arise. Ordinarily, avoidance of monopolistic exploitation by price control exercised by the government is practically infeasible.

This conclusion has clearly been drawn in US antitrust policy. The Supreme Court, 1935 in the above-cited Socony Vacuum case, found price control of a cartel to be alien to a market economy. Much earlier, in 1914, Mr Justice Holmes in the Harvester case declared price control applied to a dominant firm to be a 'problem beyond human ingenuity' and dismissed it by saying (Bork 1965, p. 842),

The reason is not the general uncertainties of a jury trial but that the elements necessary to determine the imaginary ideal are uncertain both in nature and degree of effect to the acutest commercial mind.

Consequently, in the US, price control is exercised only for regulated industries where monopolies are permitted subject to government supervision (see Section 3.4 below).

To my mind, primarily because of the logical problems involved, price control within the framework of the German regulation of cartels of 1923 remained practically ineffective. The same applies to monitoring for exploitative abuse of a dominant position according to the present law against restraints of competition in Germany. In fact, the Federal Cartel Office has practically stopped the prosecution for abusive pricing of dominant firms. During 1973–75 it opened 314 procedures. The number dropped to only 14 for 1986–87, to 7 from 1988–89, and to 14 from 1990–91. Just as in the US, price control is confined to public enterprises and to the sector of regulated industries.[23]

Exclusive Dealing

Exclusive dealing applies if a firm endows a dealer with the exclusive right to sell in a particular region under conditions that he or she refrains from selling competing products. For evaluating exclusive dealing arrangements from the viewpoint of competition policy, two aspects must be kept in mind. First, the vertical extent of an enterprise, that is, the number of successive stages of operations under the roof of a single firm, depends on a cost benefit analysis as suggested by Coase (1937). Given competition, an additional operation is internalized if the marginal costs inside the organization fall short of the marginal transactions costs incurred by relying on the market. Second, as suggested by Alchian and Demsetz (1972), a firm can be visualized as a network of contractual relationships. This implies that a close similarity exists between a vertically integrated enterprise and a succession of various stages of production connected by contracts providing for exclusive dealing. Hence vertical integration and exclusive dealing can be analyzed by adopting the same theoretical framework.

Given this insight, if competition exists, objections can be raised neither

---

[23] The stated reasons for the retreat of the Federal Cartel Office from prosecuting abusive pricing are threefold. First, the preconditions laid down in § 19, 4 KartellG are very demanding. There is only a very small number of dominant firms outside the sector of the economy where entry is subject to government regulation. Second, a reference market where effective competition exists is hard to find. Third, the courts, in cases brought before them upon prosecution by the Federal Cartel Office, required prices to substantially exceed the fictitious prices which were to be expected under effective competition.

against vertical integration nor exclusive dealing. For competition policy concerns arise only in the case of monopolistic market power and where exclusiveness is imposed by dominant firms. That may involve monopolistic exploitation or barriers to entry or both. Barriers to entry may arise if exclusive dealing entails foreclosure effects.

Exclusive dealing may serve to enforce monopolistic price discrimination to improve profitability which entails a welfare loss. That can be shown as follows. Monopolistic price discrimination is feasible only if markets can be separated such that trading between them is prevented. This can be achieved by an arrangement of exclusive dealing by which the dealer must not sell the product outside his protected region. The producer is thus able to have his product sold at different prices in the various regions. It pays for him if the markets differ with respect to the price elasticity of demand. The price is highest in the market where the price elasticity of demand is lowest.

Graphically monopolistic price discrimination is depicted in Figure 3.1. On markets A and B the inverse demand functions $p_A = A - q_A$ and $p_B = B - q_B$ apply, respectively. The slope has been assumed to equal one since the slope is irrelevant for explaining price discrimination. It is, however, assumed that $A > B$. Hence at each price the price elasticity of demand is lower on market A than on market B. Consequently, as demonstrated in Figure 3.1, profit maximization yields outputs q_A^* and q_B^* such that $p_A > p_B$. The resulting

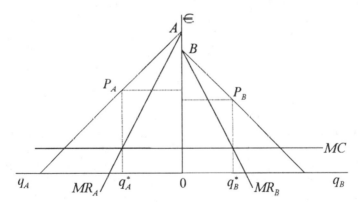

Figure 3.1 Monopolistic price discrimination

profit is higher than the profit which would result from charging the same price in both markets.[24] Since the static welfare loss equals half the monopoly

[24] Total profits are $\sum \Pi = \left[(A - c)^2 + (B - c)^2 \right] / 4$. For a unique price on both markets to derive one has to start from the inverse demand function $p = (A + B - Q)/2$, where $Q = q_A + q_B$, which results from horizontally adding both inverse demand functions. Maximized profits

profit the welfare loss entailed by price discrimination exceeds the loss arising if prices are equal in both markets.

From this point of view exclusive dealing which leads to price discrimination should be prohibited. However, exclusive dealing may also serve as a device to entice the dealer to actively promote sales of the producer by advertising at the point of sales, by displaying the product so that it attracts the attention of shoppers, by permanent availability and sundry services for customers.

Exclusive dealing may also entail a foreclosure of a noncoincident market (Bernheim and Whinston 1998). Assume a manufacturer who agrees to exclusive dealing with a retailer to serve market no. 1. Subsequently a second market comes into existence. In the case of economies to scale the incumbent manufacturer of market no. 1 can serve the second market at lower average costs than a competitor entering only the second market. He may thus be foreclosed from the second market by virtue of exclusive dealing applying to the first market.

Evaluating exclusive dealing thus requires the careful weighing of pros and cons against each other. An example has been the decision by the Federal Cartel Office to disallow exclusive dealing of VW with authorized service providers on the ground that the exclusive dealing arrangement led to the exclusion of about half of all suppliers of spare parts (Kamecke 1998, p. 154). Although, on appeal, the Federal Court of Justice agreed with this reasoning, the decision of the Federal Cartel Office was repealed. The Court recognized the right of VW to use exclusive dealing in order to secure high quality service, reliability of spare parts, and thus to maintain the image of VW. The Court put more weight on this aspect than on the involved restraint of competition.

In the EC an additional aspect comes into play. Many exclusive dealing contracts within the EC were imposed on dealers to prohibit the re-export of the respective commodity. Hence exclusive dealing re-establishes borderlines which were to be abolished by founding the European common market. Therefore, in the EC exclusive dealing which impedes trade between Member States is illegal. The leading case has been Consten and the German firm Grundig. Consten was appointed exclusive distributor in France of Grundig's radios and televisions. Consten was not allowed to deliver any Grundig products directly or indirectly outside France. In return Grundig had to refrain from selling its products directly or indirectly to anyone in France except Consten. Moreover Grundig imposed on all its other distributors and dealers

---

would amount to $\Pi_0 = \left[(A-c)+(B-c)\right]^2/8$ which clearly fall short of $\Sigma\Pi$ achieved by adopting price discrimination, since $\Sigma\Pi - \Pi_0 = (A-B)^2/8 > 0$ if $A \neq B$.

obligations not to deliver outside their respective territories. By imposing export bans on each dealer Grundig sought to protect Consten absolutely from imports of Grundig products from outside France (that is, 'parallel imports'). Consequently Grundig products obtainable more cheaply elsewhere in the EC could not be sold on the French market. The decision of the EC Commission which disallowed the Grundig system of exclusive dealing was upheld by the European Court of Justice 1966 on the grounds that it 'in its nature' restricts competition. The Court said, that the system 'results in the isolation of the French market and makes it possible to charge for the products in question prices which are sheltered from all effective competition'. Thus the vertical arrangement had the same effect as market sharing arrangements which used to be practiced in the chemical industry (Kamecke 1998, p. 144) and demarcation contracts between public utilities like electricity, gas and water.

The EC Regulation no. 17 of 1962 requests firms to notify all contracts covered by Article 81 EC Treaty to the EC Commission. This applies both to horizontal and vertical agreements, that is, in particular to exclusive dealing. Under certain conditions, specified in Article 81 section 3, the prohibition of restraints of competition may be declared inapplicable. The wording of the law implies a specific decision to be taken by the Commission, by which a restraint of competition which would be illegal according to Article 81 section 1 is exempted from the *per se* verdict.[25] In practice, given an immense number of notifications, the EC Commission has in most cases issued a so-called comfort letter which saves the firms from being prosecuted for a violation of the law, subject to subsequent examination.

Resale Price Maintenance

Vertical restraints are strengthened by resale price maintenance. The manufacturer fixes the retail price and the retailer commits himself to charge the stipulated price. Evaluating this arrangement requires various aspects to be taken into account.

---

[25] Given the workload implied by this procedure the EC Commission, in the White Paper No. 99/027 of April 28, 1999, has proposed to replace the present procedure by interpreting Article 81 section 3 as providing for legal exemptions. Firms should be allowed to decide by themselves whether a contract infringes the law against restraints of competition, subject to being attacked by the EC Commission in serious cases, by national authorities or by private parties. As forcefully argued by Mestmäcker (1999) and Möschel (2000) adopting the proposal of the Commission would in practice amount to abandoning the *per se* verdict against cartels, because the conditions under which an exemption can be granted according to Article 81 section 3 are extremely vague such that in particular private parties will hardly be able to succeed in court procedures.

The manufacturer expects retailers to provide services and to promote sales of the respective product and offers an adequate margin in return. A retailer would be left uncompensated if the customer left the shop after having been advised regarding the characteristics of the product and turned to another retailer who, without providing the services, sells at a lower price. Given this risk, retailers will not be ready to offer services, in particular to hold adequate inventories to guarantee availability, which the manufacturer expects to be provided (Marvel 1994). On the other hand, the manufacturer's advertising benefits retailers, too. Resale price maintenance thus involves an exchange of mutual advantages.

An alternative interpretation suggests that retailers are interested in collusion, the enforcement of which is shifted to the manufacturer who obligates the retailers to maintain a certain price (Yamey 1954). Thus a situation arises where monopoly power can be exercised at successive stages of production. To evaluate whether it favors or disfavors consumers one may consider a model of successive monopolies, the result of which carries over to the case of successive oligopolies (Greenhut and Ohta 1979) but need not be considered here in particular.

The model is illustrated in Figure 3.2. Assume two successive stages of production with constant marginal costs c_M and c_R, respectively, and a linear demand curve DD'. As a matter of simplification assume that the output at both stages can be measured in a single unit. Output can then be shown on the horizontal axis by q. Prior to vertical integration, at each stage of production, the monopoly price obtains which follows from equalizing marginal costs and marginal revenue. The demand curve at the first, that is,

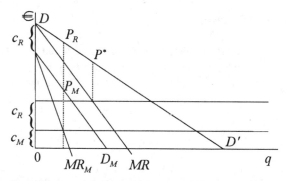

Figure 3.2 A model of successive monopolies

the upstream, stage results from vertically deducting marginal costs c_R from marginal revenue MR associated with final, that is, downstream, demand. Equalizing marginal revenue MR_M, associated with the derived demand curve D_M, with marginal costs c_M, yields the monopoly price P_M. Adding the marginal costs of the retail stage gives the total incremental costs of retailing, that is, purchase price plus c_R. Equalizing it with marginal revenue yields the final price P_R. By contrast, after vertical integration, the merged enterprise, which now covers both manufacturing and retailing, would charge a price P^* which results from equalizing total marginal costs $c_M + c_R$ with marginal revenue MR. Obviously, following vertical integration the price consumers have to pay is lower and final output is higher.[26]

If the same outcome shall be achieved by contractual arrangements which involve both exclusive dealing and resale price maintenance the participants must agree on the distribution of the joint profit. Usually considerations of fairness are invoked to fix margins for the manufacturer and retailers which are commensurate with their respective performance.

Now compare the equilibrium following from vertical integration of successive monopolies with an equilibrium which would result if a monopoly exists only at the manufacturing stage whilst retailers are subject to perfect competition. In this case the final price equals the purchase price of retailers plus their marginal costs. The derived demand curve faced by the manufacturer is $p = a - c_R - bq$. Maximizing profits then yields an output $q = [a - (c_M + c_R)]/2b$ which exactly equals the one to be expected in the case of vertical integration. The monopoly profit, however, accrues entirely to the manufacturer whilst in the case of vertical integration it must be shared between manufacturer and retailers.

This reasoning leads to the conclusion that the manufacturer cannot be interested in selling to cartelized retailers. The manufacturer would be ill-advised to enter an arrangement which would create monopolistic market power for retailers. Thus interpreting resale price maintenance as a device to stabilize collusion among retailers, as suggested by Yamey, is hardly convincing, unless collusion is required to entice retailers to increase promotional efforts. This, however, can also be done without collusion. Resale price maintenance and exclusive dealing is thus more likely to be adopted for promotional reasons. The additional expenses of retailers are likely to increase

---

[26] The integrated firm starts from the inverse demand function $p = a - bq$ and maximizes profits $\Pi = pq - (c_M + c_R)q - F$ where $F = F_M + F_R$ are fixed costs. This yields the output $q = [a - (c_M + c_R)]/2b$. Prior to vertical integration profits at the final stage are $\Pi_R = (.a - bq)q - (c_R + p_M)q - F_R$. Maximizing with respect to output q yields $p_M = a - c_R - 2bq$. Hence profits of manufacturing are $\Pi_M = (a - c_R - 2bq)q - c_M q - F_M$. Again, maximizing with respect to q leads up to $q = (a - c_R - c_M)/4b$. Total profits arising at both separately run stages are $\Pi_R^* + \Pi_M^* = (a - c_R - c_M)^2/8b - F$, whereas following vertical integration final output is $q = (a - c_R - c_M)/2b$ and maximized profits amount to $\Pi^* = (a - c_R - c_M)^2/4b - F$.

sales and can thus be expected to yield higher profits. This interpretation is supported by empirical evidence uncovered by Ippolito and Overstreet (1996). According to their finding, the sales of the US firm Corning Glass Works declined following the prohibition of resale price maintenance.

Although the depicted arrangement may be conducive to favoring consumers it cannot unequivocally be recommended. Services provided by retailers are certainly welcomed by some consumers, particularly in the case of technologically sophisticated commodities. For other products, however, no special service is actually required. That applies in particular to branded goods which are heavily advertised by manufacturers. Quite a few consumers do not demand services and prefer to buy products at low prices. Generally, imposed resale price maintenance thus fails to cope with the wishes of consumers and hinders retailers from satisfying differential demands. This applies in particular to resale price maintenance enforced by a dominant firm. In addition the frequently adopted practice of selling branded products with resale price maintenance and simultaneously offering no-name, but physically identical, products at lower prices, may be deemed to constitute fraud.

In the US resale price maintenance was declared illegal in 1911 by the Supreme Court in the case of Dr Miles Medical Company v. John D. Park and Sons Company. The decision relied on the argument that a sale implies the property right in the commodity to pass entirely to the buyer. 'Where commodities have passed into channels of trade and have been sold by complainant to dealers at prices satisfactory to complainant, the public is entitled to whatever advantage may be derived from competition in the subsequent traffic' (Neale 1966, p. 341). A reversal of policy occurred when, to support small business, 1937 the Miller–Tydings Act and 1952 the McGuire Act (Fair Trade Act) legalized resale price maintenance in most States of the US. A first restriction occurred when in 1973, in the case of the Corning Glass Works, the prohibition of resale price maintenance by the Federal Trade Commission was upheld by the court. In 1975 the fair trade legislation (Miller–Tydings Act and McGuire Act) was repealed by Congress. The history of resale price maintenance in the US reveals that from the very beginning it aimed at protecting retailers from allegedly excessive competition. This, of course, is the same reason which has always been advanced in defense of cartels. The theoretical analysis above, however, suggests that resale price maintenance may actually fail to accomplish this aim and rather tends to favor monopolistic market power in manufacturing.

In Germany resale price maintenance until 1973 could legally be practiced by producers who are subject to competition. Since 1973 resale price maintenance is illegal except for the sale of books and pharmaceutical products which are subject to government price regulation. In the legal history pertaining to resale price maintenance the eventual prohibition has been justified as follows. Large retailers, given their buying power, used to disregard resale price maintenance and undersold small retailers who, being virtually power-less *vis-à-vis* manufacturers, had to abide by the contracts. Whilst resale price maintenance could, and has been, enforced on small retailers, most manu-facturers were too weak to enforce resale price maintenance on large retailers. Hence the buying power of large retailers entailed an unfair distortion of competition both at the retail level and in manufacturing. The legal conse-quence has been a general prohibition. However, producers have still been allowed to recommend retail prices which do not bind retailers. These rec-ommendations are subject to be monitored by the Federal Cartel Office. An abuse is deemed to exist if the recommendation is conducive to raise prices, to prevent prices from declining, or if recommendations are not observed and thus entail deceiving consumers.

Tying Contracts

A tying involves two commodities or services to be supplied together. Tying may occur for technological reasons. It may also, in the case of complemen-tarity in demand, be arbitrarily adopted. One of the commodities is sold cheaply to entice demand whilst the other product is sold at a high price. For competition policy tying practices pose a problem only if they are exercised by dominant firms and infringe upon economic freedom of competitors. Ac-tually arbitrary tying is an option available only to dominant firms.

Legally tying is treated differently in the US and the EC. Neither in Ger-many nor in the EC is tying subject to *per se* prohibition. In the US tying, according to court decisions within the scope of the Sherman Act, is illegal *per se* if it applies to different commodities. The problem whether commodi-ties are different came up in the recent Microsoft case regarding the operating system and the internet explorer. Illegality is also predicated on monopolistic market power to exist in the tying product market and on tying to be imposed by coercion. A justification by invoking a *rule of reason* does not exist (Monopolkommission 1992, pp. 462ff). By contrast, in Germany a justifica-tion is possible if cost savings can be proved to be achievable. In Germany tying is illegal if imposed by a dominant firm and if competition is restrained unless cost savings can be shown to outweigh the unfavorable effects of the restraint of competition (Monopolkommission 1992, p. 456).

A typical case in the US was American Can Company which held a market share of 40 per cent in tins and about 50 per cent for closing machines which are an essential equipment of the canning industry. The machines were leased at a rental and they were not to be used 'for any purpose except therewith to close cans which the lessee shall have bought from the lessor'. This tying arrangement was declared illegal by the authorities and later on by court decision (Neale 1966, p. 156). A case from the EC has been Tetra Pak which had developed a very efficient technique for aseptic filling of UHT milk for which it held a market share of some 90 per cent. Dairies would lease the machines but were obligated to buy the cartons from Tetra Pak. Thus competing suppliers of cartons were effectively excluded. The justification offered by Tetra Pak that the process of aseptic filling was highly complex, and that securing quality would require only cartons supplied by Tetra Pak to be used, was dismissed by the EC Commission in a decision later on upheld by the Court of First Instance of the European Court of Justice.

Predatory Pricing

Prices which do not cover costs may be compatible with normal competition. They may, however, also amount to illegal monopolizing. A firm entering a market must ordinarily displace competitors. To be successful the entrant must acquire customers which previously had bought from incumbents. This requires either the prices charged by the entrant to be lower or the quality of his product to appeal to the preferences of consumers better than products they used to buy before. For achieving success it is frequently necessary to incur initial losses by selling at prices which do not cover costs or to expend money for advertising for building up a goodwill. Initial losses may in particular be justified if the entrant can expect costs to decline caused by learning by doing.

Predatory pricing requires, as suggested by Areeda and Turner (1975), that prices fall short of marginal costs. Because of practical difficulties to identify marginal costs it has been suggested that average variable costs should be used as the benchmark instead. As explained by Baumol (1996), the rationale of the Areeda–Turner test is that through predatory pricing conducted by a dominant firm a more efficient competitor should not be eliminated. Hence average 'avoidable costs' should be used as the relevant benchmark. Avoidable costs include, in addition to variable costs, product-specific fixed costs which are not sunk and are thus avoidable if production is stopped.[27]

For monopolizing by predation to be successful it is necessary that entry of new competitors or re-entry of displaced incumbents must be forestalled. Only in this case can initially incurred losses be recouped once incumbency has been achieved. Accordingly, in the US the Supreme Court has clarified in the case Brooke Group v. Brown Williamson Tobacco Corporation that the requirement for illegal predation to be assumed is twofold. First, the price

---

[27] Baumol correctly points out that total average costs are irrelevant for identifying predation since for a multiproduct firm, because of overhead costs, total average costs of a particular product cannot be defined.

must not cover costs, and, second, initial losses must be likely to be subsequently compensated by higher prices (Cabral and Riordan 1997, p. 155). Aggressive pricing is to be classified as normal business practice if the firms involved start at a level playing field.

A case of this kind occurred in the US market for TV sets. The Japanese firm Matsushita had been selling TV sets in the US for a considerable time at prices lower than in Japan, and was accused of predatory pricing and dumping. The Supreme Court argued, however, that an intent to monopolize could be presumed only in the case of an intertemporal discrimination such that initial losses are going to be recovered by subsequent profits. As Matsushita had been selling at low prices in the US for more than two decades without succeeding in displacing US firms, the majority of the Court dismissed the accusation of predatory intent (Utton 1995, pp. 112f).

Predatory strategies are of concern for competition policy if practiced by dominant firms or cartels aiming at strengthening their dominant position. The same applies if monopoly profits are used for financing predatory activities on neighboring markets. In Germany firms with superior market power *vis-à-vis* small and medium-sized competitors must not infringe upon competitors in an unfair manner (§ 20, 4 KartellG). As an example the law defines unfair infringement as a case where a firm occasionally sells below its purchase price, unless it can be justified. The burden of proof is with the dominant firm. In the EC Tetra Pak, which held a market share of some 90 per cent for aseptic packaging of UHT milk and fruit juice, by resorting to predatory practices tried to encroach on markets for non-aseptic packaging – particularly in Italy – where Tetra Pak held much lower market shares. The EC Commission considered this to constitute an abuse of a dominant position. The crucial point has been that monopoly power in one market was used to attain a dominant position in a neighboring market, too. In the US such conduct qualifies as monopolizing behavior in the meaning of the Sherman Act.

The accusation of having achieved monopoly power by predatory pricing has in particular been leveled against John D. Rockefeller to justify the divestiture of the Standard Oil Trust. Against assuming predation to be of relevance for competition policy, McGee (1958) has argued that predatory pricing is not a rational conduct because it hurts the predator more than the prey. Therefore the threat of predation, according to his view, is not credible.[28] Instead of adopting predation it is preferable to resort to acquiring smaller competitors at a price which partially includes future monopoly profits. How-

---

[28] McGee, moreover, claimed that the files of the court proceedings in the Standard Oil case would contain no proof whatever of intent to monopolize by resorting to predation. However, as shown by Scherer (1980, p. 336), this can very well be proved by using alternative sources.

ever, if McGee were right a great many competitors would come forth to put their firm on sale, moreover, numerous new firms would be founded just to be offered for sale. This would be entirely unattractive for the incumbent. He cannot be interested in paying a price covering future monopoly profits. The price to be paid in the case of acquiring a competitor will be determined by the ability to threaten and, by adopting predation, to enforce a favorable price once the prey is on the verge of bankruptcy. Exactly this has happened both in the Standard Oil case and Tobacco case (Burns 1986) where bogus independent firms were in charge of predatory activities.

In fact, it has not only been in the US that predation occurred. As reported by Kestner and Lehnich (1927, p. 72), quite a few cartels in Germany provided for the systematic underselling of outsiders. In a case ultimately decided by the Imperial Court (Reichsgericht) a cartel of suppliers of gasoline had decided to raise prices. When an independent service station at Benrath, a suburb of Düsseldorf, maintained the previous prices, the cartel ordered all member stations of oil companies to keep gasoline prices lower than those of the outsider. He was thus facing the alternatives either to follow suit or to close down. According to the Court the action undertaken by the dominant cartel aimed exclusively at imposing damage on the competitor and had to be interdicted as being unfair in the meaning of the law against unfair competition (Mestmäcker 1984, pp. 162f).

A spectacular fight of a cartel against an outsider has been reported by Yamey (1972, pp. 138–42). Overseas traffic between China and England used to be regulated since 1879 by a 'conference', that is, a cartel to fix freight rates and market shares. The Mogul Steamship Company had applied to be admitted as a member but had been rebuffed. Then the following happened.

> In 1885 the Conference decided 'that if any non-Conference steamer should proceed to Hankow to load independently the necessary number of Conference steamers should be sent at the same time to Hankow, in order to underbid the freight which the independent ship owners might offer, without any regard to whether the freight they should bid would be remunerative or not'. Three independent ships were sent to Hankow, two of them being Mogul ships; and the agents of the conference lines responded by sending such ships as they thought necessary. Freight rates fell dramatically. ... Apparently in the event the losses of the conference were larger than those of the outsiders, since some conference ships sailed empty from Hankow, while all the outsiders' vessels were able to load up with some cargo and did not have to sail in ballast. ... The fact that shipping companies continued to use fighting ships after the Mogul affair suggests that predatory pricing and the standing threat of such action were considered efficacious.

Although this practice clearly would be deemed illegal today the Court of Appeal and the House of Lords (Mogul Steamship Co. v. McGregor & Co.

1888) decided otherwise. Since a cartel of shippers was not illegal according the English law of the time 'The object was a lawful one. It is not illegal for a trader to aim at driving a competitor out of trade, provided the motive be his own gain by appropriation of the trade and the means he used be lawful weapons' (Kintner 1980a, S. 123).

The ability to adopt predation to gain a dominant position depends on the availability of financial means. They may be provided by monopoly profits in another industry. A case in point has been the Standard Oil Trust founded by John D. Rockefeller. Entry into the market of oil refinery, where Standard Oil eventually came to hold a monopoly, was relatively easy during the last third of the 19th century. In 1880 a refinery of considerable size could be established by spending less than $50,000 (Scherer 1980, p. 336). In fact, around 1870 there were hundreds of small refineries. The market share of Rockefeller's firm in Cleveland, Ohio, was only 4 per cent. It therefore seems difficult to understand how under these conditions a virtual monopoly with a market share of more than 90 per cent could possibly be achieved. The explanation advanced by Granitz and Klein (1996) is that the refining monopoly was stabilized by a railroad cartel. Refineries of that time had to rely on railroad transportation. Control of railroading thus could be used as a lever to acquire control of refineries.[29] Around 1870 there were three railroad companies transporting petroleum. Standard Oil stabilized the cartel by assisting in maintaining given market shares, and the cartel supported Rockefeller by charging unfavorable rates to his competitors in refinery. The control over transporting oil was later on supplemented by setting up a network of pipelines. Whilst entry into refinery remained relatively easy, transportation of petroleum was subject to entry barriers caused by indivisibilities. This example shows how vertical relationships may favor the emergence of horizontal concentration and monopolistic market power.

All these examples demonstrate that predation should be of concern to competition policy. Even if, as asserted by McGee, predation were not rational, its very occurrence causes concern because of its damaging effects. Even an insane person should be stopped from inflicting harm on other people. Actually, however, the rationality of a strategy such as the one adopted

---

[29] Later on John D. Rockefeller told the US steel industry a lesson regarding the crucial role of transportation. After the discovery of rich iron ore at Lake Superior in the Mesabi range Rockefeller was astonished that the steel industry did nothing to secure transportation. So Rockefeller himself had a fleet built to transport iron ores into Ohio and Pennsylvania. When Carnegie, as major shareholder of Carnegie Steelworks, the core of what later became the US Steel Corporation, demanded a drastic reduction of freight rates, Rockefeller stopped the fleet completely and Carnegie ran out of supplies. Rockefeller thus had demonstrated where the center of power was located. Eventually, by the intermediation of J.P. Morgan, the fleet was sold to US Steel (Ellis 1974, pp. 208ff).

by Rockefeller to build his empire has been convincingly shown by Granitz and Klein (1996). Moreover, by using game theoretic models it is possible to identify constellations where under incomplete information predation is a rational conduct (Ordover and Saloner 1989).[30] On the other hand, selling below marginal costs does not, in itself, constitute sufficient proof of predation. A proof of predatory conduct requires intent to monopolize to be shown to exist. Selling below marginal costs may follow from ordinary business behavior of multiproduct firms. Two cases stand out in particular, complementarity in demand and pricing under uncertainty, given imperfections of the capital market.

Loss-Leader Strategy by Multiproduct Firms

To analyze the consequences of complementarity in demand for multiproduct firms assume

$$Q_1 = \alpha_1 - p_1 + \gamma p_2$$

$$Q_2 = \alpha_2 - p_2 + \gamma p_1.$$

Assume $\alpha_1 > \alpha_2$, which implies that at any given price the direct price elasticity of demand for good 1 is smaller than for good 2. In this sense demand for good 1 is more urgent than for good 2. The goods are substitutes if $\gamma > 0$, that is, if raising the price of commodity j gives rise to an increase in demand for commodity i. The goods are complements if $\gamma < 0$, such that a higher price of good j reduces the demand for both commodities. Furthermore, γ must fall short of unity in absolute terms. Hence the direct price effects are assumed to outweigh the cross effects.[31]

Complementarity may be a characteristic of the commodities involved. Examples are automobiles and spare parts, computer hardware and software, filling machinery for drinks and cartons as in the Tetra Pak case, or closing-machines and tins as in the case of American Can. Complementarity may also be caused by transactions costs. A case in point is retailing where the total assortment of a store may yield complementarity in demand because moving from one store to another one involves costs for consumers. If they find a

---

[30] In the US the Supreme Court in 1993, in the case of Brooke Group Ltd. v. Brown & Williamson Tobacco Corporation sided with McGee by stating that 'discouraging a price cut ... does not constitute sound antitrust policy' and put the threshold for condemning predation at a very high level. In view of the more recent developments in economics this evaluation may, however, be in need of revision (*Business Week*, November 1998, p. 82).

[31] This assumption is also necessary to satisfy second order conditions of profit maximization.

particular commodity cheap they may be induced to buy other commodities also at this store, instead of turning to another one.

In the case of complementarity it may be profitable for a multiproduct firm to sell one commodity, which is weak in demand, at a very low price to entice increased demand for other goods, which are strong in demand. The commodity sold at a low price is called a loss-leader. Losses incurred by the sale of this good by the multiproduct firm can be recouped by a higher price for other goods. If the price for the loss-leader falls short of marginal costs a specialized supplier of this good has no chance to survive in the market. However, as will be shown, an intent to monopolize need not be present. Selling below marginal costs may be a straightforward consequence of profit maximization.

To begin with, consider a multiproduct monopoly selling into two markets. Maximizing profits

$$\Pi = (p_1 - c_1)Q_1 + (p_2 - c_2)Q_2$$

by choosing quantities or prices yields

$$p_1 = \frac{\alpha_1 + \gamma\alpha_2}{2(1-\gamma^2)} + \frac{c_1}{2}$$

$$p_2 = \frac{\alpha_2 + \gamma\alpha_1}{2(1-\gamma^2)} + \frac{c_2}{2}.$$

As shown in Table 3.4, if for illustrative purposes $\alpha_1 = 10$, $\alpha_2 = 4$,

Table 3.4 *Prices for multiproduct monopoly and oligopoly, and duopoly in market 1 ($\alpha_1 = 10$, $\alpha_2 = 4$, $c_1 = c_2 = 2$)*

Price	Monopoly		Oligopoly				Duopoly in market 1 and monopoly in market 2
			$n = 2$		$n - 20$		
γ	1/4	−1/4	1/4	−1/4	1/4	−1/4	−1/4
p_1	6.86	5.80	5.24	4.53	2.46	2.36	4.53
p_2	4.47	1.80	3.64	1.86	2.23	1.98	2.11

$c_1 = c_2 = 2$, and $\gamma = 1/4$ or $\gamma = -1/4$, respectively, in the case of complementarity, the price of commodity 2, $p_2 = 1.80$, falls short of marginal costs.

This result carries over to oligopoly where each commodity is supplied by n firms. Equilibrium prices can be shown to be[32]

$$p_i = \frac{\alpha_i + \gamma \alpha_j}{(n+1)(1-\gamma^2)} + \frac{n}{n+1} c_i, \qquad i,j = 1,2.$$

---

[32] Let demand for two commodities be depicted by

$$Q_1 = \alpha_1 - p_1 + \gamma p_2, \quad Q_1 = q_{11} + q_{12}$$
$$Q_2 = \alpha_2 - p_2 + \gamma p_1, \quad Q_2 = q_{21} + q_{22}$$

and assume for two firms ($k = 1,2$) marginal costs, $c_{ik} = c_i$, to be equal for the respective good i. This assumption is justified in the present context since we are interested to figure out which consequences are following from differences in demand. On each market Cournot competition prevails. The demand functions can be transformed into inverse demand functions

$$p_1 = \frac{\alpha_1 + \gamma \alpha_2}{1-\gamma^2} - \frac{1}{1-\gamma^2} Q_1 - \frac{\gamma}{1-\gamma^2} Q_2 =: A_1 - BQ_1 - CQ_2$$

$$p_2 = \frac{\alpha_2 + \gamma \alpha_1}{1-\gamma^2} - \frac{1}{1-\gamma^2} Q_2 - \frac{\gamma}{1-\gamma^2} Q_1 =: A_2 - BQ_2 - CQ_1.$$

Profits of firm k are

$$\Pi_k = (p_1 - c_1)q_{1k} + (p_2 - c_2)q_{2k}, \quad k = 1,2$$

Maximizing with respect to q_{1k} and q_{2k} yields a system of four equations

$$\begin{pmatrix} -2B & -B & -2C & -C \\ -2C & -C & -2B & -B \\ -B & -2B & -C & -2C \\ -C & -2C & -B & -2B \end{pmatrix} \begin{pmatrix} q_{11} \\ q_{12} \\ q_{21} \\ q_{22} \end{pmatrix} = \begin{pmatrix} -(A_1 - c_1) \\ -(A_2 - c_2) \\ -(A_1 - c_1) \\ -(A_2 - c_2) \end{pmatrix},$$

which, by somewhat tedious calculations, can be solved for the respective quantities. Then replace the coefficients A_1, A_2, B and C by the original coefficients of the inverse demand functions and add up the quantities to obtain $Q_1 = (2/3)(\alpha_1 - c_1 + \gamma c_2)$ and $Q_2 = (2/3)(\alpha_2 - c_2 + \gamma c_1)$. Inserting into the demand functions yields a system of two equations with solutions

$$p_i = \frac{\alpha_i + \gamma \alpha_j}{3(1-\gamma^2)} + \frac{2}{3} c_i, \qquad i,j = 1,2.$$

Generalization gives rise to the formula given in the text. It may be noted that a loss-leader strategy for commodity 2 to be feasible requires the demand for this good to be relatively weak. If, by contrast, $\alpha_1 = \alpha_2 = \alpha$ the price for either good is $p_i = \lfloor nc_i + \alpha(1-\gamma) \rfloor/(n+1)$ and hence exceeds marginal costs, irrespective of whether the goods are substitutes or complements.

As demonstrated in Table 3.4, irrespective of whether the products are substitutes or complements, as the number of competitors goes to infinity the price approaches marginal costs.

For a finite number of firms, in the case of substitutes, both prices exceed marginal costs. Comparing the case of multiproduct firms with the case of specialized firms suggests that prices are higher in the former case. The reason is that for a buyer facing only a multiproduct supplier instead of two independent producers the number of alternatives is reduced. Hence, the price elasticity of demand as perceived by a multiproduct firm is lower than for specialized suppliers and hence monopolistic market power is higher.

In the case of complements the price for the commodity which is relatively weak in demand may fall short of marginal costs and may thus be used as a loss-leader to stimulate demand for the other commodity which is stronger in demand. The shortfall of the price charged for the loss-leader from marginal costs declines with an increasing number of competitors. However, an intent to monopolize need not be present.

Still, complementarity in demand and the ensuing price policy of multiproduct firms may have ramifications which must be of concern for competition policy. To see why, look once more at the case of a multiproduct monopoly Obviously since the price of commodity 2 falls short of marginal costs a firm specializing in producing this commodity has no chance to survive. However, once a competitor specializing in commodity 1 enters the market, in the ensuing duopoly, the price of commodity 1 is driven down and profits of the incumbent decline. Consequently, even the loss-leader strategy may be undermined.

To illustrate the outcome assume a multiproduct incumbent facing Cournot competition by an entrant in market 1. For the case of complementarity in demand the last column of Table 3.4 shows that the price of commodity 1 is substantially reduced and a loss-leader strategy for commodity 2 does not pay any more. Given $\gamma = -1/4$ the price of commodity 2 now exceeds marginal costs and may attract entry of new competitors. However, if ceteris paribus γ were absolutely larger than 0.28 the price of commodity 2 would still fall short of marginal costs.

To entrench its own position the multiproduct monopoly will seek to ward off the entry of a specialized competitor. The multiproduct monopolist may acquire patent protection for producing commodity 2, such as, for example, a filling machine as in the Tetra Pak case or a closing machine as in the case of American Can, which is then sold, or rented, cheaply; and to impose tying on users of product 1, such as, for example, cartons or tins in the aforementioned cases. Product 1 is then protected from competition from outsiders and can be sold at an elevated price. As reported above, tying of this kind has been prohibited both in the US and the EC because it was deemed to constitute mono-

polizing. This, however, must be, and in the said cases has been, proved by
the prosecuting authorities. Beyond this, selling below marginal costs need
not, in itself, be of concern for competition policy. A general prohibition of
selling below marginal costs, as stipulated in the US by the Robinson–Patman Act and in Germany by § 20, section 4 KartellG, cannot be justified but
by reference to objectives of industrial policy, as for example the aim to protect small business.

Imperfections of the Capital Market and the 'Deep Pocket Hypothesis'

Imperfections of the capital market may be conducive to the adoption of
aggressive strategies which lends support to the 'deep pocket hypothesis'
(Tirole 1988, pp. 377ff) which, according to Edwards (1955, pp. 334f),
applies to big conglomerate enterprises.

> An enterprise that is big in this sense obtains from its bigness a special kind of
> power, based upon the fact that it can spend money in large amounts. If such a
> concern finds itself matching expenditures or losses, dollar for dollar, with a sub-
> stantially smaller firm, the length of its purse assures it of victory. ... The large
> company is in a position to hurt without being hurt.

The 'deep pocket hypothesis', with a view especially on the alleged practice
of cross-subsidization of conglomerate firms, became a major point in an
appellate court decision confirming in 1962 the Federal Trade Commission's
order that Reynolds Metals Co., the US leading producer of aluminum foil,
cancel its merger with a small firm specializing in florists' foil. 'The power of
the "deep pocket" ... suppliers in a competitive group where previously no
company was very large and all were relatively small opened the possibility
and power to sell at prices approximating cost or below and thus to undercut
and ravage the less affluent competition.'

This aspect also entered German and EC competition law regarding merger
control by assuming that market dominance may depend on access to financial resources. However, bigness alone and access to finance does not suffice
to render predation a rational strategy. The crucial aspect is diversification.
But even though diversification of a conglomerate firm may be conducive to
predatory pricing not every underselling of competitors by a large enterprise
qualifies as condemnable predation. For a diversified firm it may be quite
rational to sell some product out of its program below marginal costs if the
profits attributable to the product are negatively correlated with the return of
the so-called market portfolio of all investments in the economy (Neumann

1982, pp. 275f).[33]

For a single product firm this option is not available because capital markets are imperfect. If the capital market were perfect the optimal quantity of the commodity i should be independent on whether firm i is owned by various stockholders holding diversified portfolios or whether it is part of a conglomerate firm. In a perfect capital market, investors will be prepared to cover losses entailed by the possession of stock of a firm if holding such stock enables them to reduce the risk of their respective portfolio. Yet there is an important difference between a conglomerate and a single product firm. Capital owners without immediate control of the firm's operations cannot rule out the possibility that negative expected profits are due to bad management. They will therefore ordinarily expect a firm to be run profitably. By contrast, the management of a conglomerate with full control of operations does not suffer from the lack of information indicated. It will therefore be willing to run a subsidiary with negative expected profits if the respective line of business contributes to lowering the portfolio risk.

Besides this, there is another imperfection of the capital market frequently encountered. It rests on the existence of default risk which prevents an investor to borrow unlimited funds at the going rate of interest. For the owner of a small-scale business, it is often impossible to obtain funds exceeding even a rather low limit. There may, however, be economies of scale to be exploited which are residing in the technical skill of the owner. The owner is perfectly confident in his abilities, but he is unable to convince bankers. Since he cannot get the business financed from outside, and at the same time expects to earn profits well in excess of the normal rate of interest, he decides to invest his own capital exclusively in his own business. Such a firm, if its returns happen to be negatively correlated with the performance of the entire economy, is unable to stand the competition of large diversified firms in a line of production which so far has only been run by small owner-operated

---

[33] The present value of a line of business i of a firm under perfect competition, given uncertainty regarding the price, is

$$V_i = \frac{\bar{p}_i q_i - C(q_i) - \lambda_1 \operatorname{cov}(R_i, R_M)/\sigma_M}{r}$$

where $\bar{p}_i$ is the expected price, q_i is output of product i, $\operatorname{cov}(R_i, R_M)$ is the covariance between the return attributable to product i and the return of the market portfolio, σ_M is the standard deviation of the return of the market portfolio, λ_1 is the market price of risk, and r is the interest rate. Expected profits,

$$E(\Pi_i) = \bar{p}_i q_i - C(q_i) - rV_i = \lambda_1 \operatorname{cov}(R_i, R_M)/\sigma_M$$

are thus positive or negative, if the covariance is positive or negative, respectively.

firms and that is now invaded by conglomerates. The owners of small firms of the kind described will, of course, find the behavior of the large firms predatory. Actually, however, the emergence of multiproduct firms only removes an imperfection of the capital market.

Buying Power

Buying power poses a problem for competition policy equivalent to selling power. This applies not only in the case of monopsony but also for an oligopsony, that is, a small number of buyers facing a large number of competing sellers. Such a constellation frequently occurs between a large manufacturer or a big retailer and small suppliers. For analyzing this situation assume a linear inverse demand function

$$p = a - bQ$$

for the final product and a linear supply curve

$$w = A + BQ$$

where $Q := \sum_{i=1}^{n} q_i$ is the aggregate supply of n producers. To simplify, without loss of generality, assume one unit of input to be required for one unit of output, and let marginal costs at the final stage be zero. Given a single buyer who, at the same time, holds a monopoly, at the final stage the equilibrium is depicted in Figure 3.3. DD' is the demand curve for the input[34] and MR

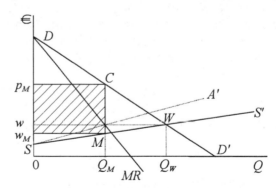

Figure 3.3   Monopoly and monopsony combined

---

[34] If marginal costs at the final stage were positive the DD'-curve would be shifted downwards by the amount of marginal costs.

depicts the associated marginal revenue. Profit maximization yields an output (and input) of Q_M where the final price charged to consumers is p_M and the input is bought at a price w_M, as determined by the intersection of the marginal revenue curve MR and the marginal expenditure curve SA'. That gives rise to profits following both from monopoly and monopsony power, the size of which is shown by the rectangle $p_M CM w_M$. By contrast, if perfect competition would prevail throughout, the equilibrium would be given by the intersection of the supply curve SS' with the demand curve DD'. The final price would be $p = w + c$ (where $c = 0$ has been assumed above). As caused by monopoly and monopsony, a welfare loss arises depicted by the triangle CMW which is composed of lost consumers' and producers' surplus.

For an oligopsony, at an equilibrium, the output is somewhat larger than Q_M but smaller than Q_W. The final price is lower and the purchase price is higher than in the case of monopsony. Correspondingly, both profits and the welfare loss are lower. The solution can be found as follows.

Profits of an oligopolist are

$$\Pi_i = (a - bQ)q_i - (A + BQ)q_i - cq_i.$$

Maximizing profits by choosing an appropriate level of output/and input) q_i yields a Cournot equilibrium where

$$q = \frac{a - c - A}{(n+1)(b+B)}, \qquad Q = \frac{n}{n+1} \frac{a-c-A}{b+B}$$

if all buyers are equal. Regarding the influence of the number of suppliers and marginal costs the following conclusions can be drawn.

- As $\partial Q / \partial n = (a - c - A)/(b+B)(n+1)^2 > 0$, the output Q is lower the smaller the number of buyers. Increasing concentration among buyers thus yields a lower purchase price w and a higher final price p.

- A reduction of marginal costs, c, yields a larger output (and input) Q and hence a lower final price and higher purchase price.

An increase in horizontal concentration at the final stage might yield a reduction of marginal costs. Hence counteracting effects arise. Whilst increased concentration at the final stage exerts a depressing effect on the purchase price, reduced marginal costs allow it to rise. Anyway, increased concentration at the final stage, ceteris paribus, is conducive to depress purchase prices. This implication of the theoretical model has been tested and confirmed by Lustgarten (1975) for the US and by Waterson (1980) for the UK.[35]

Collusion among buyers is conducive to an outcome following from monopsony. Exercising buying power is therefore subject to the *per se* ban regarding cartels. In the US the leading case has been Mandeville Island Farmers v. American Crystal Sugar Co. (Blair and Harrison 1993, p. 69) decided in 1948 by the Supreme Court. Sugar refineries in Northern California had agreed on prices for buying sugar beet which were lower than prices which could have been expected in the absence of the agreement. The Supreme Court held this agreement to be an illegal cartel. However, not all purchasing cooperations are considered to be illegal in the US. By having recourse to the doctrine of an ancillary restraint, as alluded to but not used in the Addyston Pipe case (Blair and Harrison 1993, pp. 100f), cooperative purchasing is legal if cost savings are sought to be achieved and the price agreement is indispensable for success.

The same principle applies in German cartel law. The leading case has been 'Selex-Tania' (WuW 10/86 OLG 3737ff), as decided in 1986 by the Kammergericht on appeal against a decision of the Federal Cartel Office. The Selex-Tania group was a cooperative enterprise run by about 100 retailers. Its objective was joint buying and the execution of deliveries and payments. Most participants were small and medium-sized firms. The clout of the group was, however, determined by eleven large members with a turnover around or even exceeding a billion DM, accounting for more than 50 per cent of all purchases of the group. Although members were not obliged to avail themselves of the services of the cooperation, the Court assumed that the common objective to achieve gains by joint buying excludes the freedom to compete independently and thus violates the ban against cartels. The crucial fact which rendered Selex-Tania illegal was the participation of large firms. By contrast, cooperative purchasing by small firms can be exempted from the ban against cartels if competition is not substantially lessened (§ 4 KartellG). The doctrine of ancillary restraint in US antitrust law corresponds to § 5, 2 KartellG in Germany where joint purchasing agreements may include agreements regarding pricing if this is indispensable for achieving the objective of the cooperation. The same principle applies to recently proposed rules applying for purchasing cooperation in the EC.

Increased concentration in retailing and the formation of joint purchasing cooperations has led to tough price competition among suppliers. That has given rise to the complaint that big retailers, by price discrimination and

---

[35] Lustgarten's findings have been questioned by Guth, Schwartz and Whitcomb (1976) for methodological reasons. The findings of Waterson for the UK do, however, support the validity of Lustgarten's results even if additional studies mentioned by Schmalensee (1989, p. 977) raise doubts regarding their robustness.

predation, displace even mid-sized competitors and would exploit suppliers, in particular smaller ones. Arguments of this kind had in the US led to the Robinson–Patman Act in 1936 and the prohibition of price discrimination.[36] For the same reasons the most recent legislation in Germany provided for a prohibition of selling below purchase prices.

At first sight it appears questionable whether developments regarding the relationship between manufacturing and retailing can be exclusively interpreted as following from increased monopsonistic market power. Exercise of buying power implies that the purchaser, by restricting demand, forces the supply price down along an upward sloping supply curve, which entails, as shown above, a decrease in supply and consequently also a decrease in sales of the final output. This outcome, however, is apparently contrary to what can be observed. Actually large retailers are granted lower prices for increasing sales. This observation need not contradict the implications of the theoretical model advanced above, provided that marginal costs decline, as caused by technical progress, and final demand grows. However, an alternative model may yield additional insights.

Since differential products are supplied both in manufacturing and retailing, monopolistic competition in the sense of Chamberlin can be assumed to prevail. One may then invoke the model of successive oligopolies. From the manufacturer to the final consumer double marginalization occurs. Following a vertical integration between manufacturing and retailing double marginalization would be avoided, the final price would be lower, demand would increase and the joint profit would exceed the sum of profits attainable previously by manufacturing and retailing. This result would also be attainable by entering a vertical contract and adopting a common strategy. However, it leaves the manufacturer vulnerable once he has committed himself to irreversible, that is, sunk, investments. Following a decline in demand the retailer may behave opportunistically and claim a larger share of profits by reference to alternative sources of supply. The danger of being exploited by opportunism can be avoided by the manufacturer insofar as he does not commit himself to a single retailer but diversifies his sales. For a small and even for a medium-sized firm this may be difficult since technological indivisibilities require high investments even to serve no more than a single retailer. The same applies to the relationship between a manufacturer, like an automobile company, and its industrial suppliers. Small suppliers may be unable to raise sufficient capital for maintaining several vertical relationships which would enable them to withstand the opportunism of customers. Therefore horizontal concentration on the side of demand can, in the long run, be expected to in-

---

[36] For details see Neale (1966, pp. 463ff.) and Herrmann (1984, pp. 368ff.).

duce an increase in concentration in manufacturing as well.

3.4   REGULATION, DEREGULATION AND PRIVATIZING

Both the US law and German law provides for sectoral exemptions from the *per se* rule against cartels in cases where workable competition is deemed to be unattainable. EC law does not explicitly identify sectoral exemptions but can cope with the problem by granting block exemptions within the framework of Article 81 section 3 EC Treaty. Exemptions in these cases do not rely on applying a *rule of reason* which involves weighing favorable against unfavorable effects, but rather on the presumption that competition is not feasible for technological reasons. Exempted sectors, where thus monopolies are unavoidable, must be regulated by the government to prevent abusive exercise of monopolistic market power.

The government thus assumes authority to interfere with private property insofar as it is justified by the public interest. In the US this principle has been clearly established by the Supreme Court in the landmark case Munn v. Illinois. To justify regulations issued by the State of Illinois in regard to rates set by grain elevators and warehouses the Supreme Court postulated (Viscusi, Vernon and Harrington 1995, p. 311) that

> property does become clothed with public interest when used in a manner to make it of public consequence, and affect the community at large. When, therefore, one devotes his property to a use in which the public has an interest, he, in effect, grants to the public interest in that use, and must submit to be controlled by the public for the common good.

This corresponds to the principle stated in the constitution of the Federal Republic of Germany (Article 14, 2 GG) according to which private property carries the obligation to simultaneously serve the public interest.[37] It thus grants authority to the government to interfere with private property, to prevent abusive conduct and to forestall damages caused by external effects. The power to interfere is not unlimited, however, because this would be in contradiction of the principles of a market economy. Although the German constitution does not explicitly require a well-defined economic order to be established, this has de facto been accomplished by the ratification of the EC Treaty. Whilst the German constitution does not exclude expropriations and equivalent government interventions, provided an adequate compensation is granted, their permissibility is severely limited if not completely ruled out by

---

[37] 'Eigentum verpflichtet. Sein Gebrauch soll zugleich dem Wohl der Allgemeinheit dienen.'

the EC Treaty. Article 1 of the Treaty, and again Article 98, postulate that the policy of the Member States and the EC shall be conducted 'in accordance with the principle of an open market economy with free competition, favoring an efficient allocation of resources.'

Causes for the Impossibility of Workable Competition

Workable competition may be impossible because indivisibilities yield increasing returns to scale and sunk costs which gives rise to the following concerns,

- ruinous competition
- natural monopoly
- undersupply on thin markets
- consumer protection, safety at the workplace, and environmental protection.

For economic policy different approaches are available to cope with the indicated problems, in particular public enterprises to pursue the public interest, government regulation of private firms which, following a governmentally established regulation of entry, enjoy monopoly power (see Kahn 1988, Knieps 1988, Borrmann and Finsinger 1999).

Ruinous competition may arise if, following a decline in demand or excessive entry, the inverse demand curve lies below the declining curve of average costs. Although total costs are no longer covered the individual firm may still find the price exceeds average variable costs. It may then attempt to displace competitors by reducing the price.[38] Ruinous competition may also yield a deterioration of the quality of commodities and services, for example by negligence regarding safety to reduce costs.

In particular these concerns led in the US to regulating railway traffic by the Interstate Commerce Act of 1887 and installing the Interstate Commerce Commission (ICC). Later on similar agencies were established to regulate additional sectors, public utilities (electricity, gas and water supply), trucking, telecommunication, banking and insurance. The same applies in Germany where, after the privatization of telecommunications, a special regulatory agency has been established. For the rest, European governments responded to the aforementioned concerns by founding public enterprises. They are

---

[38] The danger of ruinous competition attributable to high fixed costs has been assessed as being so grave by Eugen Schmalenbach, a prominent business economist in Germany, that he questioned the future viability of a competitive economy altogether in his book with the challenging title 'Der freien Wirtschaft zum Gedächtnis' ('In Memory of the Free Economy'), published in 1949.

expected to be operated in the public interest. Normally prices should cover average costs. If profits arise they shall be used for public causes. Since they enjoy monopoly power they are not subject to competitive pressures to apply the most efficient techniques. Hence, presumably X-inefficiency causes costs to exceed the level which could be expected under competitive conditions.

In the case of a single product firm a natural monopoly is defined to exist if average costs decline throughout and if fixed costs are sunk because of irreversible investments. In the case of a multiproduct firm, average costs cannot be defined because of overhead costs which cannot be attributed to individual products. For a natural monopoly to exist the cost function needs to be subadditive (Baumol, Panzar and Willig 1982). This applies if for outputs $q_1, q_2, ..., q_n$ the costs of joint production fall short of costs arising if each output is produced separately, that is, if $C(q_1, q_2, ..., q_n) < C(q_1) + C(q_2) + ... + C(q_n)$. Subadditivity may exist, because costs to be incurred for producing some bundle of commodities rise less than proportionally, or because external economies between the various lines of production yield economies of scope.

High fixed costs may also prevent a private supply of a certain commodity or service if the market is 'thin'. This case obtains if the inverse demand curve, which depicts the willingness to pay of consumers, lies at any imaginable level of production below the average cost curve (AC), as illustrated in Figure 3.4. This explains, for example, why thinly populated regions are not becoming connected by the private supply of traffic to economic centers or only at a quality considered inadequate by politicians. A solution may be found by providing the service by a public enterprise, the deficits of which are covered by the government budget. An alternative which is sometimes used consists in granting a monopoly to a public or private enterprise to serve

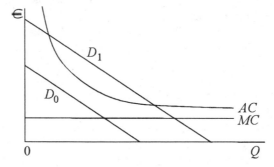

Figure 3.4   Fixed costs and a thin market

both the thin market and the thick ones, and have the enterprise cover the losses incurred on the thin market by profits earned elsewhere.

Price Control

For a natural monopoly pricing at marginal costs would yield losses since marginal costs are lower than average costs at any level of output. Therefore a first-best solution is not feasible. A single product firm must be permitted to charge a price covering average costs unless the deficit is made up by government subsidies. For a multiproduct firm Ramsey prices are a second-best solution. Total costs to be covered then requires cross subsidization. The guiding principle is to have the burden of fixed costs borne by choosing prices in such a way that the welfare loss is minimized. If the price is to exceed marginal costs the welfare loss, as measured by consumer surplus forgone, is higher the lower is the compensated price elasticity of demand. This insight yields the Ramsey rule according to which the price should exceed marginal costs at a rate inversely related to the price elasticity of compensated demand for the particular product.[39]

Price control alone is not sufficient, however, for coping with the problems associated with a natural monopoly. For example, if for a multiproduct firm Ramsey prices are fixed which for some products exceed average costs, so-called cream skimming will occur. A firm specializing in the respective product line would find it profitable to enter the market. For a Ramsey pricing scheme to be feasible it is therefore necessary to set up barriers to entry.

An additional problem arises insofar as the regulating agency does not know the cost function of the natural monopoly. Furthermore, for a public enterprise which is endowed with a monopoly by government decree pressures to reduce costs, as they exist in the case of competition, are absent. On the contrary, in quite a few cases politicians used to avail themselves of public enterprises to further causes like employment which are alien to the proper objectives of the firm. The government, and for that matter a regulatory agency, may compensate for the lack of competitive pressures by imposing price limits which are to be reduced successively. A leading role has been assumed in Britain by the so-called RPI-X regulation introduced in 1983. It requires the rate of increase of the average price of the services provided by a public enterprise to fall short of the rate of increase of the retail price index (RPI) by X per cent. The respective percentage rate is to be fixed by the regulatory authority (Armstrong, Cowan and Vickers 1994, pp. 165ff).

An indirect price control is applied in the US by fixing a maximal permissible rate of return for a regulated enterprise. This practice can be justified by presuming that private decisions are governed by time preference. According to the Golden Rule of capital accumulation (Phelps 1961), for consumption

---

[39] The Ramsey rule depends on the assumption of zero cross–price elasticities. If these are non-zero a more involved rule applies (see Atkinson and Stiglitz 1980, pp. 457–81).

per head to be maximized the rate of interest should equal the rate of growth of Gross National Product (GNP). This rule is violated if future utility is discounted by some rate of time preference and thus the rate of interest exceeds the rate of growth of GNP. If the government, in the pursuit of achieving a social optimum, ignores the private time preference, it has to impose on public enterprises a rate of interest which is less than the market rate of interest. This entices profit-maximizing firms to invest capital up to the point where the value of the marginal product of capital, or the marginal revenue times the marginal product of capital respectively, equals the permissible rate of return. Consequently, capital per employee in regulated industries is higher than in comparable private firms. This has been called the Averch–Johnson effect (Averch and Johnson 1962).

Competition fails to yield allocative efficiency if external economies and diseconomies prevail. In the case of external diseconomies total marginal costs to be borne by society are not fully borne by the producer. Hence the output of the commodity or service, the production of which causes external diseconomies, is too large, whilst the output of other products is too small, in comparison with the output required for allocative efficiency to be attained. Regulation of private production is thus desirable to enhance economic welfare. This applies in particular to traffic on roads and streets, to railroads, ocean shipping and air traffic; to the health industry for doctors, hospitals and pharmacies, it applies to security standards for machinery and other equipment, to safety at the workplace, and to environmental protection.[40] Government regulation in these fields entails barriers to entry for potential and, usually too, actual competition.

A fundamental criticism against government regulation has been advanced by invoking the 'capture theory', which has been extended and generalized by Stigler (1971) and Peltzman (1976). The capture theory starts from the observation that regulatory agencies in their activities must rely on information provided to them by the regulated industry. This is conducive for the agencies to become dependent on the industry. Therefore the capture theory claims that government regulation has turned out to be less beneficial for consumers than for the industry which has been able to attain profits higher than would have been possible under competitive conditions. Government has thus been charged with being instrumental in redistributing income in favor of regulated industries. As propounded by Stigler and Peltzman it was not accidental for regulation to be introduced following the lobbying activities of interest groups.

For these reasons regulation has become subject to severe criticism in the

---

[40] For the US see in detail Viscusi, Vernon and Harrington (1995, pp. 551–830).

US and was cut back in most industries and even completely abandoned in some of them. Insofar as monopoly power is inevitable because of economies of scale and scope, authorities in charge of competition policy must seek to prevent abuse of monopolistic market power. Since the feasibility of abuse control is severely limited, as explained in the previous section, it is imperative to create market structures which give rise to as much competition as possible. Of course, although government regulation suffers from serious shortcomings it is indispensable in the case of natural monopolies.

Privatization

Privatization is to be recommended to avoid both allocative inefficiency and X-inefficiency. Through privatization the control mechanism of the capital market is put into action. Although it certainly does not work perfectly either, it at least serves to limit inefficiencies. On the other hand privatization of a natural monopoly would entail all misgivings of monopolistic market power. This dilemma raises the question of how acute a problem is posed by natural monopolies in practice. Obviously not all public enterprises are natural monopolies. Usually only the infrastructure of the economy displays all identifying characteristics of a natural monopoly, that is, increasing returns to scale, or subadditivity in the case of multiproduct firms respectively, and sunk costs. For railways this applies to tracks and connected installments, for air traffic it applies to airports and air traffic control, for public utilities it applies to networks of electricity, gas and oil. By contrast, it does not apply to the rolling stock of railways, the aircraft, boats and the periphery of telecommunications. That suggests privatizing those parts of public enterprises which do not qualify as natural monopolies. For those parts which are in fact natural monopolies, free access for users must be guaranteed at regulated fees to be determined by government agencies or the authorities in charge of competition policy. Steps in this direction have been undertaken in the EC with respect to railways, and to the access to networks for electricity, gas and telecommunications.

Regarding thinly-populated regions where traffic, telecommunications and postal services cannot be expected to be provided by private enterprise, the government may step in to compensate for market failure by using proceeds from taxation to finance the desirable supply. Alternatively the government may grant a monopoly to either a public enterprise or a private firm committed to serving the thin market, and cover losses by monopoly profits earned in more remunerative markets. In both cases welfare losses arise, that is, by taxation since lump sum taxes are usually not feasible, or by monopoly power. Theoretically it might be possible for the government to cover the required expenditures for serving thin markets by indirect taxation equivalent to Ramsey pricing or by committing the public enterprise to charge Ramsey prices. This option, however, is usually not available in practice because of lack of the requisite data.

3.5 CONCLUSION

Has competition policy been successful? Has it been possible by prohibiting cartels, by merger control and abuse control, for dominant firms to contain ever-prevailing tendencies conducive to restraints of competition? In my view the answer is in the affirmative, even if some qualifications apply. It is certainly true that prohibitions by law cannot eradicate offenses altogether – even theft and murder do occur. On the whole, however, competition policy has been successful. Countries which apply a strict competition policy display superior international competitiveness. Not least for this reason the Member States of the EC have adopted competition policy in their countries along the lines given by EC law which, in turn, has displayed convergence with US antitrust law.

Competition policy aiming at establishing a competitive order faces the danger of degenerating into interventionism which would undermine competition. Competition policy always entails weighing favorable and unfavorable effects against each other. This assessment may, as for cartels, lead to the conclusion that a *per se* prohibition is justified because any economies which might be entailed are likely to be dwarfed by welfare losses. In less clear cases, like mergers, weighing favorable and unfavorable effects against each other is indispensable. In German competition law a two-stage procedure applies. At the first stage the Federal Cartel Office has to decide from the viewpoint of competition policy. Firms whose cause has been dismissed, have two alternative options. They may either appeal to courts or they may turn to the Minister of Economics for granting an exception justified by political reasons. This procedure entails transparency because the reasons for granting an exception must be spelled out and are thus amenable to be openly discussed. By contrast, the decisions of the EC Commission are taken in one shot. Although the decisions have to be justified by reference to the law it frequently remains unclear what the real reasons have been. Suggestions for also adopting a two-stage procedure at the EC level have not so far found sufficient support politically. In the US, actions against mergers fall into the competence of both the Department of Justice and the Federal Trade Commission. How far they are motivated by purely legal and economic considerations, and how far political deliberations are coming into play, can hardly be determined from outside.

Interventions affecting private property rights may be justified by public interest. They should not, however, engender distortions of competition and should, moreover, be confined to unequivocal cases of a natural monopoly and external effects which cannot be offset by resorting to alternative means.

For containing restraints of competition government interventions are to play the dominant role. In addition, restraints of competition can be checked by private litigation for compensating damages. The assessment of such damages, however, is extremely difficult since the incidence of restraints is unclear. Exercising monopoly power yields both a change in income distribution and efficiency losses. The impact on distribution may be ascertained with some accuracy for those people immediately affected. The total impact on distribution, however, is widespread since monopoly pricing entails a decrease of real income throughout the entire economy. The same applies to the deadweight loss of monopoly. Therefore fines imposed on violators by the government and courts are more appropriate. They serve as deterrents and at the same time compensate the public at large for damages incurred. Whilst in Europe private litigation for damages is confined to only a few cases it has become a weighty weapon to fight restraints of competition in the US. The possibility to sue for treble damages may be derived from the incidence of damages to extend immediate damages. It certainly reinforces deterrence but also implies a redistribution of income.[41] It may be justified as a reward for doing a service to the public by contributing to removing a competition restraint.

---

[41] For further discussion of the issue of treble damages see Pitofsky (1979, p. 1207).

4. The Social Framework and Competition Policy

As competition policy is a constitutive part of economic and social policy it is subject to the impact of conflicting tendencies and interests. On the one hand, under the influence of economic theory, the aspect of economic efficiency has assumed increasing weight. On the other hand, reference to the distribution of power, wealth and income has remained influential. This includes the question as to what extent market forces should be relied on or, alternatively, government regulation should be used to shape economic development. These questions will be discussed in this chapter by relating competition policy to other politics both in the national and the international context.

4.1 FREEDOM OF COMPETITION AND PROPERTY RIGHTS

Freedom of competition has been an issue of overriding importance for competition policy. In view of a prevailing inclination for resorting to restraints of competition, the difficulties of proving collusion and distinguishing between efficiency-enhancing mergers and those undertaken with intent to monopolize, the task assigned to competition policy is greatly facilitated by securing freedom of competition because it is most effective in undermining collusive intent. Freedom of competition implies that everybody is entitled to property rights and to use them according to one's own judgement. In fact the workability of markets depends on well-defined property rights. In a competitive economy everybody should thus have access to private property. As property implies exclusiveness with regard to utilizing commodities, at first sight, property appears to convey monopoly power. In fact, however, private property in itself does not engender monopolistic market power. By contrast, private property and the legitimacy of its acquisition gives rise to individual motivation driving the competitive process and thus furthers the creation of wealth. On the other hand, competition entails 'creative destruction' and thus leads to the deterioration of the welfare of losers, at least in the short run. Establishing private property therefore does not mean that each individual is protected from being disturbed by competition and the danger of suffering losses. Safeguards against this possibility would undermine the efficacy of the competitive process. Such tendencies frequently arise following government regulations which deprive individuals from using certain locations or resources. Decisions of this kind are usually justified by referring to the public interest, particularly to the need of environmental protection. In quite a few cases arguments of this kind are advanced by interest groups which find themselves in danger of being hurt by creative destruction and clothe their private interests by invoking the public interest.

Patents

The Janus-face of private property and the entailed possibility of restraints of competition is most conspicuous for patents. A patent granted for an invention provides the right of exclusive use for the holder for some stipulated period of time and simultaneously provides information to the public about the invention. The foundations for the development of patent rights were laid by the English Parliament in 1623–24. The 'Statute of Monopolies' prohibited monopolies, with a single exception, granting a monopoly for a limited time to the 'first and true inventor'.[1]

In the US a patent is conferred on somebody who proves to be the first and true inventor for 20 years. In Germany a patent, which also grants protection from imitation for 20 years, is granted to the person who is the first to apply for the patent to the Patent Office. It will be awarded, provided the invention displays sufficient 'height'. To acquire protection abroad necessitates applying for a patent in the respective foreign country. Protection throughout Europe can be obtained by applying for a patent to the European Patent Office, located in Munich, Germany. In Germany, for an invention displaying less 'height', the protection of a so-called 'Gebrauchsmuster', a kind of minor patent, can be obtained which lasts for a maximum of 10 years. The owner of a patent may license his right and can, in this case, impose limitations of use on the licensee. For keeping the property right in the patent valid the owner must pay an annually increasing fee from the third year onwards. Not least for this reason many owners of a patent abandon their right before it expires.

If an invention were free to be used by everybody there would hardly be any incentive to incur expenditures for research and development. The patent thus serves to secure compensation for the inventor by granting exclusive use. On the other hand the patent is open to public inspection. This offers the opportunity for any other person to use existing knowledge in their own re-

---

[1] Regarding the preceding and subsequent controversies about the justification of patent monopolies see Fritz Machlup (1961).

search efforts, such that the wheel need not be invented over and over again. However, since rivals may use this opportunity to develop similar products to compete with the inventor, the incentive to apply for a patent is diminished. Firms in quite a few cases, particularly in the case of process inventions, refrain from seeking patent protection in favor of keeping their knowledge secret (Simon 1996, p. 106). On the other hand, since in Europe a patent is granted to the person who applies for the patent first, an incentive is created to seek patent protection. Otherwise the same invention could be made by somebody else who, by applying for a patent, would enjoy priority.

The economic effects of patent rights are ambivalent. Although incentives for research and development are strengthened, the right for exclusive use may hamper innovative activity. Which effect, incentive or impediment, is larger cannot unequivocally be determined a priori.[2]

As exclusiveness of use is granted to the patentee for only a limited period of time, frequently the advantages of an invention cannot be fully exploited by the inventor. Moreover, inventions give rise to external economies such that the marginal benefit for the economy at large is greater than the marginal benefit accruing to the inventor. This external economy reduces economic incentives for research and development. Hence R&D activity is presumably less than optimal. This reasoning has been used to justify government subsidies for R&D. Two opposing arguments may, however, be raised. First, the inventor enjoys a lead in knowledge and may thus seek a shareholding in a firm which turns the invention into innovative activity (Hirshleifer 1971). Second, among oligopolies frequently patent races have been observed where each firm seeks to gain an edge on its rivals. This may yield excess expenditures for R&D. Consequently, across industries, a clear-cut correlation between appropriability of results from R&D and the level of expenditures does not appear to exist (Cohen and Levin 1989, p. 1095, Gual 1995, p. 13). Nevertheless, property rights conveyed by patents are likely to stimulate R&D and thus are an important lubricant for the competitive process.

A patent is abused if it is used to enforce rights beyond the proper content of the patent. According to German law (§ 17 KartellG) restrictions with regard to kind, scope, technological range of application, quantity, geographic area and period of time must not extend the proper content of the patent. The monopoly right entailed by a patent must not, in particular, be used to achieve another monopoly. In the US this principle has come to be known as the GE doctrine, first established 1948 in the case of US v. General Electric (Neale 1966, p. 265).

A patentee may make it a condition of a license that the licensee shall not

---

[2] Machlup (1961, p. 136), for illustrating the problem, pointed out that effective brakes are required to enable an automobile to be driven at high speed on a motor way.

charge a lower price than he himself chooses to charge. He must not, however, demand that the licensee abstains from underselling a product into which the licensed article enters only as one of various components (Neale 1966, pp. 263ff). An abuse is also deemed to exist if firms enter an agreement of cross licensing by which patents are put into a pool with the intent to exclude competitors. In the leading American case, US v. Hartford Empire Company, the Supreme Court 1948 (Neale 1966, pp. 278ff) considered a combination of competing patents as analogous to a financial combination. Competing manufacturers of glassware had brought their patents for glass-making machinery together in a pool and had used the combined strength of the patents to exclude entrants from the industry and to control the supply and price of glassware which was not in itself a patented product.[3]

An abuse of patent rights is also deemed to exist if additional restraints are imposed on the licensee such as tying, prohibiting the use of alternative products, a grant back condition, a condition preventing challenges to liability, or coercive package licensing.

Trademarks and Advertising

Trademarks are similar to patents by providing exclusive rights of use for suppliers of a particular article or a group of articles for which a trademark is registered with the Patent Office. Prior to granting the right the Office examines whether the trademark has sufficient power to distinguish the article or articles from other ones. Upon registration the owner of the trademark has acquired the exclusive right to use the trademark for his respective products. In Germany protection expires after 10 years but can be repeatedly renewed for another period of 10 years. Advertising by using the trademark contributes to building up a goodwill which creates an advantage for the advertiser. In fact, in numerous empirical studies the price–cost margin has been shown

---

[3] The ruling of the Supreme Court was summarized by Mr Justice Roberts as follows (Neale 1966, p. 279). 'In summary, the situation brought about in the glass industry, and existing in 1938 was: Hartford, with the technical and financial aid of others in the conspiracy, had acquired more than 600 patents. These with over 100 Corning patents, 60 Owens patents, over 70 Hazel patents and some 12 Lynch patents, had been merged by cross-licensing agreements into a pool which effectively controlled the industry. Production in Corning's field was allocated to Corning, the general container field was allocated to Owens, Hazel, Thatcher, Ball and smaller manufacturers the group agreed should be licensed. The result was that 94% of the glass containers manufactured in this country on feeders and formers were made on machinery licensed under the pooled patents. The district court found that invention of glass-making machinery had been discouraged, that competition in the manufacture and sale or licensing of such machinery had been suppressed, and that the system of restricted licensing had been employed to suppress competition in the manufacture of unpatented glassware and to maintain prices of the manufactured product.'

to be positively associated with advertising. In Germany a positive relationship has also been found between the price–cost margin and the number of trademarks held per unit of total assets of the respective firm (Neumann, Böbel and Haid 1979).

These findings have frequently been interpreted as revealing an undesirable imperfection of markets. Advertising has been presumed to exert an undue influence on consumers' preferences and, moreover, to give rise to monopolistic market power. For these reasons legal restrictions on advertising have been demanded. However, the presumption that consumers' preferences are manipulated by advertising is easily refuted. Products of a firm which suit consumers' wishes best can be successfully sold with less efforts, than products of a firm which are less appealing to consumers. Since the most suitable product requires the least advertising, competition renders the best product to be most successful in the market. Advertising for products which do not appeal to consumers' preferences does not pay.

A simple reasoning is also possible to show that advertising contributes to favor the survival of superior products. Usually producers are better informed regarding their products than consumers. To highlight the consequences of asymmetric information, assume consumers to be completely uninformed. Under this condition suppliers with the worst products, the production of which costs the least, will be most profitable. Producers with initially higher quality products will have no chance and will be induced to shift to offer inferior quality products themselves. Low-quality products thus drive out better quality products. Now assume by contrast that a supplier of a better product is able to inform buyers convincingly by advertising, a trademark for identifying his products and a guarantee of quality. If buyers find the actual quality to conform to advertised promises they may become permanent customers willing to pay a higher price for better quality. Customers will, in addition, extrapolate previous experiences to apply also to new products offered by the favored supplier (von Weizsäcker 1980, pp. 72f). The supplier will not presumably risk losing the acquired goodwill, and will continue to sell high-quality products.

The goodwill created by advertising and coming up to customers' expectations conveys a competitive advantage. Since advertising expenditures are sunk the goodwill may, like fixed costs in general, render the entry of competitors difficult. In the long run they do not, however, constitute an entry barrier in itself because building up a goodwill is an opportunity open to everybody.

Prohibition of Unfair Competition

Property rights are also protected by legislation against unfair competition, in

Germany by the 'Law against Unfair Competition' of 1909; in the US by regulations contained in the Federal Trade Commission Act (FTC Act) of 1914. Although the respective laws were enacted in Germany and the US at almost the same time the thrust of the laws differ in a remarkable way. The US law focuses on consumer protection. Business conduct is deemed unfair if it violates the Sherman Act or the Clayton Act or both (FTC 1998, pp. 6f). By contrast the German law aims also at protecting businessmen against competition which does not conform to generally accepted standards of fairness (Hefermehl 1998, p. x). Unfairness is thus defined with reference to decent behavior in business. This opens the door for collusive elements. Accordingly, rules of fair business conduct, which are permitted to be issued by trade associations (§ 24 KartellG), are to regulate business conduct in pursuance of fair competition.

Regional Policy

Restraints of competition may be caused by regulations of communities regarding settlements. These regulations may legitimately follow from the objective to minimize external diseconomies. They may, however, also be motivated by aiming at maintaining a given structure of industry, for example, by opposing the settlement of supermarkets or factory outlets at the outskirts of cities to protect traditional retailing. The city government may pursue the objective to counteract tendencies for the inner city to be vacated. Thereby it clearly creates entry barriers for new kinds of business activity. A distortion of competition is also caused by subsidies granted by cities or regional governments to further the settlement of industries.

Consumer Protection Causing Restraints of Competition

Free entry may endanger public security and health if consumers are incompletely informed by deceitful advertising of poorly qualified suppliers. In view of these risks governments usually control the entry into professions by requiring quality standards to be satisfied by applicants. In Germany examples are the required proof of adequate proficiency for the admittance to trades like plumbers and electricians, for example, the proof of adequate professional training for pharmacists, membership in a professional association of physicians for admittance to treat people covered by Social Security, satisfying certain standards for being allowed to set up a banking firm. For physicians regulations with similar effects apply in the US. Until recently the admittance to medical practice used to be predicated on the membership in the American Medical Association (AMA) which involved the possession of monopoly power (Kessel 1958). Since the decision of the Supreme Court of

1975 the learned professions are no longer exempt from antitrust. Therefore doctors are also subject to the Sherman Act (Toepffer 1997, pp. 115f). There are still restraints of competition, however, because access to liability insurance at reasonable conditions is still predicated on the membership of the AMA.

Consumer protection and safety at the workplace is also pursued by stipulating standards to be observed. Some of them are issued by the government, some by insurance companies or their associations, some by voluntary organizations of industries. Their effect is ambivalent, in particular because they entail non-tariff barriers to international trade and are thus conducive to restraints of competition.

An outstanding example has been the case of Cassis de Dijon, decided by the European Court of Justice. German legislation prevented the sale of liquor with an alcoholic content below a specified minimum. It had the effect of preventing the import into Germany of French cassis. The Court established an important principle which subsequently has been applied to various other cases. It says that the sale of any product lawfully produced and marketed in one Member State of the EC can rightfully be sold in any other Member State. This principle is subject to only a few exceptions, such as the effectiveness of fiscal supervision, the protection of public health, the fairness of commercial transactions, and the defense of consumers. The decision of the Court removed numerous non-tariff barriers between the Member States of the EC.

The Cassis de Dijon principle gives rise to competition of standards within the Common Market. Sometimes concerns are expressed that it would be conducive to a deterioration of quality because the least demanding standards would survive. This concern is unfounded, however. First, consumers can be trusted to be able to correctly assess the quality of competing products. This applies in particular if producers are obliged to provide truthful information regarding their supplies and if they are held liable for damages. Second, as explained above, advertising implies sunk costs such that competition with quality is enhanced and producers are not interested in deteriorating quality.

Network Effects

Similar problems arise in the case of networks like telecommunications. The utility of a phone increases with the number of people using phones. In addition, the cost of availing oneself of a phone decreases since economies of scale can be exploited.

Usually alternative networks can be established. Which one comes into existence and prevails may be the outcome of competition. It may alternatively arise through agreements among suppliers or by government decree.

Once one of the feasible alternatives has achieved a lead, economies of scale may yield an irreversible process of an ever-increasing market share of the leading alternative. The introduction of a standard by government decree or an agreement among suppliers – for example 220 V in Germany vs. 110 V in the US for electric appliances – creates a reliable foundation for planning and allows for enjoying economies of scale. If several standards are competing, like videos or mobile phones, the scope for enjoying economies of scale is limited. At first sight, a collective decision in favor of one alternative appears to be cheaper. For this reason in Germany cartels concerned with agreements on uniform norms and types in industry are admitted, provided expected cost savings outweigh restraints of competition involved, and the emergence or strengthening of a dominant position is not to be anticipated. A close look, however, gives rise to doubts whether collective decisions regarding the standard to be applied is unequivocally preferable. The decision causes path dependency in favor of some system whereby experiments with alternatives are cut off *ab initio*. Even if they were actually superior they will never have a chance. Admittedly, the same applies if, in the case of competing systems, path dependency and economies of scale render an alternative to lose before it has got a chance to fully unfold its advantages. It has also to be taken into account that competition between alternative systems implies the existence of private property rights, some of them incorporated in patents, which entail restraints of competition. By contrast, standards introduced by government decree are freely accessible. Still, standards of this kind introduced for the domestic market may constitute non-tariff barriers for international trade and as such, too, restrain competition.

Property Rights as Entry Barriers

How property rights may constitute entry barriers and thus be conducive to monopoly power can most forcefully be shown by looking at a bottleneck facility. A famous case in point in the US has been the Terminal Railroad Association of St Louis. St Louis can be reached from the West only by passing a narrow valley. All railroads have to use this route. In 1889 several railway companies had founded the Association as a joint venture for running the track. They agreed that outsiders should not be permitted unless by unanimous consent and payment of a fee to be determined by the Directors of the joint venture. The Supreme Court held that the group's monopoly was acquired legitimately but must not be used oppressively. The conditions in the contract were held to violate the Sherman Act and the Court ordered the joint venture to be reorganized so as to permit non-proprietary companies to use the facility on terms that were reasonable and non-discriminatory (Neale 1966, pp. 131ff).

   The justification for government intervention follows from the public interest which has to be observed as postulated in the US by the Supreme Court in the case Munn v. Illinois and in Germany by the constitutional provision that private property has to simultaneously serve the public interest. This reference, however, implies strict limitations for the legitimacy of an intervention by the government. Sometimes it has been argued, by contrast, that access to an essential facility should be granted to avoid the duplication of the facility which would entail excessive costs (Valletti and Estache 1999, p. 1). This reasoning is based on the model of an oligopoly where fixed costs give rise to a tangential solution on the declining branch of the average cost curve where no supplier is able to utilize his facility up to minimum average costs. If the individual firm were obliged to grant access to its facility for competitors at a fee fixed by a regulatory agency, so the argument runs, the product in question could be produced at lower costs. Such a regulation, however, would open the door to far-reaching government interventions and to government control of private investments. It would dilute private property, weaken incentives and thus undermine the competitive process. Even though in a competitive economy based on private property, investments which render losses cannot be excluded, in the long run competition can be relied upon to give rise to better solutions than can be expected from government interventions. Thus, for economic reasons alone, general access to privately-owned facilities must be dismissed. A regulating intervention to oblige a private owner to grant access to a bottleneck facility can be justified only if, first, the existence of the bottleneck is beyond human influence and cannot be duplicated by any effort from competitors. This applied in the case of the access by railway to St Louis. Second, access can be demanded to be granted by the owner if the exclusive right to the facility has been conferred by the government, or if establishing the facility has been supported by government subsidies. This applies to the networks for electricity, telephone, gas and water embedded in, or constructed along, public roads. Granting an exclusive right implies that the government has the power to regulate the monopoly entailed.[4] With regard to an essential facility both the German law and EC law justifies a regulating intervention along the lines applicable to an abuse of a dominant position. According to German law (§ 19, 4, No. 4 KartellG) a dominant position is deemed to be abused if a dominant firm declines access to its facilities for another enterprise which for legal or other reasons is excluded from competing with the dominant firm in downstream or upstream markets, unless the dominant firm proves that access is impossible for technological or other reasons. The dominant firm is, however, entitled to demand

---

[4] See Papier (1997) and Wallenberg (1999, p. 22) for a discussion of the respective German law and, for the 'essential facility doctrine' of EC law, Müller (1998).

an adequate user fee. The same principles apply according to EC law regarding access to an essential facility.

4.2 COMPETITION POLICY AND INTERNATIONAL TRADE POLICY

Traditionally competition policy and international trade policy have been treated as separate fields despite the fact that they are closely related. Trade policy aims at improving domestic welfare even at the expense of foreign nations. On the other hand, all countries try to fend off foreign infringements with domestic welfare. This antagonism necessarily gives rise to trade conflicts which cause welfare losses for all countries involved. Therefore, after World War II the General Agreement on Tariffs and Trade (GATT), applying to trade in commodities, and more recently the World Trade Organization (WTO), pertaining also to trade in services, have been created to reduce trade barriers and to settle trade disputes. Establishing these agreements has been driven by the insight that unimpeded international trade and the competition involved is welfare enhancing for all participating countries. In fact, substantial progress in this direction has been achieved. Nevertheless the emergence of a really global market is still a good deal down the road. The traditional stance of both trade policy and competition policy has been deplorably resistant.

Strategic Trade Policy and Export Cartels

Up to this date export cartels, unless they also pertain to domestic trade, have been exempt from being illegal. In the US the exemption is based on the Webb–Pomerene Act of 1918 and the Foreign Trade Antitrust Improvement Act. In Germany so-called pure export cartels have been exempt *per se*. Export cartels which pertain to the domestic market as well have been subject to a rule of reason and must be disallowed if they cause a substantial restraint of competition or if they are in contradiction to international treaties. The same applies to EC law since cartels are illegal only insofar as they affect trade between Member States and have as their object or effect a restraint of competition within the common market.

In the spirit of traditional trade policy, which focuses on domestic welfare alone, more recently the notion of strategic trade policy has been advanced. Whilst the classical and neoclassical trade theory has been developed on the premise of perfect competition prevailing on all markets, the theory of strategic trade policy took cognizance of numerous markets being served by oligopolies. In the most simple model, treated in Chapter 2, a duopoly is assumed with a domestic firm competing with a foreign firm where both firms are supplying a homogeneous product on a global market without any impediments to trade. If the domestic firm receives a subsidy, its marginal costs decline. This causes its market share and profits to increase at the expense of the foreign rival. Presuming the demand curve and the cost curve to be linear, it has been shown that the increase in profits of the domestic firm outweighs the subsidy. Hence strategic trade policy may yield a welfare gain for the domestic economy. This conclusion carries over to the case where domestic firms set up an export cartel supported by a subsidy from the government.

Beyond the fictitious world of models it is hardly possible for monopoly power to be exercised in exports without affecting the domestic market as well. It is, moreover, shortsighted to focus exclusively on immediate effects. Strategic trade policy will be visualized as dumping by foreign competitors. They will therefore demand protection from their government which is likely resort to anti-dumping activities, such as for example countervailing duties (Marvel and Ray 1995). This provokes conflicts conducive to additional protective moves which give rise to restraints of competition.

Dumping and Antidumping

In particular cases it is difficult to ascertain whether an increase in the market share of a foreign competitor is caused by superior efficiency or by receiving government subsidies. Of course, domestic firms will usually find competing imports to be disturbing, in particular if competition on domestic markets is restrained by barriers to entry and collusion. Domestic producers can therefore be expected to accuse rivals from abroad of dumping and to demand protection. A typical example has been the anti-dumping complaint of European producers of soda-ash decided by the EC Commission 1990. The GATT secretariat commented on this case as follows (Bourgeois and Demaret 1995, pp. 108f),

> A recent case in which the EC authorities intervened to restore competitive conditions concerns soda-ash, where domestic producers had sought anti-dumping protection to defend cartel rents against competing imports. The companies involved were convicted under EC competition law and the anti-dumping measures repealed in 1990/91.

In fact anti-dumping measures may fend off competition from abroad and thus stabilize collusion (Messerlin 1990, Messerlin and Reed 1995).[5] From

---

[5] Nieberding (1999) found for various US industries that adoption of anti-dumping measures led to an increase in monopolistic market power, quantified by the price–cost margin.

the viewpoint of competition policy, dumping may involve predation aiming at destroying a competitor. For dumping to be condemned as predation, however, the same criteria must be applied which have to be invoked generally for a dominant firm or a cartel to be found guilty of predatory conduct. This cannot be ruled out offhand. It will, however, apply only in a few cases because it would require global dominance of a single firm or an export cartel.

Another case, pointed out by Ethier (1982) does not constitute anticompetitive dumping either. Given specific factors of production and the immobility of factors involved, a business cycle downturn may yield excess output offered at prices below average costs and sold on foreign markets where a business cycle upturn occurs. In the foreign country the import may be considered as dumping. Actually, though, such a process may happen in the domestic market, too, without a restraint of trade being involved.

Competition is certainly distorted if firms receive government subsidies and are thus able to displace foreign competitors. With good reasons the EC Commission therefore has a watchful eye on government aids by Member States, as will be discussed in Section 4.4 in more detail.

Exterritorial Effects of National Competition Policy and International Competition Policy

The present tendencies of an increase in globalization suggest that competition policy should also be exercised on a global scale. A first step in this direction has been taken by allowing national competition policy to impact beyond national borders. Frequently foreign firms participate in domestic cartels. Moreover, sometimes mergers and cartels which exert an influence on the domestic economy are organized abroad. For example the dyestuff collusion, mentioned in Chapters 1 and 3, was an international cartel among chemical firms located both in the EC and abroad. Among the firms fined by the EC Commission was the British ICI, even though Britain at that time was not yet a member of the European Economic Community (EEC). More recently an international cartel pertaining to pipes for heating systems has been prohibited by the EC Commission. The most severe fine was imposed on ABB (Asea Brown Boveri Ltd.) located in Zürich, Switzerland, because the cartel had been organized from that country (FAZ October 22, 1998, p. 20). In the case Gencor/Lonrho the Court of First Instance of the European Court of Justice upheld a prohibition of a joint venture to be founded in South Africa, by the South African group Gencor and the British firm Lonrho (Christensen and Owen 1999, p. 23), for extracting platinum. A claim to exterritorial effectiveness is also contained in the German cartel law, which specifically postulates (§ 130 KartellG) that the law pertains to restraints of competition even if they originate abroad.

Politically it is still a delicate matter. National legislation can, in principle, command to be observed only within the national borders. However, a government should be able to protect its citizens from being damaged by an action exercised abroad which is illegal according to national law. Traditionally a government used to respond by adopting measures of protective trade policy. This may, however, elicit counteractions by the foreign government which may escalate into a trade war. Therefore governments have increasingly tried to forestall the emergence of conflicts of this kind by establishing international law. This tendency has led to an increasing recognition of the 'effects doctrine'. The dyestuff decision of the European Court of Justice, for instance, and other cases mentioned above, were based on applying this doctrine (Basedow 1998, pp. 17f). Likewise in the US the Supreme Court postulated in 1993 (Basedow 1998, p. 20) that it is 'well established by now that the Sherman Act applies to foreign conduct that was meant to produce and did in fact produce some substantial effect in the United States'.

A politically subtle question arises how a conflict between the laws of countries involved can be resolved. A reasonable solution to minimize the problem was proposed by the Supreme Court in 1993. It said that a true conflict between US law and foreign law only exists if in some country a behavior is mandatory which is illegal according to US law. By contrast, if the behavior in question is only admissible, without being requested according to foreign law, the foreign firm may behave in such a way as not to violate US law (Basedow 1998, p. 25). As a matter of fact, this principle allows for applying national competition law exterritorially in almost all cases pertaining to cartels. Difficulties arise for mergers and all other cases where a rule of reason has to be invoked. In these case a consensus must be sought, as for instance in the case of the merger between Boeing and McDonnell-Douglas. Accordingly the US and the EC agreed on a far-reaching 'positive comity' regarding cartels but only restrictively with regard to mergers. Positive comity implies that one partner, at the request of the other one, has to enter an investigation and inform the partner about the findings as to whether competition is restrained (Kiriazis 1998).

Even though the recognition of the effects doctrine is an important step in the right direction the development should go further. In the case of conflict, political deliberations still play a dominant role. It would be much better if a consensus regarding reasonable principles to govern international competition policy could be reached. This would allow conflicts to be resolved by invoking the law. Some proposals of this kind have been advanced.[6]

For combating collusion across national borderlines and global mergers

---

[6] A pertinent proposal has been submitted by a research group within GATT as a 'Draft International Antitrust Code' 1993. Another proposal has been advanced by F.M. Scherer (1994).

with intent to monopolize, an effective international competition policy would certainly be highly welcome. It is questionable, however, whether this can be achieved by worldwide harmonization of competition law within the framework of the WTO. Given very different national traditions regarding competition policy and industrial policy, a global consensus about the aims and instrument of competition policy which would come up to the standards presently applied in the US and the EC can hardly be expected, at least not in the near future. It is worth noting that even competition policy in the US and the EC contains a striking inconsistency insofar as, on one hand, export cartels are allowed, and on the other hand, competition law is claimed to extend beyond national borders. A first useful step for harmonizing competition policy internationally would be, following a suggestion of the American Bar Association (Scherer 1994, p. 91), to generally prohibit export cartels. For the rest, applying the effects doctrine can be expected to be conducive to some harmonization of competition policy.

4.3 FINANCIAL MARKETS AND COMPETITION ON GOODS MARKETS

The emergence of potential competition is facilitated, on one hand, by the ease of access to financial resources for new firms, and, on the other hand, it is hampered by the competitive advantages of incumbents derived from the financial resources at their command.

Sources of Finance in Alternative Systems of Financing Industry

Financial resources for new competitors may consist of equity or loans. As has been shown by Myers (1984), financing of an enterprise follows a hierarchical 'pecking order'. Internal financing by plowing back profits occupies the first rank, followed by loans and finally by issue of shares, in this order. In fact, for non-financial enterprises in the US, Canada, the UK, Germany, and France from 1978 to 1990 internal financing amounted to 40–60 per cent of total financial resources (in Germany from 1960 to 1992 even 62 per cent). Outside financing covered about 40 per cent and only a very small percentage was provided by issuing shares (Schwiete 1998, p. 93).

Outside financing may take the form of loans extended by banks or the issue of bonds. The latter alternative is an option available only for large and renowned companies, practically it is not available for small firms. Actually, in Germany, the percentage share of long-term loans taken from banks in total outside financing was much smaller for large firms than for small and medium-sized ones. In 1989 in manufacturing, trade and traffic for enterprises with annual sales of 100 Mio DM and more it amounted to 7.6 per cent of total assets, for enterprises with annual sales less than 10 Mio DM to 32.0 per cent and for mid-sized firms to 24.3 per cent (Weigand, C. 1998, p. 120). Long-term bank liabilities of public companies were lower than for single businessmen or partnerships, they were lower in industries with high level horizontal concentration than in industries with lower concentration (Weigand, C. 1998, pp. 123ff). These findings suggest that the organization of the financial sector of an economy exerts a substantial influence on shaping competition on goods markets.

Asymmetric Information as an Entry Barrier

Newly-founded enterprises usually suffer from being disadvantaged *vis-à-vis* incumbent firms. Since they cannot avail themselves of profits plowed back they are dependent on loans or issuing equity. Costs of finance are higher than for incumbents because of asymmetric information between an enterprise and providers of either loans or equity. New firms are unknown and their prospects of future profitability are usually expected to be more risky than for incumbents. Therefore, the expected return must be higher to compensate for risk. In addition, creditors usually demand collateral, that is, property pledged as security for repayment of the loan, from new firms more frequently than from well-known incumbents. Hence long-run marginal costs, which include the costs of financing investments, are higher than for incumbents. Given equal costs of production incumbents are thus able to maintain a larger market share. Entry pays if the expected return exceeds the opportunity costs of capital, that is, the return which an alternative investment would yield. Investing in an incumbent enterprise is thus more remunerative than investments in a new firm unless it promises excess profits due to lower costs or superior products. Otherwise an incumbent enjoys a competitive advantage and would be able to intimidate potential entrants.

Competition between Financial Systems

Regarding outside financing through loans and equity two alternative models of a financial system may be distinguished, that is, market-based and bank-based financing, respectively (Schwiete 1998, pp. 115ff, Neuberger 1999). In a market-based financial system financing of enterprises occurs by securization, that is, by issuing bonds and shares. The US and Germany may serve as respective prototypes, where the US stands for a market-based system and Germany for a bank-based system. From 1978 to 1990 long-term credits from banks amounted to 18.4 per cent of outstanding liabilities of firms in the US and 62 per cent in Germany (Schwiete 1998, p. 118).

Frequently a market-based financial system, characterized by a high degree of securization, is claimed to be the most progressive outcome of an evolutionary process. This view overlooks that the US banking system has been thoroughly regulated because of a widespread mistrust in the potential power of banks. Until quite recently, by an institutional separation between commercial banking and investment banking, by prohibiting banking across the borders of states, and the illegality of mergers between banking and insurance (Roe 1993) the field of activities open to banks has been severely limited.[7] The market-based US financial system has thus largely been framed by government regulation (Roe 1991, Schwiete 1998, pp. 120f, Neuberger 1999). A market-based financial system can therefore hardly be claimed to be superior by invoking the evolutionary law of natural selection. Which one of the alternative systems is superior can only be revealed by competition undistorted by regulatory checks. In fact, more recently some dismantling of regulating banking in the US took place and thus the actual systems converged to some extent (Blommerstein 1995).

Banking and Goods Markets

Given the crucial role of financing, restraints of competition in banking exert an influence on goods markets. A shown by Smith (1998), excess profits due to the monopolistic market power of banks raises the opportunity costs of capital and thus makes outside financing more expensive. Monopolistic market power in banking is thus conducive to adversely affecting macroeconomic stability.

This applies in particular to countries with a bank-based financial system. Mergers and acquisitions in the financial sector of the economy are therefore to be critically evaluated. Overall concentration in banking is particularly susceptible to rise if entry barriers exist because of government regulations. In fact, in Germany more recently entries of domestic suppliers into banking could not be observed. Mergers thus entailed an increase in horizontal concentration. Nevertheless horizontal concentration is still relatively low. The market share of the group of the four largest banks[8] in total banking activity, as measured by total assets of banks, in Germany in November and December 1999 amounted to no more than 14.6 per cent. By contrast the combined

---

[7] The separation between commercial banking and investment banking stipulated by the Glass–Steagall Act of 1933 has been repealed by the Gramm–Leach–Bliley Act of 1999 (Barth, Brumbaugh and Wilcox 2000). The McFadden Act of 1927 which prohibited banking across state borders was repealed in 1994 by the Riegel–Neal Interstate Banking and Efficiency Act.

[8] Deutsche Bank, Dresdner Bank, Bayerische Hypo-Vereinsbank, Commerzbank. Monthly Report of the Deutsche Bundesbank February 2000, p. 24.

market share of savings banks was 35.9 per cent and the share of cooperative banks was 13.1 per cent. At first sight these figures appear to be innocuous. However, the sum total of bank assets can hardly be considered to be the relevant market. Actually, the market is composed of various compartments, like commercial banking and investment banking for one, and among commercial banking the geographically relevant market does not comprise the entire area of Germany. Hence for an adequate evaluation of competitive conditions in banking to be achieved, detailed and careful investigations are required.

Savings banks and cooperative banks are the backbone of financing small business and medium-sized firms in Germany which, by the way, account for some two-thirds of total employment. Savings banks are run by local communities and the Federal States which makes them immune from ever going bankrupt. This guarantee confers a substantial competitive advantage on savings banks and the associated 'Landesbanken' with regard to their international activities. The implicit subsidy has been severely criticized (Sinn 1997) and has come under scrutiny by the EC Commission. Still, the Federal Government succeeded at the EC Conference 1999 in Amsterdam in having the EC Treaty complemented by a note recognizing the right of communities and Federal States to maintain a banking system covering the area of the respective jurisdiction. However, competition must not be restrained beyond what is required for the attainment of particular objectives and it must not contradict the aims of the EC. The de facto subsidy in favor of savings banks may be justified since it is conducive to opening investment opportunities on international capital markets for low and middle-income recipients, and thus compensates for disadvantages entailed by insufficient size.

Even though overall concentration in banking is low in Germany, large banks do play a prominent role in financing large firms in industry and trade. This may facilitate collusive arrangements among customers of those banks insofar as the customers belong to industries where horizontal concentration is high. Representatives of banks in supervisory boards of joint stock companies would certainly dislike the aggressive moves of enterprises which might endanger loans extended by banks and may thus be susceptible to favor collusion. To counteract these tendencies the number of board memberships is restricted by law. Collusive inclinations can, however, hardly be forestalled entirely.

The Monopolkommission (1978, pp. 44ff 281ff) emphasized that conflicts of interest may arise from the simultaneity of the shareholdings of banks, the administration of proxy voting rights ('Depotstimmrecht') and the role of creditors. Still, a general prohibition of shareholding of banks in industrial firms may go too far. The separation of ownership and control in large corporations with dispersed shareholding (Berle and Means 1932) requires mechanisms which entice managers to act in accordance with the interests of share-holders. In market-based financial systems this may be accomplished by the 'market for corporate control'.[9] In a bank-based financial system, banks, being creditors, trustees for shareholders and shareholders themselves, can be expected to monitor the conduct of managers. It would not be a wise decision to abandon one element, that is, shareholdings by banks, of a bank-based system without replacing it by an adequate alternative (Neuberger 1997).

4.4   PUBLIC POLICY AND COMPETITION POLICY

The objectives pursued by competition policy may come into conflict with other aims of public policy. They arise in particular between economic efficiency and social justice. Conflicts of this kind must be resolved. As suggested by Müller-Armack (1946) a 'Social Market Economy' should be able to accomplish this end by combining freedom of markets with social justice. Competition policy aims primarily at economic efficiency to be attained where efficiency is unequivocally defined. By contrast, social justice comprises multifarious aspects. Still, competition policy itself contributes to achieving social justice by providing for freedom of business activity, by curbing monopolistic market power and thus avoiding the introduction of monopoly rents. It thus simultaneously favors wage earners, that is, the great majority of society. The same effect follows from competition policy insofar as competition enhances technical progress and the growth of income per head. Accordingly, Adam Smith ([1776] 1950, vol. 1, pp. 90f) observed that

> it is in the progressive state, while the society is advancing to the further acquisition, rather than when it has acquired its full complement of riches, that the condition of the labouring poor, of the great body of the people, seems to be the happiest and the most comfortable. It is hard in the stationary, and miserable in the declining state. The progressive state is in reality the cheerful and the hearty state to all the different orders of the society.

It was exactly this insight which led Ludwig Erhard, the first Minister of Economics of the Federal Republic of Germany, to propagate the Social Market Economy after the ravages left by World War II. He emphasized that social justice is most effectively enhanced by opening chances of wealth creation for everybody and not just for a limited circle of privileged people.

---

[9]   See Manne (1965), Jensen and Ruback (1983) with an assessment of its effectiveness.

Government Aids

Competition may be severely distorted by subsidies. Accordingly, for the EC, Article 87 EC Treaty stipulates that

> Save as otherwise provided in this Treaty, any aid granted by a Member State or through State resources in any form whatsoever which distorts or threatens to distort competition by favoring certain undertakings or the production of certain goods shall, insofar as it affects trade between Member States, be incompatible with the common market.

This provision docs not pertain to general government activities favoring all enterprises of a Member State (EC 1995, pp. 66f). By contrast, any aid given to an individual enterprise may be deemed illegal if it confers an advantage on the recipient which under normal business conditions would not be available. Aids may be granted in quite different ways, that is, as an outright payment, exemption from taxation, sale of real estate at a price below the market, granting a public warrant or increasing equity of a public enterprise. An increase in government shareholding is deemed as an aid if a private investor would not at the same conditions have become a shareholder. This criterion, called the 'private investor test', has been applied by the Court of First Instance of the European Court of Justice 1999 in the case Neue Maxhütte Stahlwerke GmbH (FAZ February 26, 1999, p. 22). The Court ruled that government aids cannot be justified by invoking macroeconomic effects, such as for instance the saving of jobs, because for a private investor such an argument would be irrelevant.

For evaluating aid control as exercised by the EC Commission it is necessary to recognize that subsidizing industries, or even particular enterprises, may serve the public interest of the country concerned. On one hand, it is certainly true that international trade flows and trade within the common market are governed by comparative advantages and that they should not be distorted by government interventions driven by considerations of strategic trade policy. On the other hand, it has to be recognized that comparative advantages are not always falling from heaven, nor are they unchangeable. To a substantial extent comparative advantages have been created by investing in private and public, both non-human and human, capital. For this reason Article 87, 3 EC Treaty recognizes exemptions from the general prohibition of government aids, in particular for

> (a) aid to promote the economic development of areas where the standard of living is abnormally low or where there is serious underemployment;
> (b) aid to promote the execution of an important project of common European interest or to remedy a serious disturbance in the economy of a Member State;
> (c) aid to facilitate the development of certain economic activities or of certain eco-

nomic areas, where such aid does not adversely affect trading conditions to an extent contrary to the common interest;

(d) aid to promote culture and heritage conservation where such aid does not affect trading conditions and competition in the Community to an extent that is contrary to the common interest;

(e) such other categories of aid as may be specified by decision of the Council acting by a qualified majority on a proposal from the Commission.

According to Article 87, 2 EC Treaty aids are permissible if, having a social character, they are granted to individual consumers without discrimination related to the origin of the products concerned. The same applies to aids to make good the damage caused by natural disasters or exceptional occurrences, and aids granted to the economy of certain areas of the Federal Republic of Germany affected by the previous division of Germany, insofar as such aid is required in order to compensate for the economic disadvantages caused by that division.

Thus government aids may be motivated by the consideration of industrial policy and social justice. They must not, however, contradict the interest of the European Community. It is upon the EC Commission to decide on a case-by-case basis. Unless aids qualify to be exempted according to Article 87, 2 or 3 of the EC Treaty they are illegal if they noticeably interfere with trade between Member States. According to the EC Commission this applied in the case of the German Leuna Werke GmbH, a chemical enterprise in Eastern Germany, although the firm did not export into other Member States. The government aid, however, was judged by the EC Commission to enable the firm to increase domestic production and thus to foreclose the market for imports (EC 1995, p. 67). In the case of regional aids to FORD Genk, Belgium, the EC Commission required that aids do no more than just compensate for regional disadvantages (EC 1995, p. 69).

State aid control of the EC Commission must strike a balance between competition policy and industrial policy. Invoking the aims of the EC as stated in the Treaty may entail conflicts. For example, invoking the aims of regional policy, a subsidy granted by the German government to VW for setting up a new facility in Saxony has been declared incompatible with the Common Market in view of existing excess capacities in the European automobile industry. Aids given to other firms, among them Daimler and Ford, have been admitted subject to the condition that existing capacities should be dismantled (EC 1996, p. 61). It is highly questionable for the EC Commission to agree on, or dismiss, investment decisions of enterprises the eventual responsibility of which rests with the firms. Decisions of the EC Commission in those cases necessarily involve forecasts regarding future developments of the respective markets, the reliability of which is doubtful. Moreover, the decisions of the EC Commission in the cases mentioned above pertained to large firms with subsidiaries in various Member States. Therefore the incidence of government aids and their prohibition remains dubious.

Conflicts between the common interest of the EC and the objectives of national policy may engender substantial welfare losses. An outstanding example has been the European market for iron and steel, where some Member States tried to increase the market share of their national, and partly nationalized, steel industries by heavily subsidizing. State aid control, in this case conducted by the ECSC, has been largely ineffective. From 1975 to 1993 the 12 Member States granted aids amounting to 138 billion DM, of which 12.7 billion DM was given by Belgium, 23.8 billion DM by France, 27 billion DM by Britain, 44.4 billion DM by Italy, and 8 billion DM by Germany (Berthold 1994, p. 29). Despite the efforts of the EC Commission, during the early 1980s a race of subsidizing national enterprises developed. National government obviously believed that the need of inevitable curtailments of capacities in the steel industry could be shifted to other countries. Thus dismantling excess capacities could not be achieved. This episode documents the futility of strategic trade policy which in the end yields losses for everybody. It also illustrates both the necessity of aids control and the inherent difficulties.

Public Procurement

Concerns for competition policy also arise with regard to public procurement. On one hand, it may become instrumental in the framework of industrial policy by favoring national suppliers or particular regions by discriminating against foreign competitors. On the other hand, public interest demands procurement at favorable conditions for budgetary reasons. For private firms aiming at buying cheaply follows from the pursuit of self-interest. A similarly unequivocal interest does not exist for public procurement. Two problems must be considered. First, corrupt practices may arise since the monetary volumes involved usually are gigantic *vis-à-vis* the personal income of the respective public officials who have to decide. Thus the temptation to accept bribes is substantial. Second, competing suppliers may collude. To avoid both evils, corruption and collusion, usually a formal procedure is adopted, that is, submission and auction. It aims at securing an equal treatment of equals and the right to have fairness of the procedure examined by courts. According to EC law public procurements have to be openly advertised community-wide if the volume exceeds some benchmark such that an unlimited number of suppliers may submit offers. Among them the most economic one should win. Thereby reliability of the supplier must be taken into account. German law (§ 97 KartellG) requires in addition that, for promoting small business, orders should be divided if feasible.

In an auction for public procurement the task to be accomplished is described in detail. Thus a homogeneous good is defined. That gives rise to pure price competition (McAfee and McMillan 1987, Milgrom 1989). For a solution, at first the Bertrand model of pricing in oligopoly comes to mind. In this model the equilibrium price can be expected to converge towards marginal costs. However, since usually fixed costs exist, such a price will not cover average costs. Alternatively, the model of a contestable market (Baumol, Panzar and Willig 1982) appears to be more appropriate. Contestability applies since submitting an offer is hardly associated with sunk costs. Hence exit, that is, withdrawing an offer, is possible almost without additional costs. In the case of perfect contestability the price equals average costs. The price resulting from an auction can be shown to be lower the larger the number of competing suppliers (Phlips 1995, p. 72). This theoretically-derived hypothesis has repeatedly been confirmed by empirical evidence (McAfee and McMillan 1987, p. 729). Thus the requirement for public procurement to be based on a publicly advertised auction appealing to a large number of suppliers is well grounded in theory and evidence.

An offer to be submitted for an auction is frequently subject to considerable uncertainty regarding the costs. This applies in particular to large buildings to be constructed. In this case a phenomenon arises which is called 'the winner's curse'. As the business is usually given to the supplier requesting the lowest price in a so-called common value auction, a tendency arises for the winner to have underestimated the actual costs and thus to wind up with a loss. Therefore, in quite a few cases the winning supplier goes bankrupt before having completed the task.

The rigor of Bertrand competition and the danger of falling victim to the winner's curse is conducive for suppliers to enter collusive agreements. Thus submission cartels are frequent (OECD 1976, McAfee and McMillan 1992). This applies in particular where the same suppliers meet again and again. As the requested supply prices become public knowledge upon opening the bids, defectors from an agreement are immediately identified. Monitoring collusion is thus easy and defection therefore less likely.

Competition and Social Policy

Competition yields structural changes which give rise to risks for both employees and capitalists. Although 'creative destruction' opens chances it also entails losses, at least temporary ones. Not everybody is sufficiently strong to bear the brunt of those risks. Social policy, which provides support for those who find themselves on the losing side, thus contributes substantially to the stability and workability of the economy and is thus a constitutive element of a competitive order. Social policy must not, however, be reduced to encom-

passing distributive justice alone. It has also to contribute to achieving commutative justice in the meaning given by Aristotle. Rewards for efforts must
be commensurate with achievement. If social justice were to be identified
with distributive equity alone it would require income distribution to become
equal. This would destroy incentives constitutive for a competitive economy
and would hamper economic development. Economic structures would pet-
rify, and opportunities to move up the social ladder would be shut off.
Moreover, diminished growth or even stagnation and decline would cut into
financial resources available for compensating losers and would thus substantially reduce the feasible scope of social policy.

Social justice is invoked for exempting labor markets from competition
policy. The German constitution provides for all occupations to have the right
to join associations aiming at the enhancement of their economic well-being.
Hence trade unions are legal devices for the pursuit of group interests. The
same applies to the US where trade unions are also exempt from antitrust, as
well as to all other industrialized countries. Hence cartels have come into
being on both sides of labor markets. To justify this general exemption labor
markets are assumed to be characterized by labor to be weak relative to employers. This follows, first, from looking at numbers. Usually workers are
much more numerous than employers. Second, capitalists can diversify their
investments whilst employees have to offer their human capital practically
undiversified. The supply elasticity of labor is thus comparatively low which
renders workers vulnerable to being exploited by employers who enjoy
monopsonistic market power. Even in the case of a bilateral monopoly workers are in an inferior position following from relatively low supply elasticity.[10]

A similar asymmetry of power is presumed to exist for agriculture. For this
reason in the EC agriculture is partially exempt from the ordinary regulations
of competition policy. For agriculture and trading with agricultural products
the EC Treaty has established a market organization with regulated competition (Articles 32ff. EC Treaty). The major agricultural products are subject to
a system of minimum prices to which individual producers may adjust themselves competitively. Since the minimum prices have usually yielded excess
supplies the EC has to counteract by regulating output. Correspondingly to
these regulations, associations pertaining to producing, selling, storing and
processing agricultural products are exempt from the ban against cartels
unless they fix prices and exclude competition. The legal prohibition of price
fixing is to no purpose, however, since most prices are fixed within the

---

[10] The Rubinstein (1982) model of a bilateral monopoly can be used to show that it is the party
with the higher rate of time preference, that is, the urgency of satisfying immediate needs,
which ceteris paribus is the weak one.

framework of EC market organizations.

4.5 CONCLUSION

Competition is the cornerstone for a market economy to achieve maximum welfare for the great majority of people, and competition policy is indispensable for maintaining the workability of competition. Having said this, it must be admitted that competition policy is not everything. It is embedded in economic policy at large. It aims primarily at economic efficiency to be attained. Other branches of economic policy are rigged for other goals. Hence conflicts may arise.

Competition entails creative destruction. Once-leading industries decline when replaced by new ones. Although temporary losses of income and wealth in declining sectors of the economy are going to be offset in the long run by gains achievable in new industries, temporary hardships frequently arouse complaints and opposition. For society to remain stable the competitive order of the economy must be agreed on as if following from a social contract. This gives rise to the question whether cooperation should be substituted for competition as the guiding principle of economic policy, such that structural changes might be achieved as following from consensus politics avoiding social hardships entailed by competition. This idea, however, is no more than a mirage leading astray. Cooperation may be an appropriate mode of conduct within a small group like a family. It is inadequate among strangers in a global economy. Where emotional ties are absent, self-interest is much stronger than charity. Hence cooperation is conducive to seeking solutions at the expense of outsiders, as is typical for cartels and other kinds of collusion. Even for a cooperation which were free from such a tendency the outcome would usually fall short of results achievable by competition, because self-interest harnessed by competition is a much stronger driving force to seek solutions. Mainly for this reason the co-operative sector of the economy has never become more than a marginal phenomenon of a capitalist society. Many firms which are run in the legal for of a co-operative organization can hardly be distinguished from their capitalist counterparts.

The notion of a co-operative economy has frequently been associated with the expectation that altruism should displace profit-seeking behavior characteristic for a market economy, that charity is preferable to greed. From this perspective non-profit organizations are particularly welcomed. In the US these organizations account for about 10 per cent of GNP (Weisbrod 1998). This share has declined recently, however. In Germany, too, under the pressure of competition from profit-seeking firms non-profit organizations have turned to adopt methods which previously were considered foreign to them but which ultimately lead to improved efficiency.

Still, from the point of ethics many people will feel uneasy about social relationships being dominated by self-interest. They would like altruism to replace the profit-seeking behavior characteristic of a market economy, and would thus prefer charity to greed and avarice which is usually seen to go hand in hand with maximizing shareholder value. This feeling has been given vivid expression by John Stuart Mill (1871) praising the virtues of a stationary state which would provide scope for 'all kinds of mental culture, and moral and social progress' (p. 751) as opposed to the drudgery entailed by economic growth, of which Mill confessed (p. 748) that he

> was not charmed with the ideal of life held out by those who think that the normal state of human beings is that of struggling to get on; that the trampling, crushing, elbowing, and treading on each other's heels, which form the existing type of social life, are the most desirable lot of human kind, or anything but the disagreeable symptoms of one of the phases of industrial progress.

From this point of view, instead of waiting until the stationary state envisioned by Mill eventually comes to dawn upon us, alternatives to a capitalist society have been propagated and tried. Public interest has been proposed to substitute for private interest to be pursued by the government or public enterprises. The results, however, have not been too encouraging, to say the least. The main reasons are, first, the self-interest of people in charge cannot entirely be suppressed and public interest has frequently been used as a pretext to camouflage the pursuance of private interest. Second, comprehensive planning of the economy has been experienced in socialist countries to be beyond human capability and eventually in quite a few cases led to economic disaster. In the end it has to be admitted that self-interest is the most powerful driving force of human nature. To prevent it from degenerating into greed and imposing harm on other people, it must be domesticated. In history, appealing to moral obligations has been proved as being too weak. It will also be too weak in these days to prevent dominant firms from exploiting consumers and workers. It requires institutional safeguards to contain misconduct.

It has been suggested that shareholder orientation ought to be replaced by stakeholder orientation which would require the management of firms to also take into consideration the welfare of workers, suppliers and customers who, by having committed themselves to the firm by investments, have a stake in the firm. As far as the notion of stakeholder orientation goes beyond contractual obligations and institutional arrangements, as in German co-determination, it amounts to no more than an appeal to ethics. It may be of some help to alleviate social tensions, it is insufficient, however, to overcome the inherent danger of unfettered self-interest. A dominant firm, even if guided by stakeholder orientation, may still afflict the interest of third parties. To curb economic power and to harness self-interest to serve the public interest, competition appears to be the only effective expedient.

Nevertheless the question remains how the trade-off between efficiency and equity can be taken care of, and how conflicts can be resolved which come up regarding the goals of various branches of economic and social policy. Although the stationary state holds the chance to overcome the drudgery of a competitive economy, as suggested by John Stuart Mill, given self-interest as the dominant trait of human nature, a stationary state of the economy is likely to aggravate distributive conflicts. By contrast economic growth offers the chance to improve one's own well-being without necessarily imposing lasting harm on others. Moreover, in a global economy the pursuit of efficiency and adopting a strict competition policy is indispensable for the sake of survival. It is thus certainly preferable to take on the challenge rather than to throw up entrenchments which ultimately turn out to be overcome by the forces of international competition.

References

Acs, Z.J. and D.B. Audretsch (1990), *Innovation and Small Firms*, Cambridge, Mass. and London: MIT Press

Aiginger, K. and M. Pfaffermayr (1997), 'Looking at the Cost Side of Monopoly', *Journal of Industrial Economics*, **55**, 245–67

Albach, H. (1996), 'The U.K. Agricultural Tractors Information Exchange System', in H. Albach, J.Y. Jin and C. Schenk (eds), *Collusion through Information Sharing?*, Berlin: Rainer Bohn Verlag, pp. 123–35

Alchian, A.A. and H. Demsetz (1972), 'Production, Information Costs, and Economic Organization', *American Economic Review*, **62**, 777–95

Areeda, P. and D. Turner (1975), 'Predatory Pricing and Related Practices under Section 2 of the Sherman Act', *Harvard Law Review*, **88**, 697–733

Areeda, P. and D. Turner (1980), *Antitrust Law IV*, Boston: Little, Brown

Armstrong, M., S. Cowan and J. Vickers (1994), *Regulatory Reform: Economic Analysis and British Experience*, Cambridge, Mass.; London, UK: MIT Press

Arrow, K.J. (1962), 'Economic Welfare and the Allocation of Resources for Invention', in National Bureau of Economic Research (ed.), *The Rate and Direction of Inventive Activity: Economic and Social Factors*, Princeton: Princeton University Press

Ashton, T.S. (1964), *The Industrial Revolution 1760–1830*, New York: Oxford University Press

Atkinson, A.B. and J.E. Stiglitz (1980), *Lectures on Public Economics*, London: McGraw-Hill

Audretsch, D.B. (1995), *Innovation and Industry Evolution*, Cambridge, Mass.: MIT Press

Audretsch, D.B. (1999), 'Industrial Policy and Industrial Organization', in D.C. Mueller, A. Haid and J. Weigand (eds), *Competition, Efficiency, and Welfare. Essays in Honor of Manfred Neumann*, Dordrecht, Boston and London: Kluwer, pp. 223–52

Averch, H. and L. Johnson (1962), 'Behavior of the Firm under Regulatory Constraint', *American Economic Review*, **52**, 1052–69

Badura, P. (1966), 'Bewahrung und Veränderung demokratischer und rechtsstaatlicher Verfassungsstrukturen in den internationalen Gemeinschaften', *VVDStRL (Veröffentlichungen der Vereinigung Deutscher Staatsrechtsleh-*

rer) **23**, 34 ff.

Bagwell, K. and R.W. Staiger (1997), 'Collusion Over the Business Cycle', *Rand Journal of Economics*, **28**, 82–106

Bain, J.S. (1951), 'Relation of Profit Rate to Industry Concentration: American Manufacturing, 1936–1940', *Quarterly Journal of Economics*, **65**, 293–324

Bain, J.S. (1956), *Barriers to New Competition*, Cambridge: Harvard University Press

Bain, J.S. (1966), *International Differences in Industry Structure*, New Haven: Yale University Press

Baldwin, J.R. and P.K. Gorecki (1994), 'Concentration and Mobility Statistics in Canada's Manufacturing Sector', *Journal of International Economics*, **42**, 93–103

Banerjee, A. and E.W. Eckard (1998), 'Are Mega-Mergers Anticompetitive? Evidence from the First Great Merger Wave', *Rand Journal of Economics*, **29**, 803–27

Barth, J.R., R.D. Brumbaugh Jr. and J.A. Wilcox (2000), 'The Repeal of Glass–Stegall and the Advent of Broad Banking', *Journal of Economic Perspectives*, **14**, 191-204

Basedow J. (1998), *Weltkartellrecht*, Tübingen: J.C.B. Mohr (Siebeck)

Baumol, W.J. (1996), 'Predation and the Logic of the Average Variable Cost Test', *Journal of Law and Economics*, **39**, 49–72

Baumol, W.J., J.C. Panzar and R.D. Willig (1982), *Contestable Markets and The Theory of Industry Structure*, New York: Harcourt Brace Jovanovich

Baxter, W.F. (1980), 'The Political Economy of Antitrust', in R.D. Tollison (ed.), *The Political Economy of Antitrust: Principal Paper by William Baxter*, Lexington, Mass.: Lexington Books, pp. 3–49

Bellamy, C. and G.D. Child (1993), *Common Market Law of Competition*, 4th edn, edited by V. Rose, London: Sweet and Maxwell

Bergson, A. (1973), 'On Monopoly Welfare Losses', *American Economic Review*, **63**, 853–70

Berle, A.A. and G. Means (1932), *The Modern Corporation and Private Property*, New York: Macmillan

Bernheim, B.D. and M.D. Whinston (1998), 'Exclusive Dealing', *Journal of Political Economy*, **106**, 64–103

Berthold, N. (1994), *Dauerkrise am europäischen Stahlmarkt – Macht- oder Politikversagen?*, Bad Homburg: Frankfurter Institut

Bertrand, J. (1883), 'Théorie des Richesses', *Journal des Savants*, September, 499–508 (Review of 'Théorie Mathématique de la Richesse Sociale', by Léon Walras, Professeur d'économie politique à l'académie de Lausanne, Lausanne 1838 and 'Recherches sur les Principes Mathématiques de la Théorie des Richesses', by Augustin Cournot, Paris 1838)

Bittlingmayer, G. (1982), 'Decreasing Average Cost and Competition: A New Look at the Addyston Pipe Case', *Journal of Law and Economics*, **25**, 201–29

Blair, R.D. and J.L. Harrison (1993), *Monopsony. Antitrust Law and Economics*, Princeton, N.J.: Princeton University Press

Blommerstein, H.J. (1995), 'Structural Changes in Financial Markets: Overview of Trends and Prospects', in OECD 1995, *The New Financial Landscape*, Paris, S. 9–48

Böbel, I. (1984), *Wettbewerb und Industriestruktur. Industrial Organization. Forschung im Überblick*, Berlin et al.: Springer-Verlag

Böhm, F. (1948), 'Das Reichsgericht und die Kartelle', *ORDO Jahrbuch*, **1**, 197–213

Bork, R.H. (1965), 'The Rule of Reason and the Per Se Concept: Price Fixing and Market Division', *Yale Law Review*, **74**, 775–847

Bork, R.H. (1978), *The Antitrust Paradox: A Policy at War with Itself*, New York: Basic Books

Borrmann, J. and J. Finsinger (1999), *Markt und Regulierung*, Munich: Franz Vahlen

Bourgeois, J.H.J. and P. Demaret (1995), 'The Working of EC Policies on Competition, Industry and Trade: A Legal Analysis', in P. Buigues, A. Jacquemin and A. Sapir (eds), *European Policies on Competition, Trade and Industry. Conflict and Complementarities*, Aldershot, UK; Brookfield, US: Edward Elgar, pp. 65–114

Bourlakis, C.A. (1997), 'Testing Competitive Environment and the Persistence of Profit Hypotheses', *Review of Industrial Organization*, **12**, 203–18

Brander, J. and B. Spencer (1985), 'Export Subsidies and International Market Share Rivalry', *Journal of International Economics*, **18**, 83–100

Bremer, K.J. (1985), 'Die Kartellverordnung von 1923: Entstehung, Inhalt und praktische Anwendung', in H. Pohl (ed.), *Kartelle und Kartellgesetzgebung in Praxis und Rechtsprechung vom 19. Jahrhundert bis zur Gegenwart*, Wiesbaden: Franz Steiner Verlag, pp. 111–26

Brodley, J.F. (1990), 'Antitrust Law and Innovation Cooperation', *Journal of Economic Perspectives*, **4**, 97–112

Brozen, Y. (1971), 'Bain's Concentration and Rates of Return Revisited', *Journal of Law and Economics*, **14**, 351–69

Brozen, Y. (1974), 'Concentration and Profits: Does Concentration Matter?', *The Antitrust Bulletin*, **19**, 381–99

Bücher, K. (1895), 'Die wirtschaftlichen Kartelle', in *Schriften des Vereins für Socialpolitik*, Band **61**, 138–57

Bühner, R. (1994), 'Erfolge und Mißerfolge von Unternehmenszusammenschlüssen', in M. Neumann (ed.), *Unternehmensstrategie und Wettbewerb auf globalen Märkten und Thünen-Vorlesung*, Jahrestagung des Vereins für

Socialpolitik in Münster 1993, Berlin: Duncker & Humblot, pp. 23–40

Burns, M. (1986), 'Predatory Pricing and the Acquisition Costs of Competitors', *Journal of Political Economy*, **94**, 266–96

Cabral, L.M.B. and M.H. Riordan (1997), 'The Learning Curve, Predation, Antitrust, and Welfare', *Journal of Industrial Economics*, **45**, 155–69

Cason, T.N. and C.F. Mason (1999), 'Information Sharing and Tacit Collusion in Laboratory Duopoly Markets', *Economic Inquiry*, **37**, 258–81

Chamberlin, E.H. (1933), *The Theory of Monopolistic Competition*, Cambridge, Mass.: Harvard University Press

Chandler, A.D. (1977), *The Visible Hand. The Managerial Revolution in American Business*, Cambridge, Mass. et al.: Harvard University Press

Choi, E.K., C.F. Menezes and J.H. Tressler (1985), 'A Theory of Price Fixing Rings', *Quarterly Journal of Economics*, **100**, 465–78

Christensen, P. and P. Owen (1999), 'Comment on the Judgement of the Court of First Instance of 25 March 1999 in the Merger Case IV/M.619 – Gencor/Lonrho', *EC Competition Policy Newsletter*, Number 2, June, 19–23

Clark, J.M. (1940), 'Toward a Concept of Workable Competition', *American Economic Review*, **30**, 241–56

Clark, J.M. (1961), *Competition as a Dynamic Process*, Washington, DC: The Brookings Institution

Clarke, R.N. (1983a), 'Duopolists Don't Wish to Share Information', *Economic Letters*, **11**, 33–6

Clarke, R.N. (1983b), 'Collusion and the Incentives for Information Sharing', *Bell Journal of Economics*, **14**, 383–94

Coase, R.H. (1937), 'The Nature of the Firm', *Economica*, **4**, 386–405

Coates, M.B. and F.S. McChesney (1992), 'Enforcement of the US Merger Guidelines. Empirical Evidence on FTC Enforcement of the Merger Guidelines', *Economic Inquiry*, **30**, 277–93

Cohen, W.M. and R.C. Levin (1989), 'Empirical Studies of Innovation and Market Structure', in R. Schmalensee and R.D. Willig (eds), *Handbook of Industrial Organization*, vol. II, Amsterdam et al.: North-Holland, pp. 1059–107

Comanor, W.S. and F.M. Scherer (1995), 'Rewriting History: the Early Sherman Act Monopolization Cases', *International Journal of the Economics of Business*, **2**, 263–89

Cooke, A. (1973), *Alistair Cooke's America*, New York: Alfred Knopf

Cournot, A. (1838), *Recherches sur les Principes Mathématiques de la Théorie des Richesses*, Paris

Cowling, K. and D.C. Mueller (1978), 'The Social Costs of Monopoly Power', *Economic Journal*, **88**, 727–48

Cowling, K. and M. Waterson (1976), 'Price-Cost Margins and Market

Structure', *Economica* **43**, 267–74

D'Aspremont, C. and A. Jacquemin (1988), 'Cooperative and Noncooperative R&D in Duopoly with Spillovers', *American Economic Review*, **78**, 1133–7 and 'Erratum 1990', *American Economic Review*, **80**, 641

Davies, S.W. and P.A. Geroski (1997), 'Changes in Concentration, Turbulence, and the Dynamics of Market Shares', *Review of Economic Statistics*, **79**, 383–91

Deneckere, R. and C. Davidson (1985), 'Incentives to Form Coalitions with Bertrand Competition', *Rand Journal of Economics*, **16**, 473–86

Denness, J. (1998), 'Application of the New Article 2(4) of the Merger Regulation – a review of the first ten cases', *EC Competition Policy Newsletter*, no. 3, October, 30–2

Dick, A.R. (1996), 'When are Cartels Stable Contracts?', *Journal of Law and Economics*, **39**, 241–83

DiLorenzo, T.J. and J.C. High (1988), 'Antitrust and Competition, Historically Considered', 26, 423–36

Doyle, M.P. and C.M. Snyder (1999), 'Information Sharing and Competition in the Motor Vehicle Industry', *Journal of Political Economy*, **107**, 1326–64

Duménil, G., M. Glick and D. Lévy (1997), 'The History of Competition Policy as Economic History', *The Antitrust Bulletin*, Summer, 373–416

EC (1985), *Vollendung des Binnenmarktes. Weißbuch der Kommission an den Europäischen Rat*, Juni 1985

EC (1995), *Die Wettbewerbspolitik der Europäischen Gemeinschaft. XXV. Bericht über die Wettbewerbspolitik*, Brüssel/Luxemburg: EGKS-EG-EAG 1996

EC (1996), *Die Wettbewerbspolitik der Europäischen Gemeinschaft. XXVI. Bericht über die Wettbewerbspolitik*, Brüssel/Luxemburg: Europäische Gemeinschaften 1997

EC (1997), 'Bekanntmachung der Kommission über die Definition des relevanten Marktes im Sinne des Wettbewerbsrechts der Gemeinschaft', *Amtsblatt der Europäischen Gemeinschaften* vom 9.12.1997

EC (1998), *Die Wettbewerbspolitik der Europäischen Gemeinschaft. XXVII. Bericht über die Wettbewerbspolitik 1997*, Brüssel/Luxemburg: Europäische Gemeinschaften

EC (1999), *Weißbuch über die Modernisierung der Vorschriften zur Anwendung der Artikel 85 und 86 EG-Vertrag, Arbeitsprogramm der Kommission Nr. 99/027*

Eddy, A.J. (1912), *The New Competition. An Examination of the Conditions Underlying the Radical Change that is Taking Place in the Commercial and Industrial World – the Change from a Competitive to a Cooperative Basis*, Chicago, Ill.: McClury

Edwards, C.D. (1955), 'Conglomerate Bigness As a Source of Power', in Bureau of Economic Research (NBER) (ed.), *National Business Concentration and Price Policy*, Princeton: Princeton University Press, pp. 331–59

Ellis, W.D. (1974), *Land of the Inland Seas*, New York: Weathervane Books

Elzinga, K.G. (1977), 'The Goals of Antitrust: Other Than Competition and Efficiency, What Else Counts?', *University of Pennsylvania Law Review*, **125**, 1191–213

Ethier, W.J. (1982), 'Dumping', *Journal of Political Economy*, **90**, 487–506

Eucken, W. (1959), *Grundsätze der Wirtschaftspolitik*, edited by E. Eucken-Erdsiek and K.P. Hensel, Hamburg: Rohwohlt

EuGH (European Court of Justice) (1972), 'Begriff und Indizien aufeinander abgestimmten Verhaltens. Urteil des Gerichtshofes der EG vom 14. Juli 1972 ('Farbstoffe')', *Wirtschaft und Wettbewerb (WuW)*, **9**, 593–600

Feldenkirchen, W. (1985), 'Das Zwangskartellgesetz von 1933. Seine wirtschaftliche Bedeutung und seine praktischen Folgen', in H. Pohl (ed.), *Kartelle und Kartellgesetzgebung in Praxis und Rechtsprechung vom 19. Jahrhundert bis zur Gegenwart*, Wiesbaden: Franz Steiner Verlag, pp. 145–64

Fischer, C.E. (1954), 'Die Geschichte der deutschen Versuche zur Lösung des Kartell- und Monopolproblems', *Zeitschrift für die gesamte Staatswissenschaft*, **110**, 425–56

Fisher, F.M. and J.J. McGowan (1983), 'On the Misuse of Accounting Rates of Return to Infer Monopoly Profits', *American Economic Review*, **73**, 82–97

FTC (1998), 'A Brief Overview of The Federal Trade Commission's Investigative and Law Enforcement Authority', *Internet www.ftc.gov/ogc/brfovrvw.htm*

Gaskins, D.W. (1971), 'Dynamic Limit Pricing: Optimal Pricing under Threat of New Entry', *Journal of Economic Theory*, **3**, 306–22

Gaskins, D.W. (1974), 'Alcoa Revisited: The Welfare Implication of a Secondhand Market', *Journal of Economic Theory*, 7, 254–71

George, K.D. (1990), 'Lessons from UK Merger Policy', in P.H. Admiral (ed.), *Merger and Competition Policy in the European Community*, Oxford: Basil Blackwell, pp. 71–116

Geroski, P.A. (1989), 'European Industrial Policy and Industrial Policy in Europe', *Oxford Review of Economic Policy*, **5**, 20–36

Geroski, P.A. (1990), 'Innovation, Technological Opportunity and Market Structure', *Oxford Economic Papers*, **42**, 586–602

Geroski, P.A. (1994), *Market Structure, Corporate Performance and Innovative Activity*, Oxford: Oxford University Press

Geroski, P.A. and J. Schwalbach (eds) (1991), *Entry and Market Contestability. An International Comparison*, Oxford and Cambridge, Mass.: Blackwell

Gilman, J.J. (1992), 'Broken Sticks – Why Mergers May Fail to Garner Market Shares', *Managerial and Decision Economics*, **13**, 453–56

González, F.E. (1998), 'Commentaire sur L'Arrêt de la Cour du 31 mars 1998 dans l'affaire "Kali und Salz"', *EC Competition Policy Newsletter*, June, 38–42

Granitz, E. and B. Klein (1996), 'Monopolization by "Raising Rivals' Costs": The Standard Oil Case', *Journal of Law and Economics*, **39**, 1–47

Greenhut, M.L. and H. Ohta (1979), 'Vertical Integration of Successive Oligopolies', *American Economic Review*, **69**, 137–41

Grossman, P.Z. (1996), 'The Dynamics of a Stable Cartel: The Railroad Express 1851–1913', *Economic Inquiry*, **34**, 220–36

Gual, J. (1995), 'The Three Common Policies: An Economic Analysis', in P. Buigues, A. Jacquemin and A. Sapir (eds), *European Policies on Competition, Trade and Industry. Conflict and Complementarities*, Aldershot, UK; Brookfield, US: Edward Elgar, pp. 3–48

Guth, L.A., R.A. Schwartz and D.K. Whitcomb (1976), 'The Use of Buyer Concentration Ratios in Tests of Oligopoly Models', *Review of Economics and Statistics*, **58**, 488–92

Haid, A. (1999), 'European Merger Control, Political Discretion, and Efficient Market Structures', in D.C. Mueller, A. Haid and J. Weigand (eds), *Competition, Efficiency, and Welfare. Essays in Honor of Manfred Neumann*, Dordrecht/Boston/London: Kluwer, pp. 147–72

Haltiwanger J. and J.E. Harrington (1991), 'The Impact of Cyclical Demand Movements on Collusive Behavior', *Rand Journal of Economics*, **22**, 89–106

Harberger, A. (1954), 'Monopoly and Resource Allocation', *American Economic Review*, **44**, 77–92

Hart, O. and J. Tirole (1990), 'Vertical Integration and Market Foreclosure', *Brookings Papers on Economic Activity*, Special Issue, 205–76

Hayek, F.A. von (1968), *Wettbewerb als Entdeckungsverfahren*, Kiel: Institut für Weltwirtschaft

Hayek, F.A. von (1973), *Rules and Order, reprinted in: Law, Legislation and Liberty*, London: Routledge & Kegan Paul

Hazlett, T.W. (1992), 'The Legislative History of the Sherman Act Re-Examined', *Economic Inquiry*, **30**, 263–76

Hefermehl, W. (1998), 'Einführung', in *Wettbewerbsrecht und Kartellrecht*, 20th revised edn, München: C.H. Beck, pp. 9–37

Henderson, J.M. and R.E. Quandt (1958), *Microeconomic Theory. A Mathematical Approach*, New York: McGraw-Hill

Herrmann, H. (1984), *Interessenverbände und Wettbewerbsrecht*, Baden-Baden: Nomos Verlagsgesellschaft

Herrmann, H. (1986), 'Die gefährdungstatbestandliche Auslegung des § 23a Abs. 1 Nr. 1a und b GWB bei Marktverkettungsfusionen. Ein deutsch-amerikanischer Rechtsvergleich', *Recht der Internationalen Wirtschaft*, **32**, 253–69

Herrmann, H. (1989), 'Wettbewerbsgefahren der Konglomeratfusion', *Betriebsberater*, **44**, 1213–17

Hirshleifer, J. (1971), 'The Private and Social Value of Information and Reward to Inventive Activity', *American Economic Review*, **61**, 561–74

Hoppmann, E. (1966), 'Das Konzept der optimalen Wettbewerbsintensität – Rivalität oder Freiheit des Wettbewerbs: Zum Problem eines wettbewerbspolitisch adäquaten Ansatzes der Wettbewerbstheorie', *Jahrbücher für Nationalökonomie und Statistik*, **179**, 286–323

Huck, S., H.-T. Normann and J. Oechsler (2000), 'Does Information about Competitors' Actions Increase or Decrease Competition in Experimental Oligopoly Markets?', *International Journal of Industrial Organization*, **18**, 39–57

Hughes, A. (1993), 'Mergers and Economic Performance in the UK: A Survey of Empirical Evidence 1950–1990', in M. Bishop and J. Kay (eds), *European Mergers and Merger Policy*, Oxford: Oxford University Press, pp. 9–95

Hughes, J. (1973), *The Vital Few. American Economic Progress and Its Protagonists*, New York: Oxford University Press

Ippolito, P.M. and T.R. Overstreet, Jr (1996), 'Resale Price Maintenance: An Assessment of the Federal Trade Commission's Case against the Corning Glass Works', *Journal of Law and Economics*, **39**, 285–328

Jacquemin, A. (1988), 'Cooperative Agreements in R&D and European Antitrust Policy', *European Economic Review*, **32**, 551–60

Jacquemin, A. (1990), 'Mergers and European Policy', in P.H. Admiral (ed.), *Merger and Competition Policy in the European Community*, Oxford: Basil Blackwell, pp. 1–38

Jacquemin, A. (1999), 'Theories of Industrial Organization and Competition Policy. What are the Links?', in D.C. Mueller, A. Haid, and J. Weigand (eds), *Competition, Efficiency, and Welfare. Essays in Honor of Manfred Neumann*, Dordrecht/Boston/London: Kluwer, pp. 199–222

Jenny, F. (1995), 'Evolution of Antitrust Policies in France', in G. Mussati (ed.), *Mergers, Markets and Public Policy*, Dordrecht/Boston/London: Kluwer, 163–200

Jensen, M.C. and R. Ruback (1983), 'The Market for Corporate Control: The Scientific Evidence', *Journal of Financial Economics*, **11**, 5–50

Jewkes, J., D. Sawers, and R. Stillerman (1958), *The Sources of Invention*, London: Macmillan

Jin, J.Y. (1994), 'Information Sharing Through Sales Report', *Journal of*

Industrial Economics, **42**, 323–33

Jorde, T.M. and D.J. Teece (1990), 'Innovation and Cooperation: Implications for Competition and Antitrust', *Journal of Economic Perspectives*, **4**, 75–96

Kahn, A.E. (1988), *The Economics of Regulation. Principles and Institutions*, Cambridge, Mass.: MIT Press

Kamecke, U. (1998), 'Vertical Restraints in German Antitrust Law', in S. Martin (ed.), *Competition Policies in Europe*, Amsterdam: Elsevier, pp. 143–59

Kantzenbach, E. (1967), *Die Funktionsfähigkeit des Wettbewerbs*, 2nd edn, Göttingen: Vandenhoeck und Rupprecht

Kaysen C. and D.F. Turner (1959), *Antitrust Policy: An Economic and Legal Analysis*, Cambridge, Mass.: Harvard University Press

Kerber, W. (1994), *Die Europäische Fusionskontrollpraxis und die Wettbewerbskonzeption der EG*, Bayreuth: Verlag PCO

Kessel, R.A. (1958), 'Price Discrimination in Medicine', *Journal of Law and Economics*, **1**, 20–53

Kestner, F. and O. Lehnich (1927), *Der Organisationszwang. Eine Untersuchung über die Kämpfe zwischen Kartellen und Außenseitern*, 2nd edn, Berlin: Carl Heymanns Verlag

Kinne, K. (1998), 'The "Efficiency Defense" in the U.S. American Merger Policy', *HWWA Working Paper* 67

Kintner, E.W. (1980a), *Federal Antitrust Law, Vol. I, Economic Theory, Common Law, and the Introduction of the Sherman Act*, Cincinnati: Anderson Publishing Co.

Kintner, E.W. (1980b), *Federal Antitrust Law, Vol II, Practices Prohibited by the Sherman Act*, Cincinnati: Anderson Publishing Co.

Kiriazis, G. (1998), 'Positive Comity in EU/US Cooperation in Competition Matters', *EC Competition Policy Newsletter*, no. 3, October, 11–4

Kleinwächter, F. (1883), *Die Kartelle. Ein Beitrag zur Frage der Organisation der Volkswirtschaft*, Innsbruck: Verlag der Wagner'schen Universitäts-Buchhandlung

Klette, T.J. (1999), 'Market Power, Scale Economies and Productivity: Estimates From a Panel of Establishment Data', *Journal of Industrial Economics*, **47**, 451–76

Knieps, G. (1988), 'Theorie der Regulierung und Entregulierung', in M. Horn, G. Knieps and J. Müller (eds), *Deregulierungsmaßnahmen in den USA: Schlußfolgerungen für die Bundesrepublik Deutschland*, Baden-Baden: Nomos Verlagsgesellschaft, pp. 39–82

Knight, F.H. (1921), *Risk, Uncertainty and Profit*, Chicago: University of Chicago Press

Kreps, D. and J. Scheinkman (1983), 'Quantity Precommitment and Bertrand

Competition Yield Cournot Outcomes', *Bell Journal of Economics*, **14**, 326–37

Kwoka, J.E. and D.J. Ravenscraft (1986), 'Cooperation v. Rivalry: Price–Cost Margins by Line of Business', *Economica*, **53**, 351–63

Leibenstein, H. (1966), 'Allocative Efficiency vs. X-Efficiency', *American Economic Review*, **56**, 392–415

Lerner, A.P. (1933–4), 'The Concept of Monopoly and the Measurement of Monopoly Power', *Review of Economic Studies*, **1**, 157–75

Levenstein, M.C. (1997), 'Price Wars and the Stability of Collusion: A Study of the Pre-World War I Bromine Industry', *Journal of Industrial Economics*, **55**, 117–37

Lever, J. (1999). 'The Development of British Competition Law: A Complete Overhaul and Harmonization', Berlin: *WZB Discussion Papers FS IV*, 99–104

Liefmann, R. (1915), 'Monopoly or Competition as the Basis of Government Trust Policy', *Quarterly Journal of Economics*, **29**, 308–25

Liefmann, R. (1927), *Kartelle, Konzerne und Trusts*, 7th edn, Stuttgart: Ernst Heinrich Moritz (Inh. Franz Mittelbach)

Lipsey, R.G. and K. Lancaster (1956), 'The General Theory of Second Best', *Review of Economic Studies*, **24**, 11–32

Locke, J. (1690), *Über die Regierung*; (1966) *The Second Treatise of Government*, Hamburg: Rowohlt

Lustgarten, S.H. (1975), 'The Impact of Buyer Concentration in Manufacturing Industries', *Review of Economics and Statistics*, **57**, 125–32

Machlup, F. (1961), *Die wirtschaftlichen Grundlagen des Patentrechts*, Weinheim: Verlag Chemie GmbH

Maillet, P. (1984), *La Politique Industrielle*, Paris: Presse Universitaire de France

Manne, H.G. (1965), 'Mergers and the Market for Corporate Control', *Journal of Political Economy*, **73**, 110–20

Martin, S. (ed.) (1998), *Competition Policies in Europe*, Amsterdam et al.: Elsevier

Martin, S. (1999), 'Depression Cartels, Market Structure, and Performance', in D.C. Mueller, A. Haid and J. Weigand (eds), *Competition, Efficiency, and Welfare. Essays in Honor of Manfred Neumann*, Dordrecht: Kluwer, pp. 85–99

Marvel, H.P. (1994), 'The Resale Price Maintenance Controversy: Beyond the Conventional Wisdom', *Antitrust Law Journal*, **63**, 59–92

Marvel, H.P. and E.J. Ray (1995), 'Countervailing Duties', *Economic Journal*, **105**, 1576–93

Mason, E.S. (1939), 'Price and Production Policies of Large-Scale Enterprise', *American Economic Review*, **29** Part 2, 61–74

McAfee, R.P. and J. McMillan (1987), 'Auctions and Bidding', *Journal of Economic Literature*, **25**, 699–738

McAfee, R.P. and J. McMillan (1992), 'Bidding Rings', *American Economic Review*, **82**, 579–99

McGahan, A. and M.E. Porter (1999), 'The Persistence of Shocks to Profitability', *Review of Economics and Statistics*, **81**, 143–53

McGee, J.S. (1958), 'Predatory Price Cutting. The Standard Oil (N.J.) Case', *Journal of Law and Economics*, **1**, 137–69

McWilliams, A. and K. Keith (1994), 'The Genesis of the Trusts. Rationalization in Empty Core Markets', *International Journal of Industrial Organization*, **12**, 245–67

Messerlin, P.A. (1990), 'Anti-dumping Regulations or Pro-Cartel Law? The EC Chemical Cases', *The World Economy*, 465–92

Messerlin, P.A. and G. Reed (1995), 'Antidumping Policies in the United States and the European Community', *Economic Journal*, **105**, 1565–75

Mestmäcker, E.-J. (1984), *Der verwaltete Wettbewerb. Eine vergleichende Untersuchung über den Schutz von Freiheit und Lauterkeit im Wettbewerbsrecht*, Tübingen: J.C.B. Mohr (Paul Siebeck)

Mestmäcker, E.-J. (1999), 'Versuch einer kartellpolitischen Wende in der EU. Zum Weißbuch der Kommission über die Modernisierung der Vorschriften zur Anwendung der Art. 85 und 86 EGV a.F. (Art. 81 und 82 EGV n.F.)', *Europäische Zeitschrift für Wirtschaftsrecht (EuZW)*, **10**, 523–29

Milgrom, P. (1989), 'Auctions and Bidding: A Primer', *Journal of Economic Perspectives*, **3**, 3–22

Mill, J.S. (1859), *On Liberty*, (edited by C.V. Shields, The Bobbs-Merrill Company), Indianapolis and New York 1956

Mill, J.S. (1861), *Utilitarianism*, (edited by Oskar Piest, The Library of Liberal Arts), Indianapolis and New York 1957

Mill, J.S. (1871), *Principles of Political Economy*, 7th edn (edited by W.J. Ashley: Reprints of Economic Classics, New York: Augustus M. Kelley 1965)

Mishan, E.J. (1964), *Welfare Economics. Five Introductory Essays*, New York: Random House (originally *Economic Journal 1960*, **70**, 197–256)

Monopolkommission (1978), *Fortschreitende Konzentration bei Großunternehmen, Hauptgutachten 1976/77*, Baden-Baden: Nomos Verlagsgesellschaft

Monopolkommission (1986), *Gesamtwirtschaftliche Chancen und Risiken wachsender Unternehmensgrößen, Hauptgutachten 1984/1985*, Baden-Baden: Nomos Verlagsgesellschaft

Monopolkommission (1992), *Wettbewerbspolitik oder Industriepolitik. Hauptgutachten 1990/1991*, Baden-Baden: Nomos Verlagsgesellschaft

Monopolkommission (1996), *Wettbewerbspolitik in Zeiten des Umbruchs, Hauptgutachten 1994/1995*, Baden-Baden: Nomos Verlagsgesellschaft

Möschel, W. (1972), *70 Jahre Deutsche Kartellpolitik: Von RGZ 38,155 'Sächsisches Holzstoffkartell' zum BGHZ 55,104 'Teerfarben'*, Tübingen: J.C.B. Mohr (Paul Siebeck)

Möschel, W. (2000), 'Systemwechsel im Europäischen Wettbewerbsrecht? Zum Weißbuch der EG-Kommission zu den Art. 81 ff. EG-Vertrag', *Juristen Zeitung*, 55, 61–7

Mosteller, F. (1965), *Fifty Challenging Problems in Probability – with Solutions*, Reading, Mass.: Addison-Wesley

Mueller, D.C. (1986), *Profits in the Long Run*, Cambridge: Cambridge University Press

Mueller, D.C. (1990a), 'The Persistence of Profits in the United States', in D.C. Mueller (ed.), *The Dynamics of Company Profits. An International Comparison*, Cambridge: Cambridge University Press, pp. 35–57

Mueller, D.C. (1990b), 'Profits in the Process of Competition', in D.C. Mueller (ed.), *The Dynamics of Company Profits. An International Comparison*, Cambridge: Cambridge University Press, pp. 1–14

Mueller, D.C. (1991), 'Entry, Exit, and the Competitive Process', in P.A. Geroski and J. Schwalbach (eds), *Entry and Market Contestability. An International Comparison*, Oxford: Basil Blackwell, pp. 1–22

Mueller, D.C. (1995), 'Mergers: Theory and Evidence', in G. Mussati (ed.), *Mergers, Markets and Public Policy*, Dordrecht/Boston/London: Kluwer Academic Publishers, pp. 9–43

Mueller, D.C. (1996), 'Antimerger Policy in the United States: History and Lessons', *Empirica*, **23**, 229–53

Müller, M. (1998), 'Die "Essential Facility"-Doktrin im Europäischen Kartellrecht', *Europäische Zeitschrift für Wirtschaftsrecht (EuZW)*, 232–7

Müller-Armack, A. (1946), 'Wirtschaftslenkung und Marktwirtschaft', republished in Müller-Armack, A. (1976), *Wirtschaftsordnung und Wirtschaftspolitik*, 2nd ed., Bern and Stuttgart: Paul Haupt, pp. 19–170

Münter, M.T. (1999), *Wettbewerb und die Evolution von Industrien*, Bayreuth: Verlag P.C.O.

Myers, S.C. (1984), 'The Capital Structure Puzzle', *Journal of Finance*, **39**, 575–92

Nash, J. (1951), 'Non-cooperative Games', *Annals of Mathematics*, **54**, 286–95

Neale, A.D. (1966), *The Antitrust Laws of the United States of America*, Cambridge: Cambridge University Press

Needham, D. (1978), *The Economics of Industrial Structure, Conduct and Performance*, London–Sydney–Toronto: Holt, Rinehart and Winston

Nelson, R.R. and S.G. Winter (1982), 'The Schumpeterian Tradeoff Revisited', *American Economic Review*, **72**, 114–32

Neuberger, D. (1997), 'Anteilsbesitz von Banken: Wohlfahrtsverlust oder Wohlfahrtsgewinn?', *ifo-Studien*, **43**, 15–34

Neuberger, D. (1999), 'Finanzsysteme in Europa: Harmonisierung? Anglifizierung?', *Zeitschrift für Wirtschaftspolitik*, **48**, 11–26

Neumann, M. (1966), 'Vertikale Integrationsprozesse in der Industrie', *Schmollers Jahrbuch*, **86**, 665–78

Neumann, M. (1982), '"Predatory Pricing" by a Quantity Setting Multiproduct Firm', *American Economic Review*, **72**, 825–8

Neumann, M. (1990), 'Industrial Policy and Competition Policy', *European Economic Review*, **34**, 562–7

Neumann, M. (1995), 'Competition Policy in the Federal Republic of Germany', in G. Mussati (ed.), *Mergers, Markets and Public Policy*, Dordrecht/Boston/London: Kluwer Academic Publishers, pp. 95–131

Neumann, M. (1997), *The Rise and Fall of the Wealth of Nations. Long Waves in Economics and International Politics*, Cheltenham, UK; Lyme, US: Edward Elgar

Neumann, M. (1998), 'The Evolution of Cartel Policy in Germany', in S. Martin (ed.), *Competition Policies in Europe*, Amsterdam: Elsevier, pp. 41–53

Neumann, M., I. Böbel and A. Haid (1979), 'Profitability and Market Structure in West German Industries', *Journal of Industrial Economics*, **27**, 227–42

Neumann, M., I. Böbel and A. Haid (1982), 'Innovations and Market Structure in West German Industries', *Managerial Decision Economics*, **3**, 131–9

Neumann, M., I. Böbel and A. Haid (1983), 'Business Cycle and Industrial Market Power: An Empirical Investigation for West German Industries, 1965–77', *Journal of Industrial Economics*, **32**, 187–96

Neumann, M., I. Böbel and A. Haid (1985), 'Domestic Concentration, Foreign Trade and Economic Performance', *International Journal of Industrial Organization*, **3**, 1–19

Neumann, M. and A. Haid (1985), 'Concentration and Economic Performance: A Cross-Section Analysis of West German Industries', in J. Schwalbach (ed.), *Industry Structure and Performance*, Berlin: edition sigma rainer bohn verlag, pp. 61–84

Neumann, M., J. Weigand, A. Gross and M. Münter (2001), 'Market Size, Fixed Costs and Horizontal Concentration', *International Journal of Industrial Organization* (forthcoming)

Neven, D., R. Nuttall, and P. Seabright (1993), *Merger in Daylight. The Economics and Politics of European Merger Control*, London: CEPR

Nevins, A. and H.S. Commager (1981), *A Pocket History of the United States of America*, 7th revised and enlarged edn, New York: Pocket Books

Nickell, S. (1996), 'Competition and Corporate Performance', *Journal of Political Economy*, **104**, 724–46

Nieberding, J.F. (1999), 'The Effect of U.S. Antidumping Law on Firms' Market Power: An Empirical Test', *Review of Industrial Organization*, **14**, 65–84

North, D.C. (1981), *Structure and Change in Economic History*, New York: Norton

Novshek, W. (1980), 'Cournot Equilibrium with Free Entry', *Review of Economic Studies*, **47**, 473–86

Novshek, W. and H. Sonnenschein (1982), 'Fulfilled Expectations, Cournot Duopoly with Information Acquisition and Release', *Bell Journal of Economics*, **13**, 214–18

Odagiri, H. and H. Yamawaki (1990), 'The Persistence of Profits: International Comparison', in D.C. Mueller (ed.), *The Dynamics of Company Profits. An International Comparison*, Cambridge: Cambridge University Press, pp. 169–85

OECD (1976), *Collusive Tendering*, Paris

OECD (1987), *Revenue Statistics 1965-86*, Paris

OECD (1989), *Historical Statistics 1960-87*, Paris

Olson, M. (1965), *The Logic of Collective Action. Public Goods and the Theory of Groups*, Cambridge, Mass.: Harvard University Press

Ordover, J.A. and G. Saloner (1989), 'Predation, Monopolization, and Antitrust', in R. Schmalensee and R.D. Willig (eds), *Handbook of Industrial Organization*, vol. I, Amsterdam: Elsevier, pp. 537–96

Ordover, J.A., G. Saloner and S.C. Salop (1990), 'Equilibrium Vertical Foreclosure', *American Economic Review*, **80**, 127–42

Papier, H.-J. (1997), 'Durchleitungen und Eigentum', *Betriebs-Berater*, **52**, 1213–20

Parsons, D.O. and E.J. Ray (1975), 'The United States Steel Consolidation: The Creation of Market Control', *Journal of Law and Economics*, **18**, 181–219

Peltzman, S. (1976), 'Toward a More General Theory of Regulation', *Journal of Law and Economics*, **19**, 211–40

Phelps, E.S. (1961), 'The Golden Rule of Accumulation: A Fable for Growthmen', *American Economic Review*, **51**, 638–43

Phlips, L. (1995), *Competition Policy: A Game-Theoretic Perspective*, Cambridge: Cambridge University Press

Piore, M.J. and C.F. Sabel (1984), *The Second Industrial Divide*, New York: Basic Books

Pitofsky, R. (1979), 'The Political Content of Antitrust', *University of Pennsylvania Law Review*, **127**, 1051–75

Popper, K.R. (1957), *The Poverty of Historicism*, London: Routledge & Kegan Paul

Porter, M.A. (1990), *The Competitive Advantage of Nations*, New York: Free Press

Posner, R.A. (1975), 'The Social Costs of Monopoly and Regulation', *Journal of Political Economy*, **83**, 807–27

Posner, R.A. (1976), *Antitrust Law: An Economic Perspective*, Chicago, Ill.: University of Chicago Press

Posner, R.A. and F.H. Easterbrook (1981), *Antitrust*, 2nd edn, St.Paul: West Publishing

Pryor, F.L. (1972), 'An International Comparison of Concentration Ratios', *Review of Economics and Statistics*, **54**, 130–40

Raith, M. (1996), 'A General Model of Information Sharing in Oligopoly', *Journal of Economic Theory*, **71**, 260–88

Ravenscraft, D.J. (1983), 'Structure-Profit Relationships at the Line of Business and Industry Level', *Review of Economics and Statistics*, **65**, 22–31

Reinganum, J.F. (1989), 'The Timing of Innovation: Research, Development, and Diffusion', in R. Schmalensee and R.D. Willig (eds), *Handbook of Industrial Organization*, vol. I, Amsterdam: Elsevier, pp. 849–908

Rhoades, S.A. and J.M. Cleaver (1973), 'The Nature of the Concentration/Price–Cost Margin Relationship for 352 Manufacturing Industries: 1967', *Southern Economic Journal*, **1973/74**, 90–102

Riordan, M.H. (1998), 'Anticompetitive Vertical Integration by a Dominant Firm', *American Economic Review*, **88**, 1232–48

Riordan, M.H. and S. Salop (1994), 'Evaluating Mergers: A Post Chicago Approach', *Antitrust Law Journal*, **63**, 513–68

Robertson, A. (1996), 'The Reform of UK Competition Law – Again?', *European Competition Law Review*, **17**, 210–18

Robinson, J. (1933), *The Economics of Imperfect Competition*, London: Macmillan

Roe, M.J. (1991), 'A Political Theory of American Corporate Finance', *Columbia Law Review*, **91**, 10–67

Roe, M.J. (1993), 'Foundations of Corporate Finance: The 1906 Pacification of the Insurance Industry', *Columbia Law Review*, **93**, 639–84

Röper, B. and P. Erlinghagen (1974), *Wettbewerbsbeschränkung durch Marktinformation?*, Köln et al.: Carl Heymanns Verlag

Rotemberg, J.J. and G. Saloner (1986), 'A Supergame-Theoretic Model of Price Wars During Booms', *American Economic Review*, **76**, 390–407

Rubinstein, A. (1982), 'Perfect Equilibrium in a Bargaining Model', *Econometrica*, **50**, 97–109

Salant, S.W., S. Switzer and R.J. Reynolds (1983), 'Losses from Horizontal Merger: The Effects of an Exogenous Change in Industry Structure on

Cournot–Nash Equilibrium', *Quarterly Journal of Economics*, **98**, 185–99

Salinger, M. (1988), 'Vertical Mergers and Market Foreclosure', *Quarterly Journal of Economics*, **103**, 345–56

Salinger, M. (1990), 'The Concentration–Margins Relationship Reconsidered', *Brooking Papers on Economic Activity, Microeconomics*, 287–335

Salop, S.C. and D.T. Scheffman (1983), 'Raising Rivals' Costs', *American Economic Review (Papers and Proceedings)*, **73**, 267–71

Scherer, F.M. (1980), *Industrial Market Structure and Economic Performance*, 2nd edn, Chicago: Rand McNally

Scherer, F.M. (1994), *Competition Policies for an Integrated World Economy*, Washington: The Brookings Institution

Scherer, F.M. and D. Ross (1990), *Industrial Market Structure and Economic Performance*, 3rd edn, Boston; Houghton Mifflin

Schmalenbach, E. (1949), *Der freien Wirtschaft zum Gedächtnis*, Köln: Westar Verlag

Schmalensee, R. (1989), 'Inter-Industry Studies of Structure and Performance', in R. Schmalensee and R.D. Willig (eds), *Handbook of Industrial Organization*, vol. II, Amsterdam: Elsevier, pp. 951–1009

Schmidt, I. (1999), *Wettbewerbspolitik and Kartellrecht*, 6th edn, Stuttgart: Lucius & Lucius

Schmoller, G. (1906), *Schriften des Vereins für Socialpolitik*, Band **116**, 237–71

Schumpeter, J.A. (1912), *Theorie der wirtschaftlichen Entwicklung* (5th edn 1952), Berlin: Dunckcr & Humblot

Schumpeter, J.A. (1942), *Capitalism, Socialism and Democracy*, New York: Harper

Schwalbach, J. and A. Schwerk (1999), 'Stability of German Cartels', in D.C. Mueller, A. Haid and J. Weigand (eds), *Competition, Efficiency, and Welfare, Essays in Honor of Manfred Neumann*, Dordrecht/Boston/London: Kluwer, pp. 101–25

Schwiete, M. (1998), *Finanzsysteme und wirtschaftliche Entwicklung*, Berlin: Duncker & Humblot

Selten, R. (1973), 'A Simple Model of Imperfect Competition Where Four are Few and Six are Many', *International Journal of Game Theory*, **2**, 141–201

Servan-Schreiber, J.-J. (1967), *Le défi américain*, Paris: Denoel

Shepherd, W.G. (1972), 'The Elements of Market Structure', *Review of Economics and Statistics*, **54**, 25–38

Shepherd, W.G. (1984), 'Contestability vs. Competition', *American Economic Review*, **74**, 572–87

Simon, H. (1996), *Die heimlichen Gewinner (Hidden Champions)*, 3rd edn, Frankfurt/New York: Campus Verlag

Sinn, H.-W. (1997), *Der Staat im Bankwesen. Zur Rolle der Landesbanken in Deutschland*, München: C.H. Beck

Sleuwaegen, L. and H. Yamawaki (1988), 'The Formation of the European Common Market and Changes in Market Structure and Performance', *European Economic Review*, **32**, 1451–75

Smiley, R.H. (1995), 'Merger Activity and Antitrust Policy in the United States', in G. Mussati (ed.), *Mergers, Markets and Public Policy*, Dordrecht/ Boston/London: Kluwer, pp. 45–79

Smith, A. ([1776] 1950), *An Inquiry into the Nature and Causes of the Wealth of Nations*, Cannan Edition, London: Methuen

Smith, R.T. (1998), 'Banking Competition and Macroeconomic Performance', *Journal of Money, Credit, and Banking*, **30**, 793–815

Sombart, W. (1921), *Die deutsche Volkswirtschaft im neunzehnten Jahrhundert und im Anfang des 20. Jahrhunderts*, 5th edn, Berlin: Georg Bondi

Souam, S. (1998), 'French Competition Policy', in S. Martin (ed.), *Competition Policies in Europe*, Amsterdam et al.: Elsevier, pp. 205–27

Stackelberg, H. von (1934), *Marktform und Gleichgewicht*, Wien and Berlin: Julius Springer

Stigler, G.J. (1964), 'A Theory of Oligopoly', *Journal of Political Economy*, **72**, 44–61

Stigler, G.J. (1971), 'The Theory of Economic Regulation', *Bell Journal of Economics*, **2**, 3–21

Stiglitz, J.E. (1994), *Whither Socialism?*, Cambridge, Mass.: MIT Press

Sutton, J. (1991), *Sunk Costs and Market Structure*, Cambridge, Mass.: MIT Press

Sutton, J. (1997), 'Gibrat's Legacy', *Journal of Economic Literature*, **35**, 40–59

Sutton, J. (1998), *Technology and Market Structure: Theory and History*, Cambridge, Mass.: MIT Press

Symeonidis, G. (1998), 'The Evolution of UK Cartel Policy and Its Impact on Market Conduct and Structure', in S. Martin (ed.), *Competition Policies in Europe*, Amsterdam et al.: Elsevier, pp. 55–73

Symeonidis, G. (1999), *In Which Industries is Collusion More Likely? Evidence from the UK*, Centre of Economic Research, Discussion Paper No. 2301

Tawney, R.H. (1926), *Religion and the Rise of Capitalism*, New York: Harcourt, Brace and Company (reprinted and published as a Mentor Book, New York 1948)

Telser, L.G. (1971), *Competition, Collusion, and Game Theory*, London: Macmillan Press Ltd.

Tirole, J. (1988), *The Theory of Industrial Organization*, Cambridge, Mass.: MIT Press

Toepffer, J. (1997), *Krankenversicherung im Spannungsfeld von Markt und Staat*, Bayreuth: Verlag P.C.O.

Traugott, R. (1998), 'Zur Abgrenzung von Märkten', *Wirtschaft und Wettbewerb*, **10/1998**, 929–39

Tsoraklidis, L. (1999), 'La Commission approuve le nouveau système d'échanges d'informations entre producteurs de tracteurs et machines agricoles', *EC Competition Policy Newsletter*, number 3, October

Tullock, G. (1967), 'The Welfare Costs of Tariffs, Monopolies and Theft', *Western Economic Journal*, **5**, 224–32

Utton, M.A. (1995), *Market Dominance and Antitrust Policy*, Aldershot, UK; Brookfield, US: Edward Elgar

Utton, M. (2000), 'Fifty Years of U.K Competition Policy', *Review of Industrial Organization*, **16**, 267–85

Valletti, T.M. and A. Estache (1999), *The Theory of Access Pricing: An Overview for Infrastructure Regulators*, Centre for Economic Policy Research Discussion Paper No. 2133

Varian, H.R. (1984), *Microeconomic Analysis*, 2nd edn, New York and London: W.W. Norton & Co.

Veljanovski, C. (1995), 'Merger and Monopoly Policy in the U.K.', in G. Mussati (ed.), *Mergers, Markets and Public Policy*, Dordrecht/Boston/London: Kluwer, pp. 133–62

Vives, X. (1984), 'Duopoly Information Equilibrium: Cournot and Bertrand', *Journal of Economic Theory*, **34**, 71–94

Viscusi, W.K., J.M. Vernon and J.E. Harrington, Jr (1995), *Economics of Regulation and Antitrust*, 2nd edn, Cambridge, Mass.: MIT Press

Wallenberg, G. von (1999), 'Der Anspruch auf Netzzugang muß die Grundrechte beachten', *Frankfurter Allgemeine Zeitung*, 19.2.1999, 22

Waterson, M. (1980), 'Price–Cost Margins and Successive Market Power', *Quarterly Journal of Economics*, **94**, 135–50

Weber, M. (1956), *Wirtschaft und Gesellschaft. Grundriß der verstehenden Soziologie*, 1. Halbband, edited by. J. Winckelmann, 4th edn, Tübingen: J.C.B. Mohr (Paul Siebeck)

Weigand, C. (1998), *Der Einfluß der Bankkreditvergabe auf den Unternehmenswettbewerb unter besonderer Berücksichtigung der Finanzierungsprobleme kleiner und neu gegründeter Unternehmen*, Hamburg: Dr. Kovac

Weigand, J. (1996), *Innovationen, Wettbewerb und Konjunktur*, Berlin: Duncker & Humblot

Weisbrod, B.A. (ed.) (1998), *To Profit or Not to Profit: The Commercial Transformation of the Non-Profit Sector*, Cambridge, Mass.: Cambridge University Press

Weiss, L.W. (1971), 'Quantitative Studies of Industrial Organization', in M.D. Intriligator (ed.), *Frontiers of Quantitative Economics*, Amsterdam:

North-Holland, pp. 362–411

Weizsäcker, C.C. von (1980), *Barriers to Entry. A Theoretical Treatment*, Berlin: Springer-Verlag

White, L.J. (2000), 'Present at the Beginning of a New Era for Antitrust: Reflections on 1982–1983', *Review of Industrial Organization*, **16**, 131–49

Williamson, O.E. (1968), 'Economies as an Antitrust Defense: The Welfare Tradeoffs', *American Economic Review*, **58**, 18–36

Williamson, O.E. (1969), 'Economies as an Antitrust Defense: Reply', *American Economic Review*, **59**, 954–9

Willig, R.D. (1976), 'Consumer's Surplus Without Apology', *American Economic Review*, **66**, 589–97

Wissenschaftlicher Beirat beim Bundesministerium für Wirtschaft (1987), 'Wettbewerbspolitik, Gutachten vom 6. 12. 1986', *Sammelband der Gutachten von 1973 bis 1986*, Göttingen: Otto Schwartz & Co., pp. 1359–91

Wissenschaftlicher Beirat beim Bundesministerium für Wirtschaft (1987), 'Stellungnahme zum Weißbuch der EG-Kommission über den Binnenmarkt vom 21./22. Februar 1986', *Sammelband der Gutachten von 1973 bis 1986*, Göttingen: Otto Schwartz & Co., pp. 1333–58

WuW (1995), 'EG-Informationen: Europäische Fusionskontrolle', *Wirtschaft und Wettbewerb*, **45**, 385-7

Yamawaki, H. (1985), 'Dominant Firm Pricing and Fringe Expansion: The Case of the U.S. Iron and Steel Industry, 1907–1930', *Review of Economics and Statistics*, **67**, 429–37

Yamey, B.S. (1954), *Economics of Resale Price Maintenance*, London: Pitman

Yamey, B.S. (1972), 'Predatory Price Cutting: Notes and Comments', *Journal of Law and Economics*, **15**, 129–42

Young, A.A. (1915), 'The Sherman Act and the New Anti-Trust Legislation', *Journal of Political Economy*, **23**, 201–20

Index

ABB 177
abuse control 25, 38, 99, 102, 135, 163, 164
abuse of a dominant position 16, 37, 38, 39, 40, 41, 43, 135, 136, 145, 174
abuse of monopolistic market power 5, 37, 45, 98, 99, 134, 163
abusive exploitation 135
acquisition 33, 36, 41, 110, 111, 112, 118, 121, 123, 124, 125, 127, 128, 134, 166, 181, 183
actual competition 17
Acs, Z.J. 92, 192
Addyston Pipe 34, 100, 102, 156
Admiral, P.H. 197, 199
advertising 20, 73, 79, 83, 90, 138, 140, 144, 169, 170, 171, 172
agriculture 102, 188
Aiginger, K. 88, 192
AKZO 125
Albach, H. 107, 192
Alcatel/Telettra 129
Alchian, A.A. 136, 192
Alcoa 33, 120, 133
altruism 189, 190
American Can Company 143
American Column and Lumber Company 106
American Medical Association 171
American Tobacco Company

100, 129
ancillary restraint 102, 156

anti-dumping 176
antitrust viii, 2, 30, 31, 32, 33, 34, 35, 36, 37, 44, 47, 103, 104, 110, 115, 121, 128, 132, 135, 148, 156, 164, 172, 188
Areeda, P. 134, 144, 192
Areeda–Turner test 144
Armstrong, M. 161, 192
Arrow, K.J. 53, 92, 192
Ashton, T.S. 6, 192
asymmetric information 170, 180
AT&T 129
Atkinson, A.B. 161, 192
attractiveness of collusion 70
auction 186, 187
Audretsch, D.D. 14, 32, 92, 192
Aufholfusion 123
average costs 7, 8, 9, 13, 14, 17, 18, 26, 57, 62, 63, 73, 74, 85, 92, 100, 138, 145, 159, 160, 161, 174, 177, 187
average variable costs 8, 49, 57, 74, 84, 88, 101, 144, 159
Averch, H. 162, 192
Averch–Johnson effect 162

Badura, P. 29, 192
Bagwell, K. 27, 193
Bain, J.S. 64, 74, 82, 193, 194
Baldwin, J.R. 84, 193
Banerjee, A. 119, 193

banking 30, 102, 159, 171, 181, 182
banks 179, 180, 181, 182
barriers to entry 6, 18, 65, 66, 82, 85, 104, 112, 120, 122, 124, 129, 133, 134, 137, 161, 162, 176
Barth, J.R. 181, 193
Basedow, J. 178, 193
basis point system 109
Baumol, W.J. 10, 17, 36, 144, 160, 187, 193
Baxter, W.F. 119, 193
Bellamy, C. 105, 193
benevolent dictator 29, 62
Bergson, A. 86, 193
Berle, A.A. 182, 193
Bernheim, B.D. 138, 193
Berthold, N. 186, 193
Bertrand, J. 48, 193
Bertrand case 78
Bertrand competition 48, 71, 107, 108, 187
Bertrand industry 108
Bertrand model 48, 59, 61, 187
Bertrand–Nash equilibrium 59, 60, 71, 72, 73
Bishop, M. 199
Bittlingmayer, G. 26, 100, 194
Blair, R.D. 156, 194
block exemption 102, 133, 158
Blommerstein, H.J. 181, 194
Böbel, I. 27, 74, 81, 84, 89, 90, 92, 170, 194, 204
Böhm, F. 25, 37, 194
Bork, R.H. 3, 16, 32, 33, 101, 102, 134, 135, 194
Borrmann, J. 159, 194
Bourgeois, J.H.J. 176, 194
Bourlakis, C.A. 81, 194
BP/Gelsenberg 126
Brander, J. 54, 194

Bremer, K.J. 37, 194
Britain viii, 26, 124, 127, 161, 177, 186
Brodley, J.F. 132, 194
bromine cartel 31
Brooke Group v. Brown & Williamson Tobacco Corporation 144, 148
Brown Shoe Company 121
Brozen, Y. 82, 194
Brumbaugh, R.D. Jr 181, 193
Bücher, K. 25, 194
Bühner, R. 128, 194
Buigues, P. 194, 198
Burns, M. 146, 195
business cycle 24, 26, 27, 81, 100, 101, 103, 112, 177
business cycle upswing 27, 100, 101, 103, 112
buying power 11, 12, 143, 154, 156, 157

Cabral, L.M.B. 145, 195
capital accumulation 161
capital market 13, 148, 152, 153, 163, 182
capture theory 162
cartel viii, ix, 1, 5, 6, 11, 23, 24, 25, 26, 27, 29, 31, 33, 34, 37, 38, 39, 42, 43, 44, 45, 63, 67, 68, 70, 71, 72, 73, 74, 85, 100, 101, 102, 103, 105, 113, 118, 130, 133, 134, 135, 136, 139, 142, 145, 146, 147, 156, 158, 163, 173, 175, 176, 177, 178, 179, 187, 188, 189
cartel law 38, 43, 156, 177
Cason, T.N. 107, 195
Cassis de Dijon 172
Celler–Kefauver Antimerger Act 34, 110
cellophane fallacy 117

Central Ohio Salt Co. v. Guthrie 31

Chamberlin, E.H. 47, 58, 61, 157, 195

Chandler, A.D. 34, 195

Chicago School 16, 32

Child, G.D. 105, 193

children of distress 24, 26, 27

Choi, E.K. 67, 195

Christensen, P. 177, 195

Clark, J.M. 25, 28, 32, 51, 195

Clarke, R.N. 107, 195

Clayton Act 31, 34, 35, 36, 38, 41, 110, 120, 121, 125, 171

Cleaver, J.M. 79, 206

Clorox Chemical Company 123, 125

Coase, R.H. 133, 136, 195

Coates, M.B. 126, 195

Coca Cola Enterprises/Amalgamated Beverages GB 116

Cohen, W.M. 168, 195

collusion viii, 6, 11, 39, 48, 64, 65, 67, 68, 69, 70, 71, 72, 73, 75, 76, 78, 79, 82, 85, 90, 99, 102, 103, 104, 105, 106, 107, 108, 109, 113, 117, 123, 130, 140, 141, 166, 176, 177, 178, 182, 186, 187, 189

Comanor, W.S. 129, 195

combined market share 17, 79, 84, 100, 102, 112, 119, 121, 122, 182

comfort letter 139

Commager, H.S. viii, 6, 204

common law 31

commutative justice 16, 188

compensated demand curve 87

compensating variation of income 87, 91

competition as a process of discovery 14, 29, 98

competition as institution 5

competition policy viii, ix, x, 1, 2, 3, 5, 6, 15, 17, 23, 28, 29, 30, 32, 34, 36, 37, 38, 39, 41, 42, 43, 44, 45, 46, 47, 48, 66, 67, 74, 85, 90, 97, 98, 99, 101, 104, 108, 115, 122, 127, 128, 129, 130, 131, 132, 135, 136, 137, 143, 145, 147, 151, 152, 154, 163, 164, 166, 175, 177, 178, 179, 183, 185, 186, 188, 189, 191

competitive equilibrium 10, 14, 26, 86 100

complementarity in demand 143, 148, 151

concentration ratio 81, 113

concept of power 10

concerted practice 39, 40, 103, 104, 105

conglomerate 36, 37, 110, 111, 112, 121, 123, 128, 152, 153, 154

conglomerate merger 36, 110, 111, 112, 123, 128

conjectural variation 75, 77, 78

conspiracy 5, 33, 104, 119, 169

constructivistic approach 29

consumer protection 160, 171

consumer surplus 86, 89, 91, 161

consumption per head 162

contestability doctrine 17, 121, 124

contestable markets 36

Continental Can 40, 41

Cooke, A. 35, 195

cooperation 69, 71, 107, 130, 131, 132, 133, 156, 189

cooperative purchasing 156

co-operative economy 189

Corning Glass Works 142

cost differences 52

cost function 9, 49, 50, 51, 56, 58, 61, 67, 70, 108, 160, 161
cost savings 91, 98, 119, 143, 156, 173
Council of Ministers 102
Cournot, A. 48, 57, 195
Cournot case 76
Cournot competition 48, 51, 54, 57, 61, 62, 69, 70, 108, 134, 150, 151
Cournot equilibrium 47, 49, 50, 51, 52, 53, 63, 69, 70, 73, 88, 104, 155
Cournot industry 108
Cournot model 48, 51, 61, 98, 134
Cournot oligopoly 89, 107
Cournot–Nash 61, 69
Cowan, S. 161, 192
Cowling, K. 75, 79, 80, 88, 90, 195
creative destruction 3, 5, 7, 24, 166, 187, 189
cross-price elasticity 58, 77

Daimler and Chrysler 129
Daimler Benz/MBB 127
D'Aspremont 132, 196
Davidson, C. 71, 119, 196
Davies, S.W. 84, 196
deep pocket hypothesis 152
Demaret, P. 176, 194
Demsetz, H. 136, 192
Deneckere, R. 71, 119, 196
Denness, J. 131, 196
Depotstimmrecht 182
deregulation 2, 36, 129, 158
Diamond International Corporation v. Waltershöfer 115
Dick, A.R. 27, 196
DiLorenzo, T.J. 7, 25, 51, 196
direct price elasticity of demand 78, 148
distortion of competition 39, 43, 130, 143, 171
distribution of market shares 19, 20, 21, 66, 112, 118
distributive justice 16, 188
diversification 110, 152
divestiture 129, 145
dominant design 15
dominant position 37, 38, 39, 40, 41, 43, 115, 120, 122, 123, 125, 126, 127, 132, 133, 135, 136, 145, 147, 173, 174
Doyle, M.P. 109, 196
Dr Miles Medical Company v. John D. Park and Sons Company 142
Du Pont de Nemours & Co. 115
Duménil, G. 32, 196
dumping 145, 176, 177
duopoly 49, 52, 53, 59, 64, 68, 69, 104, 122, 149, 151, 175
dyestuff 105, 177, 178

Easterbrook, F.H. 134, 206
EC viii, ix, 21, 23, 30, 38, 39, 40, 41, 42, 43, 45, 64, 98, 99, 100, 102, 103, 105, 106, 107, 108, 110, 114, 115, 116, 118, 122, 124, 127, 128 129, 131, 132, 135, 138, 139, 143, 144, 145, 151, 152, 156, 158, 163, 164, 172, 174, 175, 176, 177, 178, 179, 182, 184, 185, 186, 188, 194, 195, 196, 198, 200, 202, 209
EC merger control regulation 41, 110, 122, 127, 129, 131
EC Treaty 39, 40, 41, 102, 105, 131, 135, 139, 158, 182, 184, 185, 188
Eckard, E.W. 119, 193

economic freedom 1, 2, 3, 4, 5,
25, 45, 143
economic welfare 1, 3, 4, 5, 23,
28, 29, 32, 42, 45, 99, 130, 134,
162
economies of scale 2, 31, 38, 63,
98, 126, 153, 163, 172, 173
ECSC 30, 39, 63, 99, 103, 109,
186
ECSC Treaty 39
Eddy, A.J. 105, 196
Edwards, C.D. 152, 197
effects doctrine 178, 179
efficiency defense 125, 126, 127
elasticity of conjectural variation
75, 76, 77, 78
elasticity of supply 12
Ellis, W.D. 147, 197
Elzinga, K.G. 33, 197
empirical evidence 67, 74, 78, 98,
121, 128, 142, 187
entry barriers 80, 133, 147, 170,
171, 173, 180, 181
Erlinghagen, P. 106, 206
erosion of profits 14, 15
essential facility 174
Estache, A. 174, 209
Ethier, W.J. 177, 197
Eucken, W. 2, 6, 28, 37, 197
Eucken–Erdsieck, E. 197
EuGH 197
European Community 30, 39, 40,
45, 103, 109, 125, 185
European Court of Justice 40, 43,
104, 105, 107, 108, 123, 124,
139, 144, 172, 177, 178, 184,
197
evaluation of cartels 24
evolutionary process 4, 15, 95,
111, 112, 181
exclusive dealing 34, 102, 118,
129, 136, 137, 138, 139, 141

exempted sectors 102
exemptions from the per se rule
158
export cartel 175, 176, 177, 179
export ratio 81
external effects 158, 165
externalities 2, 94, 132
exterritorial effects 128, 177

Fair Trading Act 43
Federal Cartel Office 38, 105,
107, 113, 115, 116, 123, 124,
127, 129, 130, 133, 138, 143,
156, 164
Federal Minister of Economics
129
Feldenkirchen, W. 26, 197
financial markets 179
financial systems 180, 181, 183
Finsinger, J. 159, 194
Fischer, C.E. 26, 197
Fisher, F.M. 84, 197
fixed costs 9, 17, 24, 26, 28, 49,
52, 57, 59, 62, 63, 65, 73, 75,
77, 85, 92, 98, 101, 104, 134,
141, 144, 159, 160, 161, 170,
174, 187
foothold acquisition 123
FORD Genk 185
foreclosure 133, 134, 137, 138
France 30, 44, 45, 64, 81, 83,
127, 138, 179, 186
free entry 61, 62, 63, 64, 65, 73,
82, 85, 112
freedom of competition 44, 166
freedom of competitors 134, 135,
143
freedom of contract 1, 23
freedom of economic activity 25
FTC 115, 171, 195, 197
full function cooperative joint
venture 131

game theory 3, 27, 47, 104
Gaskins, D.W. 15, 35, 120, 197
GATT 28, 118, 175, 176, 178
Gebrauchsmuster 167
George, K.D. 110, 116, 197
Geroski, P.A. 14, 63, 84, 92, 196,
    197, 203
Gewerbefreiheit 25
Gibrat's Law 18, 19
Gilman, J.J. 20, 198
Glick, M. 32, 196
globalization viii, ix, 28, 63, 129,
    177
González, F.E. 123, 198
goods markets 179, 180, 181
goodwill 144, 169, 170
Gorecki, P.K. 84, 193
government aid 30, 177, 184,
    185, 186
Gramm–Leach–Bliley Act 181
Granitz, E. 147, 198
Greenhut, M.L. 140, 198
Gross, A. 65, 162, 204
Grossman, P.Z. 31, 198
growth of the market 62, 64, 65
Gual, J. 168, 198
Guth, L.A. 156, 198
GWB 30, 38, 102, 105, 106, 124

Haid, A. 27, 42, 81, 82, 84, 90,
    92, 125, 127, 170, 192, 198,
    199, 201, 204, 207
Haltiwanger, J. 27, 198
Harberger, A. 89, 94, 198
Harrington, J.E. 27, 158, 162,
    198, 209
Harrison, J.L. 156, 194
Hart, O. 134, 198
Hart–Rodino–Scott Pre Merger
    Notification Act 113
Hartford Empire Company 169
Harvester case 135

Hayek, F.A. von 4, 101, 198
Hazlett, T.W. 32, 198
Hefermehl, W. 171, 198
Henderson, J.M. 58, 198
Hensel, K.P. 197
Herfindahl index 18, 20, 76, 78,
    79, 80, 81, 121, 122, 123, 124
Herrmann, H. 126, 157, 198, 199
heterogeneous market 47, 70, 71,
    73, 77, 108, 119
High, J.C. 7, 25, 39, 51, 73, 160,
    196
Hirshleifer, J. 168, 199
Holzmann and Hochtief 116
homogeneous oligopoly 75
homogeneous market 64, 70, 71,
    73, 119
Hoppmann, E. 2, 199
horizontal concentration 17, 18,
    19, 20, 27, 63, 64, 65, 74, 76,
    78, 79, 80, 81, 82, 83, 84, 85,
    92, 98, 110, 112, 113, 114,
    118, 121, 122, 123, 132, 134,
    147, 155, 157, 180, 181, 182
horizontal merger 36, 110, 112,
    114, 121, 128
horizontal size of the market 48,
    62, 110
Horn, M. 200
Huck, S. 108, 199
Hughes, A. 111, 199
Hughes, J. 35, 199
human capital 7, 188

ICI 177
imitation 16, 82, 85, 167
immediate entrant 115
import quota 56, 118
import ratio 81
income distribution 16, 93, 165,
    188
increase in the market 176

increasing returns to scale 63, 100, 159, 163
incumbent 17, 57, 70, 82, 98, 104, 126, 133, 138, 146, 151, 180
indivisibilities 13, 63, 85, 98, 147, 157, 159
industrial economics x, 44, 47, 99
industrial organization viii, 78
industrial policy ix, 1, 2, 28, 29, 30, 36, 38, 41, 42, 44, 103, 126, 127, 152, 179, 185, 186
information exchange 31, 105, 106, 107, 108, 109
innovation 7, 8. 14, 15, 16, 24, 29, 51, 53, 54, 61, 70, 92, 98, 101, 111, 133
international competitiveness ix, 30, 164
international trade policy x, 26, 27, 28, 175
interventionism 36, 37, 164
Intriligator, M.D. 209
inverse demand curve 9, 48, 49, 62, 64, 70, 88, 159, 160
inverse demand function 58, 61, 68, 73, 89, 107, 137, 141, 150, 154
investment 10, 39, 96, 113, 180, 181, 182, 185
invisible hand 5
Ippolito, P.M. 142, 199
Italy 64, 81, 145, 186

Jacquemin, A. 41, 127, 128, 132, 194, 196, 198, 199
Jenny, F. 44, 127, 199
Jensen, M.C. 183, 199
Jewkes, J. 92, 199
Jin, J.Y. 108, 192, 199
Johnson, L. 162, 192
joint purchasing agreement 156

joint venture 130, 131, 132, 173, 177
Jorde, T.M. 132, 200
justice 2, 16, 38, 109, 183, 185, 188

Kahn, A.E. 159, 200
Kamecke, U. 138, 139, 200
Kantzenbach, E. 28, 200
KartellG 38, 39, 102, 110, 122, 126, 129, 133, 134, 135, 136, 145, 152, 156, 168, 171, 174, 177, 186
Kaysen, C. 2, 114, 200
Keith, K. 26, 202
Kerber, W. 129, 200
Kessel, R.A. 171, 200
Kestner, F. 73, 146, 200
Kinne, K. 121, 125, 126, 200
Kinney Shoe Company 121
Kintner, E.W. 6, 31, 33, 115, 120, 133, 147, 200
Kiriazis, G. 178, 200
Klein, B. 147, 148, 198
Kleinwächter, F. 24, 200
Klette, T.J. 92, 200
Knieps, G. 159, 200
Knight, F.H. 6, 7, 28, 51, 200
Kreps, D. 48, 200
Kwoka, J.E. 79, 201

labor-augmenting technical change 95
laissez-faire 1, 2, 5, 23, 27, 28, 35
Lancaster, K. 97, 201
Law Against Restraints of Competition 37, 38, 40, 41, 106
Law Against Unfair Competition 39, 171
legislation x, 25, 31, 32, 33, 42, 45, 113, 124, 142, 157, 170, 172, 178

Lehnich, O. 73, 146, 200
Leibenstein, H. 90, 201
Lerner, A.P. 9, 10, 12, 76, 201
Leuna Werke GmbH 185
level playing field 1, 145
Levenstein, M.C. 31, 201
Lever, J. 42, 201
Levin, R.C. 168, 195
Lévy, D. 32, 196
Liefmann, R. 11, 26, 27, 201
Linseed Oil Company 105
Lipsey, R.G. 97, 201
Locke, J. 3, 201
long-run total average costs 74
loss-leader strategy 148, 150, 151
Lustgarten, S.H. 156, 201

Machlup, F. 167, 168, 201
Maillet, P. 29, 201
Mandeville Island Farmers v.
    American Crystal Sugar Co.
    156
Manne, H.G. 183, 201
Maple Flooring Manufacturers'
    Association 106
marginal costs 7, 9, 10, 13, 48,
    49, 52, 53, 54, 57, 60, 61, 62,
    65, 67, 68, 70, 71, 72, 74, 76,
    77, 78, 79, 84, 85, 86, 88, 91,
    97, 100, 101, 104, 117, 134,
    135, 136, 140, 141, 144, 148,
    149, 150, 151, 152, 154, 155,
    157, 161, 162, 176, 180, 187
marginal expenditure curve 12,
    155
marginal revenue 9, 49, 98, 141,
    155, 162
market dominance 119, 122, 124,
    125, 135, 152
market economy 1, 23, 28, 32,
    42, 43, 45, 46, 112, 135, 158,
    189, 190

market leader 123
market performance 98, 122, 123,
    126
market power 2, 10, 11, 15, 18,
    35, 46, 63, 75, 76, 77, 79, 82,
    84, 85, 90, 92, 93, 98, 99, 112,
    113, , 117, 118, 121, 134, 137,
    141, 142, 143, 145, 147, 151,
    157, 158, 163, 166, 170, 176,
    181, 183, 188
market share 11, 15, 17, 18, 19,
    20, 21, 35, 36, 52, 54, 66, 67,
    74, 75, 76, 78, 79, 82, 83, 84,
    92, 100, 102, 105, 107, 108,
    109, 110, 112, 118, 119, 120,
    121, 122, 124, 125, 129, 133,
    134, 143, 145, 146, 147, 173,
    176, 180, 181, 186
market size 63
market structure 1, 29, 46, 47, 63,
    64, 74, 75, 77, 82, 83, 84, 85,
    98, 125, 130, 163
market transparency 103, 107
Martin, S. 45, 103, 200, 201, 204,
    208
Marvel, H.P. 140, 176, 201
Mason, C.F. 107, 195
Mason, E.S. 74, 201
Matsushita 22, 145
McAfee, R.P. 187, 202
McChesney, F.S. 126, 195
McGahan, A. 82, 202
McGee, J.S. 145, 147, 148, 202
McGowan, J.J. 84, 197
McGuire Act 142
McMillan, J. 187, 202
McWilliams, A. 26, 202
Means, G. 182, 193
Menezes, C.F. 67, 195
Mercedes Benz/Kässbohrer 128
merger viii, ix, 29, 32, 33, 34, 35,
    36, 38, 40, 41, 43, 44, 45, 63,

64, 71, 79, 85, 91, 98, 99, 100,
101, 103, 110, 111, 112, 113,
114, 115, 116, 119, 120, 121,
122, 123, 124, 125, 126, 127,
128, 129, 130, 131, 152, 164,
166, 177, 178, 181
merger control 36, 38, 40, 41, 43,
44, 45, 91, 110, 112, 113, 119,
120, 122, 123, 124, 127, 128,
129, 131, 152, 164
Merger Guidelines 116, 117, 121,
124, 125, 126
Messerlin, P.A. 176, 202
Mestmäcker, E.-J. 39, 139, 146,
202
method of discovery 101, 130
Microsoft viii, 143
Milgrom, P. 187, 202
Mill, J.S. 3, 4, 5, 190, 191, 202
Miller–Tydings Act 142
minimal efficient size 11, 63
Mishan, E.J. 86, 202
mobility of market shares 84
Möschel, W. 25, 26, 139, 203
Mogul Steamship Company 146
monopolistic competition 47, 58,
61, 157
monopolistic exploitation 33,
135, 137
monopolistic price discrimination
137
monopolization 35, 45, 119
monopolizing 18, 38, 100, 119,
135, 144, 145, 152
Monopolkommission 22, 62, 65,
111, 125, 128, 130, 143, 182,
202, 203
monopoly ix, 5, 6, 8, 9, 10, 11,
12, 14, 15, 16, 17, 18, 23, 31,
33, 34, 35, 37, 46, 47, 51, 53,
54, 57, 62, 67, 76, 81, 82, 86,
87, 88, 89, 90, 91, 92, 93, 94,

95, 96, 97, 98, 119, 120, 129,
135, 137, 140, 141, 145, 147,
149, 151, 154, 155, 159, 160,
161, 163, 165, 166, 167, 168,
171, 173, 174, 176, 183, 188
monopoly power 5, 10, 12, 15,
16, 17, 24, 34, 35, 37, 81, 82,
86, 89, 90, 91, 92, 95, 96, 97,
119, 140, 145, 159, 160, 163,
165, 166, 171, 173, 176
monopoly profit 16, 87, 88, 90,
91, 92, 138, 141, 145, 147, 163
monopoly rent 10, 17, 87, 88, 90,
183
monopsony ix, 11, 12, 46, 154,
155, 156
Mosteller, F. 20, 203
Mosteller model 65, 66, 111, 122
Mosteller's Law 19, 20, 21, 22,
23
Mueller, D.C. 15, 83, 88, 90, 110,
125, 128, 192, 195, 198, 199,
201, 203, 205, 207
Müller, M. 174, 203
Müller-Armack, A. 37, 183, 203
Münter, M.T. 15, 65, 203, 204
multiproduct firm 144, 148, 149,
151, 154, 160, 161, 163
Munn v. Illinois 158, 174
Mussati, G. 199, 203, 204, 208,
209
Myers, S.C. 179, 203

Nash, J. 47, 203
Nash equilibrium 98, 108
National Cooperative Research
Act (NCRA) 132
natural monopoly 10, 98, 135,
159, 160, 161, 163, 165
Neale, A.D. 25, 31, 34, 36, 100,
101, 106, 142, 144, 157, 168,
169, 173, 203

Needham, D. 89, 203
Nelson, R.R. 92, 203
Nestlé/Perrier 123, 129
network effects 172
Neuberger, D. 180, 181, 183, 204
Neue Maxhütte Stahlwerke
    GmbH 184
Neumann, M. 27, 29, 65, 73, 81,
    84, 90, 92, 95, 96, 97, 113, 134,
    152, 170, 192, 194, 198, 199,
    201, 204, 207
Neven, D. 116, 204
Nevins, A. viii, 6, 204
Nickell, S. 92, 205
Nieberding, J.P. 176, 205
Normann, H.-T. 108, 199
North, D.C. 5, 205
Northern Securities Company 34,
    35
Novshek, W. 61, 107, 205
Nuttall, R. 117, 204

Odagiri, H. 83, 205
OECD 96, 97, 187, 194, 205
Oechsler, J. 108, 199
Ohta, H. 140, 198
oligopoly ix, 6, 28, 48, 64, 75,
    76, 78, 84, 88, 89, 104, 107,
    108, 130, 149, 150, 174, 187
Olson, M. 28, 205
open price system 105
opportunity costs 74, 89, 180,
    181
Ordo Liberal School 37
Ordover, J.A. 134, 148, 205
output 6, 7, 9, 11, 13, 48, 49, 50,
    51, 52, 54, 56, 57, 59, 62, 63,
    64, 65, 67, 68, 74, 74, 75, 85,
    86, 88, 89, 97, 99, 100, 101,
    103, 104, , 108, 122, 130, 134,
    140, 141, 153, 154, 155, 157,
    161, 162, 177, 188

Overstreet, T.R. Jr 142, 199
Owen, P. 177, 195

Panzar, J.C. 10, 17, 36, 160, 187,
    193
Papier, H.-J. 174, 205
Parsons, D.O. 134, 205
patent 90, 102, 132, 151, 167,
    168, 169, 173
Peltzman, S. 162, 205
per se 34, 38, 99, 100, 102, 103,
    118, 139, 143, 156, 158, 164,
    175
per se prohibition 38, 100, , 143,
    164
perfect competition ix, 6, 7, 10,
    11, 16, 18, 28, 46, 47, 51, 57,
    74, 81, 88, 89, 90, 91, 97, 117,
    122, 141, 153, 155, 175
persistence of profits 14, 124
Pfaffermayr, M. 88, 192
Phelps, E.S. 161, 205
Philip Morris case 41
Phlips, L. 51, 107, 119, 187, 205
Piore, M.J. 24, 63, 205
Pitofsky, R. 2, 32, 34, 165, 205
Pohl, H. 194, 197
Popper, K.R. 4, 29, 206
Porter, M.A. 30, 82, 202, 206
Posner, R.A. 3, 32, 90, 134, 206
potential competition 17, 122,
    124, 125, 179
predation 144, 145, 146, 147,
    148, 152, 157, 177
predatory pricing 144, 145, 146, ,
    152
presumption 59, 80, 92, 100, 104,
    116, 123, 124, 158, 170
preventive merger control 113,
    114, 129
price competition 11, 48, 54, 104,
    156, 187

price control 34, 44, 101, 135, 136, 161
price discrimination 34, 137, 138, 156
price elasticity 9, 10, 75, 76, 77, 78, 88, 89, 92, 97, 117, 137, 148, 161
price–cost margin 9, 27, 74, 75, 76, 77, 78, 79, 80, 81, 84, 85, 90, 98, 116, 117, 121, 124, 169, 170
prisoners' dilemma 69
private investor test 184
private property 158, 164, 166, 167, 173, 174
privatization 159, 163
process of discovery 14, 29, 99
process innovations 53
Procter & Gamble/Clorox 123, 125
product differentiation 119
product innovation 7, 111
production possibility frontier 90
profit 5, 10, 11, 12, 13, 14, 16, 17, 49, 50, 52, 55, 57, 58, 59, 60, 61, 62, , 67, 69, 70, 74, 75, 78, 83, 88, 90, 91, 93, 108, 137, 141, 148, 149, 157
profit maximization 11, 50, 58, 59, 67, 68, 78, 108, 137, 148, 149
profit maximum 12, 60
profitability 7, 14, 15, 53, 54, 57, 61, 70, 74, 75, 79, 82, 83, 84, 85, 103, 106, 108, 109, 112, 119, 128, 134, 137, 180
prohibition of cartels 38, 44, 100, 102, 106, 129
property right x, 1, 10, 142, 164, 166, 167, 168, 170, 173
Pryor, F.L. 64, 206
public interest 5, 25, 26, 34, 43, 102, 126, 127, 158, 159, 160, 165, 167, 174, 184, 186, 190, 191
public policy 31, 183
public procurement 186, 187
public utilities 30, 102, 139, 159, 163

Quandt, R.E. 58, 198
quasi rent 7, 14, 16, 17

R&D 54, 79, 95, 102, 131, 132, 168
R&D cooperation 132, 133
railroad express cartel 31
Raith, M. 107, 206
Ramsey rule 161
random effect 16, 18, 19, 66, 122
rationalization cartel 102, 133
Ravenscraft, D.J. 79, 201, 206
Raymond Barre 44
reaction curve 49, 50, 59, 60, 72
recession 24, 26, 27, 81, 100, 101, 103, 112
Reed, G. 176, 202
regional policy 171, 185
regulation 2, 29, 36, 44, 45, 109, 121, 131, 136, 142, 158, 159, 161, 162, 166, 174, 181
Reinganum, J.F. 92, 206
relevant market 58, 64, 77, 114, 115, 116, 117, 118, 119, 120, 122, 125, 182
rent 7, 10, 14, 16, 17, 87, 88, 89, 90, 93
rent seeking 90, 93
repeated game 69, 113
resale price maintenance 139, 141, 142
research 42, 44, 54, 92, 95, 131, 132, 167, 168, 178
research and development 54, 92,

95, 167, 168
restraint of competition ix, 1, 2,
3, 6, 16, 17, 19, 21, 26, 28, 29,
30, 31, 32, 33, 36, 37, 38, 39,
40, 41, 43, 45, 64, 65, 67, 97,
98, 99, 107, 111, 114, 122, 126,
130, 132, 133, 136, 138, 139,
140, 143, 164, 165, 166, 167,
171, 172, 173, 175, 176, 177,
181
restraints of trade viii, x, 21, 28,
30, 33, 34, 37, 42, 46, 132, 177
Reynolds, R.J. 70, 119, 206
Reynolds Metals Co. v. FTC 115,
152
Rheinmetall 123
Rhoades, S.A. 79, 206
Riegel–Neal Interstate Banking
and Efficiency Act 181
Riordan, M.H. 134, 145, 195, 206
rivalry 7, 11, 48, 67
RobertsonA. 43, 206
Robinson, J. 47, 61, 206
Rockefeller, John D. 6, 35, 145,
147
Roe, M.J. 181, 206
Röper, B. 106, 206
Ross, D. 100, 207
Rotemberg, J.J. 27, 206
RPI-X regulation 161
Ruback, R. 183, 199
Rubinstein, A. 188, 206
ruinous competition 25, 44, 101,
105, 159
rule of reason 35, 41, 85, 99, 101,
102, 112, 113, 118, 125, 132,
143, 158, 175, 178

Sabel, C.F. 24, 63, 205
Salant, S.W. 70, 119, 206
Salinger, M. 80, 134, 207
Saloner, G. 27, 134, 148, 205,

206
Salop, S.C. 134, 205, 206, 207
Sapir, A. 194, 198
Sawers, D. 92, 199
Scheffman, D.T. 134, 207
Scheinkman, J. 48, 200
Schenk, C. 192
Scherer, F.M. 35, 63, 74, 100,
129, 145, 147, 178, 179, 195,
207
Schmalenbach, E. 159, 207
Schmalensee, R. 74, 84, 156,
195, 205, 206, 207
Schmidt, I. 107, 207
Schmoller, G. 25, 207
Schumpeter, J.A. 3, 7, 24, 92,
207
Schwalbach, J. 14, 73, 197, 203,
204, 207
Schwartz, R.A. 156, 198, 210
Schwerk, A. 73, 207
Schwiete, M. 179, 180, 181, 207
Seabright, P. 116, 204
securization 180, 181
self-interest 5, 6, 29, 67, 186,
189, 190, 191
Selten, R. 24, 207
separation of ownership and
control 182
Servan-Schreiber 44, 207
shareholder 11, 135, 147, 184,
190
shareholder value 11, 135, 190
Shephard's lemma 87
Shepherd, W.G. 82, 122, 207
Sherman Act 30, 31, 32, 33, 34,
35, 36, 38, 41, 100, 101, 103,
113, 119, 120, 125, 135, 143,
145, 171, 172, 173, 178
Simon, H. 132, 168, 207
Sinn, H.-W. 182, 208
size distribution 18, 19, 66, 110

size of the market 48, 62, 78, 80
Sleuwaegen 64, 81, 208
Smiley, R.H. 110, 119, 124, 125, 208
Smith, A. 5, 6, 30, 45, 93, 96, 109, 183, 208
Smith, R.T. 181, 208
Snyder, C.M. 109, 196
social framework x, 166
social indifference curves 86
social policy 166, 187, 188, 191
Socony Vacuum case 100, 101, 103, 135
Sombart, W. 27, 68, 208
Sonnenschein, H. 107, 205
Souam, S. 44, 208
Spencer, B. 54, 194
spontaneous order 4
stability of collusion 67
stable money 1
Stackelberg, H. von 47, 208
Stackelberg case 56, 57, 58, 122
Staiger, R.W. 27, 193
stakeholder 190
Standard Oil Company 6, 35
static efficiency trade-off 91
static welfare loss 86, 92, 94, 96, 98, 137
Stigler, G.J. 68, 77, 78, 79, 162, 208
Stiglitz, J.E. 17, 32, 161, 192, 208
Stillerman, R. 92, 199
strategic trade policy 54, 55, 175, 184, 186
structural crisis cartel 103
Structure–Conduct–Performance paradigm 74, 75, 78, 84
subsidy 1, 30, 54, 55, 56, 66, 103, 112, 161, 168, 171, 174, 176, 177, 182, 184, 185
substitutes 2, 9, 59, 115, 117,

148, 150, 151
successive monopolies 140, 141
successive oligopolies 140, 157
sunk costs 10, 66, 103, 159, 163, 172, 187
supply elasticity 118, 188
Supreme Court 34, 35, 36, 101, 103, 104, 106, 115, 117, 120, 121, 123, 125, 135, 142, 144, 145, 148, 156, 158, 169, 171, 173, 174, 178
Sutton, J. 19, 48, 63, 208
Switzer, S. 70, 119, 206
Symeonidis, G. 42, 43, 70, 106, 113, 208
systems of financing industry 179

tariffs 56, 118
Tawney, R.H. viii, 5, 32, 208
taxes 55, 82, 96, 97, 118, 163
Tebbit doctrine 43
technical progress 8, 43, 45, 128, 131, 157, 183
Teece, D.J. 132, 200
Telser, L.G. 68, 208
Terminal Railroad Association of St Louis 173
Tetra Pak 144, 145, 148, 151
The Sugar Institute 106
theory of second-best 97, 98
thrust-upon doctrine 120
time preference 95, 97, 161, 188
Tirole, J. 48, 82, 132, 152, 198, 208
Toepffer, J. 172, 209
Tollison, R.D. 193
trade mark 129, 169
trade policy vii, x, 26, 27, 28, 54, 55, 175, 176, 178
trade unions 10, 90, 188
transport costs 58
Traugott, R. 115, 209

treble damages 33, 132, 165
Trenton Potteries case 100, 101
Tressler, J.H. 67, 195
trusts viii, 1, 6, 11, 25, 26, 27, 32,
34, 47, 63
Tsoraklidis, L. 107, 209
Tullock, G. 90, 209
Turner, D.F. 2, 114, 134, 144,
192, 200
tying contracts 34, 143

UK 30, 42, 43, 70, 83, 90, 92,
106, 107, 108, 110, 111, 113,
116, 118, 127, 128, 156, 179
undertakings 39, 40, 41, 43, 114,
127, 129, 130, 184
undistorted competition 5, 21,
112, 122, 130
United Kingdom 42, 45
United States viii, 3, 6, 31, 44,
118, 121, 178
US v. E.I. Du Pont de Nemours &
Co. 115, 117
US v. United Shoe Machinery
Corp. 120
US Steel 35, 129, 134, 147
Utton, M.A. 42, 43, 145, 209

Valletti, T.M. 174, 209
value judgement 16, 91, 93
variable costs 8, 9, 49, 57, 74, 84,
88, 101, 144, 159
Varian, H.R. 87, 209
variance of market shares 18, 20,
66
VEBA/Gelsenberg 126
Veljanovski, C. 43, 127, 209
Vernon, J.M. 158, 162, 209
vertical mergers 123, 133
vertical size of the market 48, 62
Vickers, J. 161, 192
Viscusi, W.K. 158, 162, 209

Vives, X. 107, 209
Von's Grocery Company 121

Wallenberg, G. von 174, 209
Waterson, M. 75, 79, 80, 156,
195, 209
Webb–Pomerene Act 175
Weber, M. 10, 209
Weigand, C. 180, 209
Weigand, J. 65, 81, 92, 192, 198,
199, 201, 204, 207, 209
Weisbrod, B.A. 189, 209
Weiss, L.W. 74, 84, 209
Weizsäcker, C.C. von 62, 170,
210
welfare x, 1, 2, 3, 4, 5, 16, 23, 25,
28, 29, 32, 42, 45, 85, 86, 87,
88, 89, 90, 91, 92, 93, 94, 95,
96, 97, 98, 99, 108, 119, 130,
134, 137, 138, 155, 161, 162,
163, 164, 166, 175, 186, 189,
190
welfare loss ix, 16, 85, 86, 87, 88,
89, 90, 91, 92, 93, 94, 95, 96,
98, 108, 119, 137, 138, 155,
161, 163, 164, 175, 186
welfare optimum 2, 28, 97
welfare maximization 3
Whinston, M.D. 138, 193
Whitcomb, D.K. 156, 198
White, L.J. 100, 117, 132, 139,
210
wide oligopoly 28
Wilcox, J.A. 181, 193
Williamson, O.E. 91, 92, 126,
144, 148, 210
Willig, R.D. 10, 17, 36, 88, 160,
187, 193, 195, 205, 206, 207,
210
Winckelmann, J. 209
Winter, S.G. 92, 203
Wissenschaftlicher Beirat beim

Bundesministerium für
Wirtschaft 210
WMF 123
workable competition 28, 158,
159
World Trade Organization 175
WTO 28, 118, 175, 179
WuW 125, 156, 197, 210

X-inefficiency 90, 91, 128, 160,
163

Yamawaki, H. 35, 64, 81, 83,
205, 208, 210
Yamey, B.S. 140, 141, 146, 210
Yarn Spinners' Association 43
Young, A.A. 11, 210